FLOYD ON FRANCE

Keith Floyd's culinary expertise was first revealed in 1985 with *Floyd on Fish*. He has since presented eight more television series. Apart from brief spells in the Army and wine trade, he has spent most of his life cooking in restaurants in Britain and France. He now runs a pub, 'Floyd's Inn (sometimes)', near Totnes in Devon. Keith Floyd's other bestselling books include *Floyd on Fire, Floyd on Fish, Floyd on Britain and Ireland, Floyd's American Pie, Floyd on Oz, Floyd on Spain* and *Far Flung Floyd*.

FLOYD ON FRANCE

*Learn to Cook
the Keith Floyd Way*

BBC Books

This book is for Leo of the 'Café de France' and for Claude Arnaud of the Saint-Hubert restaurant and my friends in L'Isle sur la Sorgue.

Special thanks to:
David Pritchard (though he does not always deserve it!); Clive North; Andy MacCormack; Tim White; Steve Williams; Frances Wallis; Debby Donlin; Albert Gassier; Monique and Pierre Conil; Alexandra Golding; Jacques-Yves Cadiou; Soyo Graham-Stuart; Judith Wells.

Published by BBC Books,
a division of BBC Enterprises Ltd
Woodlands, 80 Wood Lane, London W12 0TT

ISBN 0 563 37001 7

Technical illustrations: Will Giles and Sandra Pond
Typeset by Phoenix Photosetting, Chatham, Kent
Printed in England by Clays Ltd, St Ives plc

CONTENTS

BBC COOKERY SERIES

Floyd on Fire
Floyd on Fish
Floyd on France
Michael Barry's Food & Drink *Cookbook*

INTRODUCTION

This book is not a directory nor a textbook of French cooking; nor does it reflect the enormous skills of the great modern French chefs like Joel Robuchon or Paul Bocuse who, along with so many others, have lifted French cuisine to dazzling heights of excellence. My book, *Floyd on France*, is a highly personal selection of some favourite dishes that I have enjoyed over long periods spent in France.

The recipes that I have chosen to include in *Floyd on France* show a strong regional bias, and for the main part are the kind of dishes that you would eat if you stayed with a French family or might enjoy in simple but well-run, often family-run, hotels and restaurants. Before I go over the top in praise of simple French provincial cooking, I must say that it is, like many things, an endangered species: you need only read Elizabeth David's *French Provincial Cooking*, written nearly thirty years ago, and then take a trip around France today looking for the dishes she so beautifully recommended to discover how things have changed – for the worse. Fast food has marched into the country like an invading army and the French – never slow to look for the main chance – have embraced it willingly, thus further helping to erode the tradition of country cooking. Fashion has also played its part; the introduction of Nouvelle Cuisine swept chefs and diners alike off their feet in waves of gastronomic euphoria – for a while it looked as though the slow-simmering heavy winter stews and the succulent roasts were to become a thing of the past. But with the help of men like Henri Gault the excitement generated by Nouvelle Cuisine has been stemmed, checked, and re-appraised. Now cooks are returning to their roots for inspiration, to revise and modernise the classics of their culinary heritage whilst staying closer to the earth – working with the produce of their region. This is a good and exciting development which creates an environment in which classic provincial cooking – the subject of this book – can live more easily, in the hope of continued support and growth.

An indication of the concern shown by the French towards the erosion of their local culinary traditions may be seen in the actions of many regional tourist boards, who have formed or encouraged the formation of 'save our cooking' groups: hotels and restaurants are awarded accolades and given publicity and support if they go out of their way to produce regional specialities. Help and encouragement is also given to French gastronomy, at all levels, by both local and national government; keen as they are to make money, the French realise that standards must be maintained and constantly upgraded. It is a pity that the same does not happen in Britain. When I become king or emperor, or even minister of tourism, there will be swingeing changes, I can tell you. I digress. But all the bureaucratic assistance in the world will do little without the willing cooperation of the cooks and hoteliers themselves. And if there is one single factor that elevates French cooking above its rivals, it is the fierce pride that the French cook takes in his or her work.

The pride, so evident in the professional environment, is also to be found in the domestic kitchen. The average French home, unlike its equivalent in Britain, does not have a sumptuous modern fitted kitchen, crammed, like some gastronomic space-shuttle, with the latest state-of-the-art social technology. Nor does it have shelves groaning with cookery books! Instead you will find utensils lovingly maintained: a salad shaker (no Frenchman or Frenchwoman would waste good olive oil on a wet lettuce and risk a diluted vinaigrette), a special pan for omelettes, a griddle just for grills, a fish kettle, sharp knives, a big earthenware pot especially for the daubes or chicken casseroles, a sauce separator, a huge enamel pot *à faire tout* (cook-all) so beloved of the French for soups, and a steamer for asparagus. And if this sounds like a catalogue for a kitchen shop, well, it doesn't feel that way there – just the rudimentary (as the French would say) tools of the trade.

Then there is the larder. Here you would find a piece of home-cured bacon (rather than a packet of sliced streaky) hanging ready for cutting into lardons or batons so indispensable for the myriad stews and potées. If it is a country larder, you might find a whole cured ham and sausage, permanently on hand for an hors d'oeuvre or a light lunch or supper. Cured pig's ears and trotters may hang from the ceiling, ready to pop into soups or stews, in preference to the ubiquitous stock cube. But there will be packets of instant Madeira jelly or aspic, jars of tomato purée and sea salt. There will be supplies of lard, duck or goose grease and a variety of oils from sunflower to olive for salads and shallow-frying. Dry stores will include vermicelli and other pasta, rices, pulses, and a variety of dried white beans. There will be home-made, or at least locally acquired, preserves of duck or goose, terrines and pâtés, jars of preserved fruit and bottles of eau de vie, vinegars and herb-flavoured oils. There will always be onions, shallots and, of course, garlic. The freezer will store carcasses, giblets and calf's feet for enriching or for making soups or simple meals of beans and vegetables. There will be containers of homemade fish soup. And, despite all this, there is no clutter; no studied arrangement of artifacts and bottles with posh labels. Probably the cooker will be old and simple, the walls plain, and there will be a cloth on the table, covered by a workaday oilcloth at all times. There will be a bon-bon or cubitainer of wine from the cooperative for day-to-day drinking and a few bottles of something good from the region for high days and holidays. And always a bottle or two of sparkling wine or champagne, which the French love to drink with a simple dessert after a celebration dinner.

Though huge supermarkets do big business in France and frozen food is as prevalent there as anywhere else, the French cook still shops on a daily basis, probing, prodding, equally pleased to buy tripe or foie gras, best fillet steak or the cheapest cut of ham. There is no snob attitude towards what we often think of as the lesser cuts!

Cooking is an art and patience a virtue. Patience is an essential attribute for all good cooks; patience, and the all-important ability to shop first and *then* decide on the dish to cook, which will depend on season, price, availability, and so on. These are the hallmarks of a successful and practical cook. There is no mystery. Careful shopping, fresh ingredients and an unhurried approach are nearly all you need. There is one more thing – love. Love for food and love for those you invite to your table. With a combination of these things you can be an artist – not perhaps in the representational style of a Dutch master, but rather more like Gauguin, the naive, or Van Gogh, the impressionist. Plates or pictures of sunshine taste of happiness and love. This is the philosophy of the French and it is my philosophy.

Finally, I would like to leave you with the thought that we have had in the last few years Cuisine Nouvelle, Cuisine Moderne, Cuisine Verte, Cuisine à L'eau. Brilliant though they all are, it is time to welcome the newest cooking: retro cuisine – Floyd's way (get it?).

NB Remember, dear friends, that cooking is an art not a science: all the timings and ingredients are approximate and should not be regarded as gospel handed down from on high. And oven temperatures are approximate, too. I only cook in low, medium-hot, or very hot ovens! Temperatures vary from oven to oven, so don't treat the temperature guides I give with the recipes as infallible – your knowledge of your own oven is the most reliable indicator.

THE PRINCIPAL GASTRONOMIC REGIONS OF FRANCE

Alsace

Alsace, a fruit-growing region in the east of France, is celebrated for its jams and preserves, and for its fruit liqueurs. Choucroute (pickled cabbage) and foie gras are local delicacies.

Auvergne

The green mountain pastures of the Auvergne on the eastern slope of the Massif Central are famous for cheeses, among them Cantal and Bleu d'Auvergne. Regional dishes include Coq au vin, sheep's trotters, and ham with lentils.

Basque Country

The Basque Country lies in the Pyrenees, with its coastline on the Atlantic. It is famous for its mountain-cured hams and for its fish dishes. Strong seasoning characterises Basque cuisine, as in Piperade, a dish of sautéed peppers, onions and tomatoes cooked with eggs.

Brittany

The jagged coastline of Brittany juts out into the Atlantic, and its excellent seafood – particularly its lobsters, mussels and oysters – is particularly enjoyed. The other great speciality of the region are its crêpes and galettes.

Burgundy

Burgundy is a bit of France we all rush through on the way south. Stop next time – it's a beautiful and varied countryside and its cuisine is famous for its beef, and for its red wine sauces. Snails are also a speciality.

Charentes

The Charentes estuary just north of Bordeaux is the home of Cognac and is also renowned for its seafood, particularly oysters and mussels: Mouclade and Chaudrée are brilliant dishes that should not be missed.

Languedoc

Squeezed between the Massif Central and the Mediterranean, Languedoc is yet another region of mountain and coast. Delicious lamb pies, known as Petits pâtés de Pézenas, come from here. It is also famous for Cassoulet, one of the great country dishes of France.

Lorraine

Lorraine, in the Vosges mountains in north-eastern France, is a region of dairy farms and orchards, with a cuisine to match. Its most famous dish is the much-abused Quiche. If properly made, it's out of this world.

Normandy

Much of the Normandy countryside is like the west of England, particularly Devon and Hereford, with lush meadows, black and white half-timbered cottages, and cider apple orchards. Cream and Calvados (the local applejack) feature in the regional cuisine.

Périgord

Périgord on the western slopes of the Massif Central, is one of the most heavily wooded areas of France, and its cuisine is full of the earthy flavours of its forests; walnuts, delicious mushrooms, magnificently flavoured truffles. Preserved goose and foie gras are local specialities.

Provence

The cusine of Provence is based on sun, olive oil and garlic – all of them poured forth in unstinted measures. Its rich fish stews are famous – Bouillabaisse, Bourride and Brandade de morue among them. Tomatoes, aubergines and courgettes are used in generous abundance too.

Savoy

The cuisine of the French Alpine region of Savoy is relatively uncomplicated, relying mainly on fresh local produce – cheeses (Emmenthal, Reblochon, Beaufort), freshwater fish from the lakes, forest mushrooms and fruit.

STOCK AND SAUCES

Most of the sauces that follow are simplicity itself to prepare, despite all those myths about curdling mayonnaises, particularly if you follow my quick and easy, foolproof instructions. So don't be afraid to try them.

The sauces here relate to specific dishes described later in the book, but why not risk a bit of experimentation of your own? A well-chosen sauce can lift a good, honest dish into something really brilliant – the important thing to remember, though, is never to swamp the meat or fish with the sauce that is supposed to be accompanying it. Three or four tablespoons per helping should generally be quite enough.

BASIC FISH STOCK

1 kg (2 lb) fish trimmings
  (bones, head, etc.)
1 onion, chopped
1 carrot, chopped
Celery leaves or 1 leek,
  chopped

1 tablespoon peppercorns
150 ml (5 fl oz) dry white
  wine
1 bouquet garni

Put all the ingredients in a large pan, add 1 litre (2 pints) water and bring to the boil. Simmer for 30 minutes.

Strain through muslin or a very fine sieve and taste. If it is too bland, return to the heat and reduce until the flavour is to your liking.

BÉCHAMEL SAUCE

50 g (2 oz) butter
3 tablespoons flour
500 ml (17 fl oz) milk
Salt and pepper
1 slice onion

1 bayleaf
1 slice carrot
1 sprig parsley
Pinch of grated nutmeg

Melt the butter and stir in the flour. Cook gently for 2 or 3 minutes without burning.

Put all the remaining ingredients in a separate pan, bring the milk to the boil, then remove from the heat and leave to stand for 5 minutes. Strain.

Pour the milk into the flour and butter over a low heat, stirring with a whisk. Simmer gently for 20 minutes, whisking occasionally until you have a thick creamy sauce.

VELOUTÉ

A velouté is a basic white sauce which can be made from either, say, chicken or veal stock, or from fish stock.

SERVES 6

40 g (1½ oz) butter	*600 ml (1 pint) fish stock*
40 g (1½ oz) flour	*(see opposite page)*

Melt the butter in a pan and stir in the flour until you have a smooth white paste. Pour in the boiling fish or meat stock, stirring as you do so. Bring to the boil and allow to simmer for about 40 minutes. Strain through a fine sieve.

This simple sauce can now be served on its own, or enriched with cream or flavoured with grated cheese, or used in a more sophisticated sauce, such as *Shellfish Sauce* (see page 19).

WHITE WINE SAUCE for FISH

This sauce is fairly simple to prepare, but has a sophisticated flavour. For a meat dish, chicken or veal stock can be used instead of fish stock.

SERVES 6

25 ml (1 fl oz) strong fish stock (basic fish stock reduced by at least two-thirds, so that when chilled it sets like a jelly)

600 ml (1 pint) fish velouté (see preceding recipe)
2 egg yolks, beaten
75 g (3 oz) butter

Mix the strong fish stock and the velouté together and simmer gently until reduced by one-third. Over a very low heat beat in the egg yolks followed by the butter in little pieces.

SHALLOT VINAIGRETTE

SERVES UP TO 8

150 ml (5 fl oz) wine vinegar
3 shallots, finely chopped

1 tablespoon nut oil
2 pinches of salt
Pepper

Beat everything together and leave at room temperature for a couple of hours before stirring again and serving.

SHELLFISH SAUCE

This is a great sauce for things like fish terrines and plain white fish fillets.

SERVES 6

25 g (1 oz) onion, finely chopped
25 g (1 oz) carrot, finely chopped
25 g (1 oz) butter
6 freshwater crayfish with shells on, or the crushed-up shells of 1 lobster

250 ml (8 fl oz) Cognac
50 ml (2 fl oz) dry white wine
600 ml (1 pint) fish velouté (see page 17)
50 g (2 oz) tomatoes, chopped
15 g (½ oz) tomato purée
Salt and pepper

Fry the onion and carrot in butter until they turn golden. Add the crayfish, or pieces of lobster shell. Flame with the Cognac and pour in the white wine. Let this mixture reduce by about a third. Add the fish velouté and simmer gently. Next add the tomatoes and tomato purée, salt and pepper, and cook for a further 30 minutes.

Whack the whole lot through a food processor or liquidiser and strain through a very fine sieve.

BUTTER SAUCE

This is a super sauce to serve with all kinds of vegetables, white meats and fish.

SERVES 8

75 g (3 oz) shallots, finely chopped
150 ml (5 fl oz) wine vinegar

Fine salt
Pepper
300 g (10 oz) butter, cut into small pieces

Put the shallots and vinegar into a saucepan and bubble up until you have half the original quantity. Add salt and pepper. Turn down the heat and, whisking furiously all the while, add the butter, piece by piece, until you have a nice creamy sauce, which must be served immediately.

FRESH TOMATO SAUCE

1 onion, finely chopped
5 cloves garlic, crushed
4 tablespoons olive oil
750 g (1½ lb) ripe tomatoes, roughly chopped
1 tablespoon white sugar

2 tablespoons fruit-flavoured vinegar (preferably raspberry)
1 tablespoon parsley, chopped
1 tablespoon basil, chopped
Salt and pepper

Sauté the onion and garlic in olive oil until they are golden. Add the rest of the ingredients and about 300 ml (10 fl oz) water and simmer gently for at least 30 minutes.

This can be eaten hot or cold, as required.

Easy mayonnaise

If you are to serve the mayonnaise straight, you must use the best olive oil that you can afford. If you intend to add herbs to it, as for Tartare Sauce, substitute a blander corn or nut oil for part of the olive oil. People get really upset about making simple mayonnaise. It's quite easy: here is the all-purpose, never-fail Floyd technique. (The traditional method is given in the following recipe.)

6 eggs (at room
   temperature)
Juice of 1 or 2 lemons
1 teaspoon wine vinegar

Salt and pepper
1 litre (2 pints) olive oil (at
   room temperature)

Break the eggs into a food processor or liquidiser and add all the other ingredients except the oil. Turn the machine on to maximum for 30 to 40 seconds until the eggs are really foaming. Pour the oil in evenly for a couple of minutes with the machine still on.

If by any chance the mayonnaise is too thick, turn the machine on again at half-speed and dribble in some tepid water. This is a large amount of mayonnaise, I know, but you can bottle the remainder.

TRADITIONAL MAYONNAISE

1 egg yolk (at room
   temperature)
1 teaspoon mustard
175 ml (6 fl oz) nut oil

1 teaspoon cider vinegar
3 pinches of salt
Finely ground pepper

In a bowl mix the egg yolk and mustard together with a
wooden spoon. Keep stirring while you add the oil in a thin
stream until you have the right consistency. Stir in the vinegar and salt and pepper.

EASY HOLLANDAISE SAUCE

Cookery writers and chefs of yesterday terrified the living
daylights out of people with their old wives' tales about egg
liaison sauces. Ignore all this and follow me.

750 g (1½ lb) unsalted
   butter
6 eggs

Juice of 1 lemon
Pepper

Melt the butter in a pan with a pouring lip. Put the eggs
(unseparated) with the lemon juice and pepper into a food
processor and turn on. Pour the hot melted butter evenly into
the whisking eggs until the sauce has thickened. To keep
warm, place over a pan of recently boiled water.

   And that, my little gastronauts, is that. For variations you
can add blanched sorrel leaves, finely chopped fresh mint and
other herbs as you wish.

AÏOLI

---

8 cloves garlic
2 egg yolks
450 ml (15 fl oz) good-
    quality olive oil

Juice of 1 lemon
Salt and pepper

Crush the garlic into a pestle and mortar; then, with a whisk, stir in the egg yolks. Drizzle the olive oil in, stirring constantly, until you have a thick yellow mayonnaise. Stir in the lemon juice and add salt and pepper to taste.

Alternatively, put all the ingredients except the olive oil into a food processor or liquidiser, turn on and drizzle in the oil. This method is not as good as the former, but much quicker.

ROUILLE

---

2 large cloves garlic, finely
    chopped
Stale bread, soaked in
    water and squeezed out
    to the size of a large
    walnut

2 red chillies, finely chopped
2–3 tablespoons olive oil

Grind the chopped garlic to a paste in a pestle and mortar. Add the nut of bread and the chopped chillies and pound until smooth. Whisk in the olive oil, until the mixture looks like a smooth shiny red mustard.

PRESERVED DISHES

I know everybody has a deep freeze and they are great. You can make *Coq au Vin* or pâtés and you can pick vegetables from your garden and pop them into your freezer and that's fine – it makes life easy. But, you know, there is no way that a freezer can ever replace or indeed even help to create the wonderful food, the conserves and preserves of our grandmothers' larders.

So why don't we sometimes, when by happy chance we have a rabbit we cannot eat that day, or see a tree full of chestnuts on a late summer Sunday walk, preserve these little dreams for use at some other time? I, for example, hate frozen peas and have never eaten a fresh garden pea that was properly cooked or tasted nice, but I have to admit that I really love those tinned French peas that have lettuce in them and are pale green – almost grey – in colour and, according to the worthy executives of large food companies, are unsaleable in this country because of their pallor. The old motto (ho-ho), 'Never mind the quality, feel the colour', still presides in this country, but even better than tinned French peas (petits pois) are home-preserved peas.

What about making wonderful quince jelly to serve later with a winter roast leg of pork or saddle of hare? What about potted pork (rillettes), tasty and fatty, spread on thick toast? I am trying to tell you about the joy of preparing food in a natural and pure way, which will give you both satisfaction to make and great pleasure to eat.

THE SIMPLE ART OF STERILISING

If you are going to preserve food, you must sterilise it, and there are some elementary and vital rules to follow.

1 Make sure that your steriliser is in perfect condition: that is, it's not rusty or damaged in any way. And make sure it's perfectly clean.

2 Because you are going to put all your preserved foods in glass jars, make sure that each time you use them you have a brand new rubber ring.

3 Only ever use the freshest and purest – in short the best – ingredients.

4 Always ensure that the glass jars are immaculately clean and dry before use.

5 Never fill the glass jars to the top. Always leave space of about 2 or 3 cm (½ to 1 in.).

6 Follow precisely the temperatures and cooking durations given in the recipe. The second the required temperature has been reached, turn down the heat a fraction so that the temperature remains constant.

7 Always ensure that the glass jars are well covered with water in the steriliser.

8 Always keep preserved foods in a cool dry place – if possible, with a constant temperature: that is, a larder. Never let them be exposed to direct bright light, be it sunshine or electricity.

OK, that's enough polytechnic-type lecturing. What follows now are a few of my own favourite preserved dishes.

COULIS DE TOMATES
Puréed Tomatoes

———

It is always hard to get that sweet sunshine feeling of super-ripe tomatoes into dishes like Spaghetti Bolognese, a tomato omelette, or just a plate of fresh pasta or a pizza in the middle of winter, when tomatoes are hard and tasteless. So, puréed tomatoes preserved in the height of summer are a useful ingredient for many winter dishes.

1 kg (2 lb) sweet ripe tomatoes, quartered	*1 clove garlic*
	1 bouquet garni
1 onion	*Salt and pepper*

Put all the ingredients into a pan without water and cook over a low heat, stirring from time to time. After 45 minutes, remove the onion and the bouquet garni and purée the tomatoes.

Pour into glass jars and sterilise for 30 minutes at 100°C (212°F).

KETCHUP À LA TOMATE
Tomato Ketchup

———

Homemade tomato ketchup is really something else. My late grandfather, Harold Margetts, threw the household into confusion when, once or twice a year, he decided to make this excellent sauce. But it was worth it because it really cheers up a slice of cold meat when you cannot be bothered to cook or, indeed, even a cheese sandwich, and it's brilliant with a

slice of crisply cooked belly of pork. It leaves the stuff in
supermarkets right in the second division and struggling for
relegation.

You make as much or as little as you like. We will assume:

1 kg (2 lb) tomatoes, peeled,
de-seeded and finely
chopped
500 g (1 lb) onions, finely
chopped
1 kg (2 lb) red peppers, de-
seeded and finely chopped
Oil for frying
75 g (3 oz) sugar

3 large cloves garlic, finely
chopped
Salt and pepper
1 chilli, finely chopped
1 tablespoon mustard powder
1 tablespoon paprika
2 wine glasses vinegar
Large pinch of powdered
cloves

Cook the three vegetables in oil for about 45 minutes, or until
they are soft and purée-like. Strain through a fine sieve to
make sure that there are no seeds left. Put back into the pan.
Add all the other ingredients and cook over a low heat for
about 2 hours, stirring from time to time with a wooden
spoon, until you have a thick red sauce. Taste it at this stage.
You might like to increase the hot spiciness, or add a dash of
vinegar, or sweeten it up with a spoonful or two of sugar.

Now, here is the real artisanal bit. You do not use the
rubber-ringed preserving jars for this; instead you use some
posey looking wine bottles which you have, of course,
thoroughly washed in boiling water and dried. Fill the bottles
to within about 5 cm (2 in.) from the top. Cork the bottles
with new corks that you have dipped two or three times into
boiling water and dried. Next, tie string around the neck of
the bottles and corks (as if they were champagne corks)
so that they don't come out, and sterilise for 20 minutes at
100°C (212°F).

I hope somebody in your household has the kind of writing that will look really good on the little label you are going to stick on the bottle when the sauce has cooled!

MARRONS EN CONSERVE
Preserved Chestnuts

Make an incision into the skin of each chestnut. Drop them into boiling water for 5 minutes to blanch. Lift off both skins: the tough outside and soft inner skin. Put them into a 1 litre (2 pint) glass jar with nothing else. Seal the jar and sterilise for 1½ hours at 150°C (302°F).

CITRONS CONFITS
Preserved Lemons

These are really good for putting on fish and chicken kebabs. They are used a lot in Moroccan cookery, and are great in stews and curries.

Lemons   *Salt*

Wash and dry the lemons and cut into quarters. Salt the insides and push the fruit back together. Put into a glass jar and pour in cold water until you have covered about two-thirds of the lemons. Sterilise for 1 hour at 100°C (212°F).

Marmelade d'OIGNONS
Onion Marmalade

Like the pickled cherries (p. 31), this is terrific with cold meat and charcuterie. It is also good on little squares of toast to nibble with an aperitif.

1 kg (2 lb) onions, finely sliced	*2 bayleaves*
4 tablespoons olive oil	*1 teaspoon ground black pepper*
125 g (4 oz) caster sugar	*1 teaspoon salt*
300 ml (10 fl oz) white wine vinegar	*2 tablespoons tomato purée*
4 cloves	*Large pinch of cayenne pepper*

Sauté the onions in the olive oil until they become translucent. Add all the other ingredients, cover and cook gently for about 1 hour. Check the seasoning and add a little more sugar, salt or pepper as necessary. Continue cooking gently until the mixture has reached a marmalade-like consistency. When cool, pour off any oil and store in jars.

HUILE AUX HERBES
Spicy Herb Oil

This is really useful for all grills, especially for barbecues. In Provence there is a bottle of this oil on every table in every pizzeria, because the natives like to shake a dash or two over the pizzas as they eat them.

30 black peppercorns
6 bayleaves
3 sprigs rosemary
4 sprigs thyme
4 red chillies

4–5 sage leaves
1/2 teaspoon fennel seeds
20 coriander seeds
Best-quality olive oil

Put all the herbs and spices into a 1-litre wine bottle. Fill with olive oil and seal with a cork. Leave for 2 weeks before using.

PETITS POIS À L'ÉTUVÉES
Preserved Fresh Peas

It is best to pick the peas when they are young and small. You might win a prize at the village produce show for peas as big as marbles, but you won't make friends with people's tummies!

500 g (1 lb) peas (shelled
    weight)
65 g (2½ oz) butter
6 tiny onions, peeled

1 small lettuce, or the heart
    of a bigger one, cut into
    quarters
15 g (½ oz) salt
15 g (½ oz) sugar

Put all the ingredients into a saucepan with a lid and cook over a low heat. Do not add any water because the peas will cook in their natural juices with the butter. Shake the pan from time to time, so that they cook evenly. (By the way, do not stir with a spoon or a fork, because it will damage the peas.) When they are cooked, put the peas into glass jars and sterilise for 1½ hours at 150°C (302°F).

CERISES AIGRES DOUCES
Pickled Cherries

These sweet-sour pickled cherries make an excellent accompaniment to any cold roast meats, pâtés, terrines and so on, and are good to nibble while you are drinking an aperitif.

2.25 kg (5 lb) cherries in perfect condition	10 black peppercorns
Sugar	3 cloves
1.4 litres (2½ pints) white wine vinegar	1 bayleaf
	Salt

Trim the stalks of the cherries so that there is only 6 mm (¼ in.) protruding from the fruit. Wash and dry the cherries thoroughly, put into glass jars and sprinkle lightly with sugar.

Meanwhile, bring 1 litre (2 pints) of the vinegar to the boil with the peppercorns, cloves and bayleaf, add a little salt and boil for a further 5 minutes or so. Allow to cool. Pour the liquid over the cherries and leave to marinate for 24 hours.

The next day, strain the marinade from the cherries, re-heat it, add the remaining vinegar and boil for 5 minutes. Allow to cool, cover the cherries and seal the jars.

Leave for at least 1 month before eating.

RILLETTES DE PORC
Potted Pork

———

This is a very simple dish. Really it is a meat spread and is absolutely terrific spread over pieces of hot toast. You will find it on menus, particularly in the Loire valley and throughout France generally. It can be made from goose, duck or rabbit.

1 kg (2 lb) shoulder of pork, diced
750 g (1½ lb) fresh pork fat, diced

75 g (3 oz) salt
15 g (½ oz) pepper

Put the meat and fat into a heavy pan and cook gently for about 4 hours. When the pieces of meat are very well cooked, but not burned or brown, pour off the fat and reserve. Shred the meat using a couple of forks; do not use a food processor because it turns the meat into a paste. Add lots of salt and pepper. Put the shredded meat into glass jars and allow to cool.

Melt the reserved fat and cover the meat with it. Cool again. Seal the jars and store in a cool place.

Pickled Cherries (see page 31) go very well with this dish.

CONFIT D'OIE
Preserved Goose

It's very simple and well worthwhile to preserve a goose. You can use it in a *Cassoulet* (see page 209); you can simply re-heat it in the oven and serve with a bitter salad of endives, watercress and red lettuce; you can use the grease to enrich a soup or casserole; or you can even pop a piece of it into a simple soup, like the *Vegetable Soup* on page 48, to make it into a substantial dish.

All you need is a plump and fatty goose and some sea salt. Joint the goose first into prime pieces – that is, leg and breast – and reserve all the fat. These would be the pieces to use for a cassoulet or a main-course dish. Then butcher the other bits – pieces of carcass, wings and so on – into uniform morsels, so that they can be preserved apart from the prime cuts and used for, say, enriching soups.

Cover the goose pieces in sea salt and leave for 48 hours in a cool place. Melt all the goose fat in a large pan and simmer the pieces in it for about 2 hours or until, when pricked, no blood runs from them. Remove the pieces and strain the goose fat through a fine sieve. Now put, say, 1 leg and 1 breast into a preserving jar, and perhaps 5 or 6 lesser morsels into another jar, and cover them with melted strained fat – continue this until you have used up all the goose. (If by any chance there is not enough goose fat to go round, mix in some melted best-quality lard.)

Now sterilise the jars for 1½ hours at 102°C (216°F). They will keep for 2 or 3 months in a cool place; or, of course, you could freeze them if the storage jars are the type that can be frozen.

FROMAGE DE TÊTE
Brawn

Brawn is no longer popular in Britain, which is a pity because, chopped up and served with sliced gherkins, chopped fresh parsley, capers and a dash of vinaigrette, it makes a wonderful starter. You often find brawn on inexpensive French menus.

½ pig's head	1 large onion
4 pig's trotters	Salt and pepper
1 pig's tail	2 bayleaves
1 wine glass vinegar	2 cloves garlic
1 litre (2 pints) dry rosé wine	2 shallots

Rinse the meat under running water for a long time. Cover with fresh water, add the vinegar and bring to the boil. Strain off any scum which has accumulated on top. Take out the meat and re-cover in fresh water and half the wine. Add the onion, salt, pepper and 1 bayleaf. Simmer gently until the meat falls easily away from the bones. Allow to cool.

Remove all the meat from the bones and shred it. Strain the stock. Put the meat only back into a saucepan and add the remaining wine. Put the garlic, shallots and remaining bayleaf into a little muslin bag and add to the saucepan. Cook for 20 to 30 minutes, or until the liquid is well reduced, so that when cold it turns to jelly. Throw away the muslin bag. Pop the contents of the pan into glass jars and sterilise for 1½ hours at 110°C (230°F). Allow to cool and refrigerate.

TERRINE DE LAPIN
Rabbit Terrine

Here is the rabbit dish I was talking about in the introduction
to this section.

1 kg (2 lb) rabbit meat.	*Salt and pepper*
White wine	*Pinch of dried mixed*
1 calf's foot	*Provençal herbs*
1 sprig thyme	*800 g (1¾ lb) belly of pork,*
Bayleaves	*minced*
2 shallots, finely chopped	*Thin slices bacon*
1 onion, chopped	

Remove the bones from the rabbit and reserve. Cut the meat
into cubes and marinate for at least 2 hours in white wine.

In the meantime, prepare a stock with the calf's foot, rabbit
bones, thyme, 1 bayleaf, shallots, onion and 1 litre (2 pints)
water. Season with salt and pepper and leave to simmer and
reduce until you have a cup or two of really strong stock.

Mince the rabbit meat, season with salt and pepper and a
pinch of dried Provençal herbs. Mix with the minced pork
and put into glass jars. Put a bayleaf and a thin slice of bacon
on top of each one.

Sterilise for 2 hours at 100°C (212°F).

PÂTÉ ET GELÉE DE COINGS
Quince Jellies and Quince Jelly

---

5 kg (10 lb) firm ripe   Sugar
  quinces, peeled and
  quartered

For the jellies:
Reserve the pith and pips from the quartered quinces by placing them in a bowl and covering with water to prevent discoloration. Put the quince quarters in a large saucepan and cover with water, bring to the boil and simmer for about 20 to 30 minutes until tender. Drain the fruit and reserve the liquid. Push the fruit through a fine sieve or purée in a liquidiser. Return the purée to the pan and add the same weight in sugar. Simmer over a low heat, stirring constantly until the mixture is a deep coppery gold.

Pour the mixture on to several platters. Allow to cool and cover with teatowels. Leave undisturbed for 2 to 3 weeks. Cut into pieces and roll in sugar. The jellies can be kept indefinitely in airtight jars.

These and other fruit jellies are often made for Christmas and eaten as one of the thirteen Christmas desserts.

For the jelly:
Strain the reserved pips and pith and add to the liquid that the quinces were cooked in. Boil for 20 minutes and strain through a fine cloth (an old pillowcase is ideal for this if you don't have a proper jelly bag). Squeeze the cloth well to ensure that you've got all the pieces.

Return the quince juice to the saucepan and add the same weight in sugar. Boil for a further 20 minutes and test by

putting a small teaspoonful on to a cold plate. It should set
and be a lovely coppery colour. Pour into sterilised jars and
seal. Great with meat and game. (From Auvergne.)

PÂTÉ DE FRUIT
Blackcurrant or Blackberry Fruit Pâté

This is the French home-made version of Melton-Mowbray
fruits made with pure fruit and sugar with no colouring or
flavouring added. It is indispensable as one of the thirteen
desserts (representing Jesus and the twelve apostles) that are
eaten in France at Christmas. Naturally you make them well
before Christmas and store them in a cool dry place in airtight
tins.

You will need enough fresh fruit to produce 500 g (1 lb)
pure fruit concentrate. Discard any stalks, leaves or general
debris. Cook in a little hot water until the fruit is pulped.
Squeeze the fruit through muslin – no pips or bits of skin
must remain!

For every 500 g (1 lb) fruit concentrate you need 500 g
(1 lb) caster sugar. Heat them together in a pan until the
preparation thickens and peels off the sides of the pan. Cover
a shallow tray or trays with crystallised sugar and pour the
mixture in so it's about 1 cm (½ in.) deep. Allow it to level
out and sprinkle the top with more crystallised sugar. Leave
the tray(s) in a cool airy place for 4 or 5 days until dry. Cut
into little rectangles and store in airtight tins until you want to
eat the fruit pâté, which would probably be that same day if I
were you.

POIRES AU VIN ROUGE
Pears in Red Wine

——

This is a jolly useful emergency dessert.

1 stick cinnamon
Pinch of black pepper
1–2 cloves
1 kg (2 lb) pears, peeled,
  quartered and de-pipped

1 litre (2 pints) good red
  wine (remember that
  wine not good enough to
  drink is not good enough
  to cook with)

Tie the spices into a little muslin bag and put with the pears into a stainless-steel or enamel saucepan. Cover with red wine. Bring to the boil, then turn down the heat and leave to simmer for 20 minutes or until the pears have taken on the colour and flavour of the wine.

Allow to cool. Remove the muslin spice bag and put the pears into a glass jar. Cover with wine and sterilise at 85°C (185°F) for 10 minutes.

SOUPS

H ave you ever analysed what television adver-
tisers do to attempt to convince us of what a
home is? It's a place with a glowing artificial fire
with imitation wood; it's a poky bathroom with
scalding hot water; it's a gleaming lavatory basin; it's loft
insulation or windows with a feather floating down them. It's
electric cookers and deep freezes full of unmentionable produce; it's pieces of raw meat bubbling in some sauce mix
stirred in smilingly by some naïve actress. A home isn't any of
those things. A home is a place where a pot of fresh soup
simmers gently on the hob, filling the kitchen with the soft
aroma of lentils and ham bones and filling your heart, and
later your tummy, with joy.

And what about those terrible ads in colour supplements,
where you add little bits to a tin of liquid they call soup – ugh!

I would travel night and day, running all the way, for a
good homemade soup, fresh bread, wine and cheese. So
throw away your tins and packets, dear gastronauts, and have
a whirl at some of these recipes.

BOUILLABAISSE DE PÊCHEUR
Fisherman's Soup

SERVES 4

2 leeks, chopped
1 onion, chopped
1 head garlic, minced
1 small handful parsley,
   chopped
2 tomatoes, peeled, de-
   seeded and chopped
Fennel fronds, chopped
1 bayleaf
Cayenne pepper
Olive oil for frying

1 tablespoon tomato purée
Salt and pepper
Pinch of saffron
1 kg (2 lb) mixed fish
   (conger eel, rascasse,
   rockfish, weever), gutted
   and washed
4 medium potatoes, peeled
   and thickly sliced
Garlic croutons

In a large saucepan, gently fry the leeks, onion, garlic, parsley, tomatoes, fennel, bayleaf and cayenne pepper in the oil. Add the tomato purée and 2 litres (3½ pints) cold water. Season with salt and pepper and sprinkle in the saffron. Add all the fish and cover with the potato slices. Bring to the boil and cook over a high heat until the potatoes are done. Serve with garlic croutons. (From Provence.)

SOUPE DE POISSON À LA SÉTOISE
Fish Soup with Vermicelli

SERVES 4

1 kg (2 lb) fish (bass,
  whiting, dab, mullet,
  hogfish, small crabs,
  langoustes)
2 onions, chopped
4 cloves garlic, minced
2 leeks, chopped
2 tomatoes, peeled, de-
  seeded and chopped

Olive oil
1 bottle dry white wine
1 red pepper, de-seeded and
  chopped
1 bouquet garni
Salt and pepper
125 g (4 oz) vermicelli
Aïoli (see page 23)

Gut and wash the fish and cut into chunks. Split the langoustes down the middle. The crabs should be cooked whole.

Fry the onions, garlic, leeks and tomatoes in the olive oil. Add the wine, red pepper, bouquet garni and 750 ml (1¼ pints) water. Bring to the boil and add all the fish. Return to the boil and simmer, covered, for 15 minutes.

When the fish are cooked, remove them and keep warm. Sieve the court bouillon and bring back to the boil. Season with salt and pepper and add the vermicelli. Serve as soon as the vermicelli are done. Serve the fish afterwards with the *Aïoli* or a *tomato sauce*. (From Languedoc.)

Soupe de Poisson à la Floyd
Floyd's Fish Soup

WILL MAKE A FEAST FOR 6

*1.1 kg (2¼ lb) mixed fish
(which must include
gurnard or red mullet,
small soft-shelled crabs,
conger eel, John Dory, a
handful of langoustines, a
piece of dogfish)*
2 leeks, chopped
*2 large ripe tomatoes,
chopped*
2 onions, chopped
*2 large cloves garlic,
crushed*

Olive oil for frying
1 bayleaf
1 frond fennel
*1 teaspoon grated orange
rind*
Salt and pepper
125 g (4 oz) small vermicelli
1 sachet saffron
Rouille (see page 23)
Aïoli (see page 23)
*150 g (5 oz) Gruyère cheese,
grated*

Gut and wash the whole fish and chop into pieces about 6 cm
(2½ in.) long – head, bones and all. Fry the leeks, tomatoes,
onions and garlic in the oil until soft but not brown. Add 2.3
litres (4 pints) water to the vegetables and bring to the boil.
Now add all the fish, the bayleaf, fennel and orange rind and
cook rapidly for another 15 minutes.

Remove the fish and allow the soup to simmer gently.
Meanwhile, crush or grind the fish in a liquidiser and return
it to the soup. Stir it well and strain the lot through a fine sieve
into another pan. Throw away any bits left in the sieve. The
soup should be smooth, not lumpy, and have no bones or bits
of shell in it.

Bring this strained soup to the boil, season to taste with salt
and pepper and add the vermicelli and saffron. Once the

vermicelli are cooked, the soup is ready. (It is sensible to make the soup well in advance, otherwise you will be exhausted by the time you eat it – in which case do not add the vermicelli until just before serving or it will swell and become glutinous, overwhelming the soup.).

Let your guests add their own *Rouille*, according to their taste, and help themselves to grated cheese, which they also stir in. Tell them to spread the *Aïoli* on bread and dunk it in.

BISQUE DE CREVETTES
Shrimp Bisque

SERVES 6

1 kg (2 lb) live grey shrimps	*200 g (7 oz) tomatoes,*
1 litre (2 pints) milk	*peeled and diced*
325 g (11 oz) potatoes,	*2 cloves garlic, crushed*
peeled and diced	*Salt and pepper*
	Croutons

Chuck everything in a large saucepan and bring to the boil. Simmer uncovered for 1 hour. Whizz in a liquidiser or food processor and pass through a fine sieve.

Serve hot with croutons fried in butter. Couldn't be simpler! (From Charente.)

Soupe de POISSON
Fish Soup

SERVES 6

2 cloves garlic, minced
1 carrot, chopped
1 leek, chopped
2 sticks celery, chopped
2 tomatoes, peeled, de-
  seeded and chopped
2 tablespoons olive oil
1 onion, finely sliced
1 frond fresh fennel or ½
  coffeespoon dried fennel

1 bayleaf
1 kg (2 lb) mixed fish
  (mullet, conger eel,
  girella, hogfish, etc.),
  gutted and washed
Pinch of saffron
Salt and pepper
2 handfuls vermicelli
Gruyère or Parmesan
  cheese, grated

In a large saucepan fry the garlic, carrot, leek, celery and tomatoes in the olive oil. Allow to brown slightly before adding the onion, fennel and the bayleaf. Pour in 2 litres (3½ pints) cold water and bring to the boil. Throw in all the fish and simmer, covered, for 20 minutes.

Process the soup in batches in a blender and carefully strain back into the saucepan. Return to the boil, add the saffron and salt and pepper to taste. Throw in the vermicelli and serve when they are done, with grated Gruyère or Parmesan cheese. (From Provence.)

SOUPE AUX HARICOTS VERTS
Green Bean Soup

SERVES 4 TO 6

Butter for frying
2 thick slices smoked bacon,
    diced
1 onion, finely chopped
1 kg (2 lb) potatoes, peeled
    and diced

1 kg (2 lb) green beans,
    topped, tailed and diced
2 sprigs savory
Salt and pepper
1 tablespoon double cream
1 handful parsley, chopped

Melt the butter in a large saucepan, add the bacon and onion and fry gently until the onions are pale gold. Add the potatoes, green beans, 2 litres (3½ pints) cold water, the savory and pepper. Simmer for 1 hour.

Before serving, put a large dollop of cream and the parsley in a serving bowl. Taste the soup and add salt if necessary. Pour the soup on to the cream and parsley and serve. (From Lorraine.)

SOUPE AUX FÈVES
Broad Bean Soup with Dumplings

SERVES 4

2 medium onions, finely
  chopped
65 g (2½ oz) lard
1.5 kg (3 lb) broad beans,
  shelled
2 sticks celery, chopped
325 g (11 oz) potatoes,
  peeled and cubed

1 bouquet garni (thyme,
  bayleaf, savory, basil,
  parsley)
50 g (2 oz) streaky bacon,
  chopped
4 cloves garlic, chopped
Salt and pepper

For the rouzole:

135 g (4½ oz) bacon,
  chopped
135 g (4½ oz) raw ham,
  chopped
2 eggs, beaten

3 cloves garlic
75 g (3 oz) dried breadcrumbs
1 sprig mint, chopped
Salt and pepper
Lard for frying

Fry the onions in the lard until transparent in a large
saucepan, then add 1.1 litres (2¼ pints) boiling water. Toss
in the broad beans, celery, potatoes, bouquet garni, chopped
streaky bacon and garlic. Season, bring to the boil and
simmer, covered, for 2 hours.

While the soup is cooking, prepare the rouzole. Mix all the
ingredients together carefully and allow to rest for 1 hour.

In a large pan fry the rouzole mixture in the lard, forming a
large pancake. When it is cooked and browned, chop into
bite-size pieces and add to the soup 10 minutes before the
cooking time is up. Remove the bouquet garni before serving. (From Languedoc.)

SOUPE AU PISTOU
Vegetable Soup with Basil and Garlic

SERVES 8

5 cloves garlic, chopped
2 tablespoons olive oil
Salt and pepper
500 g (1 lb) fresh white
haricot beans, shelled
500 g (1 lb) fresh red haricot
beans, shelled, or
500 g (1 lb) dried haricot
beans, soaked overnight
(if you can't get fresh
ones)
3 potatoes, peeled and
chopped

500 g (1 lb) courgettes,
peeled and chopped
500 g (1 lb) green beans,
topped and tailed, and
cut in half
500 g (1 lb) broad beans,
shelled
750 g (1½ lb) tomatoes,
peeled, de-seeded and
chopped
2 branches basil, chopped
2 handfuls vermicelli
Gruyère and/or Parmesan
cheese, grated

Fry 2 cloves garlic in 2 tablespoons olive oil. Add 2 litres (3½ pints) cold salted water. Bring to the boil and add the haricots. Simmer for 15 minutes, then add the potatoes, courgettes, green beans, broad beans, and tomatoes. Simmer for 25 minutes.

Meanwhile, mash the basil and remaining garlic together in a mortar and pestle, or in a blender, until you have a thick paste. Stir in a cupful of slightly cooled soup liquid. Add to the rest of the soup. Throw in the vermicelli. Adjust the seasoning and serve with grated Gruyère and/or Parmesan cheese when the vermicelli are done. (From Provence.)

SOUPE À LA SAVOYARDE
Vegetable Soup

SERVES 6

1 kg (2 lb) mixed vegetables
(carrots, leeks, turnips,
cabbage, potatoes), peeled
and roughly chopped

Salt and pepper
10 thin slices white bread
150 g (5 oz) Gruyère cheese,
grated

Bring 2 litres (3½ pints) water to the boil in a large saucepan. Add all the vegetables and salt and pepper. Allow to simmer for 30 minutes, or until all the vegetables are cooked.

Crush the vegetables with a fork and pour the soup into a large casserole. Cover with the slices of bread (overlapping if necessary), sprinkle with the cheese and pop into a hot oven until the top is brown and bubbling. (From Savoy.)

SOUPE AU POTIRON
Pumpkin Soup

SERVES 4

1.5 kg (3 lb) pumpkin flesh,
cut in chunks
5 or 6 medium potatoes,
peeled and cubed

Salt and pepper
4 tablespoons double cream
Garlic croutons

Boil the pumpkin and potatoes in 1.1 litres (2¼ pints) water for 45 minutes. Purée the mixture, add salt and pepper to taste and stir in the cream thoroughly. Serve hot with plenty of croutons rubbed with garlic. (From Auvergne.)

LE TOURIN
Garlic Soup

SERVES 6

2 large onions, finely
   chopped
100 g (3½ oz) butter
1.5 kg (3 lb) tomatoes,
   peeled and chopped
10 cloves garlic, chopped

2 large potatoes, peeled and
   diced
Salt and pepper
6 thin slices stale white
   bread

In a large saucepan brown the onions in the butter, add the other vegetables and cook for 15 minutes. Add 2 litres (3½ pints) water and the salt and pepper. Bring to the boil and simmer for 45 minutes.

Put a slice of bread in the bottom of each warmed soup bowl. Pour the soup over and serve.

In the Périgord they make a similar soup – they just fry garlic and onion in goose grease, add 1 litre (2 pints) water and about 500 g (1 lb) fresh sorrel leaves. They allow this to simmer for about 30 minutes, then stir in 4 eggs to thicken it a little and pour into dishes over slices of stale bread. (From Charente.)

SOUPE AU MILLET
Millet Soup

SERVES 4

1 onion, finely chopped	1 litre (2 pints) chicken
1 tablespoon butter	stock
4 large tablespoons millet or	Salt and pepper
porridge oats	

Gently fry the onion in the butter in a large saucepan. Add
the millet or oats when the onions have turned golden. Add
the chicken stock and simmer 15 minutes, or until the millet
is tender. Season with salt and pepper. (From Lorraine.)

SOUPE À L'OSEILLE À LA CRÈME
Cream of Sorrel Soup

SERVES 6

400 g (14 oz) large sorrel	1 branch thyme
leaves, washed	Salt and pepper
1 shallot, finely chopped	2 eggs
½ clove garlic, finely	150 ml (5 fl oz) double
chopped	cream
125 g (4 oz) butter	Croutons
1 litre (2 pints) milk	

In a large saucepan heat the sorrel, shallot and garlic in
butter. Stir constantly, until you have a homogenous green
mass. Add the milk, thyme, salt and pepper. Simmer until
the sorrel is quite tender. Remove the thyme.

Beat the eggs and cream together. Remove the soup from the heat and pour in the eggs and cream, whisking constantly. Return to a low heat and keep stirring until the soup thickens. Serve with the croutons. (From Normandy.)

SOUPE À L'AIL
Garlic Soup

SERVES 4

1 litre (2 pints) chicken stock	*2 eggs, separated*
	Salt and pepper
8 cloves garlic, minced	*4 slices slightly stale white bread, toasted*
75 g (3 oz) goose, chicken or duck fat	*75 g (3 oz) cheese, grated*
1 bouquet garni	

Bring the stock to the boil. Fry the garlic in the goose fat until golden and pour on the stock. Add the bouquet garni and simmer for 20 minutes.

Remove the bouquet garni. Beat the egg whites lightly and add to the soup. As soon as they have set, remove the soup from the heat. Whisk some of the soup into the egg yolks, little by little, and pour into the rest of the soup. Season with salt and pepper.

Put a slice of toast into the bottom of each soup bowl and cover with the grated cheese. Cut the egg whites in pieces if necessary and pour the soup over the toast. (From Languedoc.)

SOUPE AUX POIS CASSÉS
Split Pea Soup

SERVES 4 TO 6

*500 g (1 lb) split peas,
soaked overnight in cold
water*
1 lettuce, chopped
1 carrot, peeled and diced
*2 potatoes, peeled and
sliced*
2 cloves garlic, chopped

1 onion, chopped
1 bouquet garni
*250 g (8 oz) streaky bacon,
left in one piece*
Salt and pepper
1 smoked sausage
1 glass eau de vie
Croutons

Put the drained split peas, lettuce, carrots, potatoes, garlic, onion, bouquet garni, bacon and pepper into a large saucepan with 2 litres (3½ pints) cold water, bring to the boil and simmer for 1½ hours. Add the sausage 30 minutes before the end of the cooking time.

Remove the bacon and sausage from the soup and slice. Purée the soup, then return the bacon and sausage slices. Add salt, if necessary, and the eau de vie. Warm through and serve with croutons. (From Lorraine.)

SOUPE À LA CARCASSE D'OIE
Goose or Duck Soup

SERVES 6

1 cabbage, coarse outer
   leaves and core removed,
   and cut in four pieces
5 potatoes, peeled and cut
   in chunks
5 carrots, peeled and cut in
   chunks
5 turnips, chopped
2 large onions, each stuck
   with 1 clove
2 cloves garlic
1 large handful haricot
   beans, soaked overnight

Salt and pepper
1 bouquet garni (parsley,
   thyme, bayleaf)
½ glass Verjus
2 tablespoons goose or duck
   fat
1 goose or duck carcass,
   jointed
1 small onion, finely
   chopped
2 tablespoons fine semolina
Garlic croutons

Blanch the cabbage for 10 minutes in boiling water. Half-fill a large saucepan with water and add the potatoes, carrots, turnips, whole onions, garlic, haricot beans, cabbage, salt and pepper. Add the bouquet garni, half the Verjus and 1 tablespoon goose fat. Bring to the boil and simmer for 15 minutes, skimming off any froth if necessary. Add the carcass and simmer for a further 15 minutes. Meanwhile, fry the chopped onion in the remaining goose fat. Stir in the semolina and brown slightly before adding the rest of the Verjus. Pour into the soup and simmer for a further 15 minutes. Serve with the croutons. (From Périgord.)

SOUPE AUX RIVELES
Soup with Alsatian Dumplings

SERVES 6

For the soup:

500 g (1 lb) oxtail	2 turnips, chopped
500 g (1 lb) beef rib bones	Salt and pepper
2 large marrow bones, salted at both ends	Nutmeg
2 large carrots, sliced	Parsley and chervil to garnish

For the dumplings:

150 g (5 oz) flour	½ teaspoon salt
1 tablespoon nut oil	Pinch of nutmeg
3 eggs, beaten	

Put all the soup ingredients into 4 litres (7 pints) cold water. Bring to the boil and simmer for 2 hours. From time to time skim off any scum that might accumulate.

Meanwhile, combine all the dumpling ingredients in a bowl, mix well and roll into a ball. Refrigerate for 30 minutes. Roll out the chilled dough on to a floured board until it is 3–6 mm (⅛–¼ in.) thick. Cut into strips about the size of your little finger.

Strain the beef broth and discard all the bones except the 2 marrow bones. Bring the broth back to a simmer and poach the dumplings in it. They are ready when they float to the surface.

Serve boiling hot, garnished with rounds of marrow extracted from the marrow bones, and with parsley and chervil to sprinkle over each helping. (From Alsace.)

HORS D'OEUVRES
AND
LIGHT DISHES

Cooking should not become a chore. Balance your menus carefully. If you have decided on a complicated hors d'oeuvre, make sure that the dish to follow is easy. When entertaining, really try to make at least one course of the meal a day or two ahead – that way you will stand a chance of actually enjoying yourself on the occasion.

Hors d'oeuvres, of course, can be anything from a stick of celery spread with cream cheese or anchovy paste to a bowl of soup, a light and subtle fish terrine or a refined cheese soufflé. Here I have simply selected my personal favourites gleaned from scouring France at a pretty ordinary level: discovering dishes that human beings – not superstar chefs – prepare.

PÂTÉ DE TRUITES
Trout Pâté

SERVES 6

275 g (9 oz) trout, filleted
  and gently beaten
75 ml (3 fl oz) Moselle wine
1 branch parsley, chopped
1 sprig each tarragon,
  chervil, thyme and
  marjoram
2 bayleaves
1 tablespoon chives,
  chopped
1 clove garlic, chopped
1 onion, chopped
1 shallot, chopped

25 g (1 oz) flour
15 g (½ oz) butter
75 ml (3 fl oz) milk
135 g (4½ oz) fresh salmon,
  puréed
3 eggs
3–4 morel mushrooms,
  chopped and sautéed in
  butter
Salt and pepper
300 g (10 oz) flaky pastry
4 tablespoons double cream

Marinate the trout in the wine with all the herbs, garlic, onion and shallot for 24 hours.

Pre-heat the oven to gas mark 6, 200°C (400°F).

Make a thick white sauce with the flour, butter and milk. When it has cooked, mix with the salmon, 2 eggs, the morels and salt and pepper.

Carefully strain the trout, reserving the marinade ingredients (herbs, onion, shallot and garlic separate from their liquid). Roll out the pastry and line a pâté tin with it. Arrange the trout, salmon and strained herb, onion, garlic and shallot mixture in alternate layers, starting and finishing with the salmon. Cover with the rest of the pastry, seal carefully and make three small holes in the top. Decorate with the pastry left-overs. Bake in the hot oven for 45 minutes.

Remove the pâté from the oven. Beat together the remaining egg, cream, a little salt and 1 tablespoon marinade liquid and pour through the holes in the pastry. Turn off the oven and return the pâté to it for 15 minutes. Serve immediately with melted butter as a sauce. (From Lorraine.)

Soufflé de TRUITES
Smoked Trout Soufflé

SERVES 6

75 g (3 oz) butter	Salt and pepper
50 g (2 oz) flour	Pinch of thyme
300 ml (10 fl oz) milk	Pinch of nutmeg
5 egg yolks	6 egg whites, beaten until
125 g (4 oz) smoked trout	stiff
fillets, mashed to a thick	
purée with double cream	

Pre-heat the oven to gas mark 6, 200°C (400°F).

Make a white sauce with the butter, flour and milk. When it has cooled, stir in the egg yolks and fish purée. Add salt, pepper, thyme and nutmeg. Fold in the egg whites. Pour into a buttered soufflé dish.

Pop into the oven for 20 to 25 minutes, and do not open the door during the cooking time. Serve immediately. (From Périgord.)

TERRINE DE POISSON AUX HERBES
Fish Terrine with Fresh Herbs

SERVES 10

2 kg (4 lb) fillets of any
white fish, skinned
750 ml (1¼ pints) double
cream
6 egg whites, beaten until
stiff
200 g (7 oz) parsley,
chopped

100 g (3½ oz) sorrel leaves,
chopped
25 g (1 oz) salt
½ teaspoon pepper
25 g (1 oz) butter
Shellfish or Butter Sauce
(see pages 19, 20)

Pre-heat the oven to gas mark 2, 150°C (300°F).

Take half of the fish fillets and purée them in a food
processor. Tip into a very cold mixing bowl. Stir in the cream
and then carefully fold in the egg whites.

Add the parsley, sorrel, salt and pepper to the fish mixture
and then put it in a large buttered terrine. Thinly slice the
other fillets of fish and lay over the mixture. Cook in the oven
in a bain-marie for 1¼ hours.

Serve chilled with *Shellfish* or *Butter Sauce*.

TERRINE DE POISSON AUX TROIS COULEURS
Three-coloured Fish Terrine

SERVES 10

300 g (10 oz) fillets of white
fish (for example
whiting), skinned
300 g (10 oz) fillet of fresh
salmon, skinned
300 g (10 oz) fillets of
monkfish, skinned
750 ml (1¼ pints) double
cream

6 egg whites, beaten until
stiff
1 teaspoon salt
1 teaspoon black pepper
50 g (2 oz) parsley, very
finely chopped
1 sachet saffron
25 g (1 oz) butter

Pre-heat the oven to gas mark 2, 150°C (300°F).

Purée each of the three fish separately. Add one-third of
the cream, one-third of the beaten egg whites and one-third
of the salt and pepper to each puréed fish. Add the chopped
parsley to the whiting mixture and the powdered saffron to
the monkfish mixture.

Butter a terrine and fill with alternate layers of the fish.
Cook in the oven in a bain-marie for 1¼ hours.

Allow the fish terrine to rest for 5 minutes or so before
tipping it out. Serve warm in slices with, say, a *White Wine
Sauce* (see page 18).

LOTTE À L'IMPÉRATRICE
Monkfish Mould

SERVES 6

1 kg (2 lb) monkfish
Fish stock
Butter
5 eggs, beaten
1 heaped tablespoon tomato
  purée

1 glass Cognac
Pinch of cayenne pepper
Fresh tarragon, chopped
Salt and pepper

Pre-heat the oven to gas mark 4, 180°C (350°F).

Simmer the monkfish in fish stock for 20 minutes. Allow to cool, remove all the bones and skin, and cut the fish into even-sized pieces.

Butter a ring mould and arrange the fish pieces evenly inside it. Beat together the eggs, tomato purée, Cognac, cayenne pepper, tarragon and salt and pepper to taste. Pour over the fish. Bake in the oven for 30 minutes until firm.

Cool and unmould. Eat cold with a herb mayonnaise. Tastes even better the next day. (From Charente.)

MOUSSELINE DE BROCHET
Pike Mousseline

SERVES 6 TO 8

60 ml (2½ fl oz) milk
1 kg (2 lb) pike fillets,
*   boned, skinned and*
*   puréed in a liquidiser*
6 large mushrooms, peeled
*   and finely chopped*

6 egg whites, beaten until
*   stiff*
Salt
Butter
Shellfish Sauce (see page
*   19)*

Pre-heat the oven to gas mark 7, 220°C (425°F).

Add the milk to the fish purée and stir in the mushrooms. Carefully fold in the egg whites and add the salt. Butter 6 to 8 ramekins and fill them two-thirds full with the mousseline. Cook in a bain-marie in the oven for 10 to 15 minutes.

Serve with *Shellfish Sauce*. (From Burgundy.)

CREVETTES FLAMBÉES
Shrimps Flambéed in Cognac

SERVES 6

3 tablespoons butter
500 g (1 lb) live grey
*   shrimps*

1 glass Cognac

Melt the butter and, when it is bubbling, throw in the shrimps and toss them for 3 minutes over a medium heat. Add the Cognac and flame. Serve immediately. (From Charente.)

CREVETTES ÉCHAUDÉES
Poached Shrimps

If you take this book on holiday, don't forget to pack a shrimp net!

SERVES 6

4 tablespoons sea salt
3 bayleaves
1 clove garlic, cut in 4
   pieces

500 g (1 lb) live grey
   shrimps

Bring 2 litres (3½ pints) water to the boil with the salt, bayleaves and garlic. Throw in the shrimps. When they rise to the surface, they are cooked. They can be eaten hot or cold. (From Charente.)

MOULES GRILLÉES À LA FAÇON DE JACQUES-YVES
Mussels Barbecued in Pine Needles

This is another free seaside meal – but don't set the country-side on fire!

SERVES 6

2.75 kg (6 lb) mussels

To clean and beard the mussels:
1 Wash the mussels thoroughly under cold running water.

2 Scrape each one free of barnacles and seaweed, until they sparkle like black pearls.

3 Rip off the fibrous beard which protrudes between the shells.

4 Push each mussel sideways between finger and thumb – if it won't budge, it is not full of sand, so go ahead and use it. If it does, discard it.

5 Do not use any cracked or open mussels. If some mussels are open, pump them for a second or two between forefinger and thumb: if they close again they are still OK.

6 Rinse again under cold water.

To barbecue:

On a large pine plank of approximately 1 metre (3 feet) long and 1 cm (½ in.) thick, arrange the mussels on their sides, join side up, so that when they open they will be facing the plank. Start in the middle, with four mussels arranged like a four-leaf clover. In between each put another mussel. Continue until you have a large rose-shaped mosaic. Make sure that the mussels are as close together as possible. This should be done outdoors on a clear piece of ground.

Cover the mussels thickly with pine needles, to a depth of about 30 cm (12 in.). Set the pine needles alight. When the flames have died, fan the cinders away. The mussels should all be opened face down (otherwise they will be full of cinders). Repeat the process with those mussles that have not opened, if any.

Eat with bread and butter. (From Charente.)

MOULES À LA MARINIÈRE

SERVES 6

2.25 kg (5 lb) mussels,
   cleaned and bearded (see
   page 62)
Ground black pepper
8 cloves garlic, finely
   chopped
2 shallots, finely chopped

1 small bunch parsley,
   finely chopped
1 litre (2 pints) Muscadet
1 bouquet garni (thyme,
   bayleaf and tarragon)
50 g (2 oz) butter, cut in
   small chunks

Put the cleaned mussels in a large saucepan. Pepper generously. Add the chopped garlic, shallots and parsley. Pour in the wine, add the bouquet garni, cover and cook over a high heat for 8 minutes. Shake well to make sure that all the mussels are opened. Add the butter and cook for a further 5 minutes. Remove the bouquet garni. Serve the mussels immediately with their juice. (From Brittany.)

PALOURDES FARCIES
Stuffed Clams

SERVES 6

3 cloves garlic, chopped
1 shallot, chopped
300 g (10 oz) butter,
   softened
½ glass Muscadet

1 heaped tablespoon
   parsley, finely chopped
Salt and pepper
6 dozen fresh clams, opened
   and drained

Crush the garlic and shallot together, add the butter, wine, parsley, salt and pepper. Beat with a fork until all the wine is absorbed.

Stuff the clams with the butter mixture and pop under the grill for 10 minutes or so, or until the butter is bubbling. (From Brittany.)

BIGORNEAUX
Poached Winkles

This is a simple meal for free when you are taking a seaside holiday!

Winkles	*2 bayleaves*
Salt and pepper	*Sprigs thyme*

Wash the winkles well. Pop them into a saucepan and cover with cold water. Add salt and pepper, a couple of bayleaves and a few sprigs of thyme. Bring to the boil. As soon as they boil, take them off the heat and drain them. They can be eaten hot or cold with the help of a pin. (From Charente.)

SARDINES À L'AIL POÊLÉES
Deep-fried Stuffed Sardines

SERVES 6

24 whole sardines, scaled and gutted, with backbone removed	10 cloves garlic, minced
	Salt and pepper
	Flour
1 handful parsley, finely chopped	Oil for frying
	Lemon wedges

Stuff the sardines with the parsley and garlic. Season with salt and pepper. Pinch the opening of each fish together and roll in plenty of flour. Carefully fry in hot oil until brown. Drain and serve immediately with lemon wedges. (From Charente.)

SARDINES GRILLÉES
Grilled Sardines, Sprats, Anchovies or any Small Fish

Aficionados do not gut sardines. They dry them carefully, paint them with *Spicy Herb Oil* (see page 30) and pop them under a very hot grill for 3 to 4 minutes each side. You can eat them with your fingers.

TIMBALES DE COQUILLES ST JACQUES
Scallop Timbales

SERVES 6

500 g (1 lb) white fish fillets, skinned

185 ml (6½ fl oz) double cream

1 teaspoon salt

½ coffeespoon pepper

3 egg whites, beaten until stiff

50 g (2 oz) butter

275 g (9 oz) scallops

Pinch of cayenne pepper

1 clove garlic, finely chopped

1 tablespoon parsley, finely chopped

1 tablespoon tomato purée

Shellfish Sauce (see page 19)

Cooked pastry shapes to decorate

Pre-heat the oven to gas mark 2, 150°C (300°F).

First purée the fish fillets in a liquidiser and put them into a cold mixing bowl. Stir in 125 ml (4 fl oz) of the cream, season with salt and pepper and fold in the egg whites. Butter the insides of six timbales (ramekins) and partly fill with the fish mixture. Make a hole in the mixture through which later to insert the scallops. Save enough of the mixture to cover the timbales when the scallops have been added.

Fry the scallops gently in butter with the cayenne, garlic and parsley and add the tomato purée and the remaining cream. Divide amongst the timbales and cover with the reserved fish mixture. Poach in a *bain-marie* for 30 minutes.

Tip out of the timbales and serve hot with *Shellfish Sauce*. Decorate the dish with little pastry shapes.

Snails

The Romans introduced snails to the table and today they are so popular that even in Britain we eat at least 60 tonnes a year – so says Richard Hales, a leading gastronaut and snailologist. He tells me that the bulk of sales are of the ready-prepared ones, already stuffed with garlic butter. It really isn't feasible to provide live snails in quantity, though if you wander along the hedgerows and garden walls, especially after a light shower, you may find some edible ones – but check with a snail book that you have found the edible variety!

In the event of your finding live snails (easy enough in France), you must starve them in a bucket for a week, then wash them under cold fresh water, liberally sprinkle them with flour and sea salt and leave them for an hour or two. Wash them again and remove the gunge that they produce. Plunge them into boiling salted water for 8 minutes and strain. Remove from their shells with a small skewer or hat pin. Now you are ready to select one of the recipes that follow, for your delight.

Escargots charentais
Snails in Meat Sauce

SERVES 6

250 g (8 oz) minced pork
1 tablespoon lard
Salt and pepper
150 snails, starved, washed and removed from shells (see above)

1 large head garlic, minced
3 ripe tomatoes, peeled and chopped
1 small bunch parsley, minced

In a large casserole fry the meat in the lard until it has browned. Add the salt and pepper. Throw in the snails and garlic. Cover and simmer for 30 minutes, stirring occasionally. After 15 minutes add the tomatoes. Add the parsley 5 minutes before serving. (From Charente.)

ESCARGOTS À LA BOURGUIGNONNE
Burgundy Snails

SERVES 4 FOR A FEAST

8 cloves garlic, finely
  chopped
2 shallots, chopped
100 g (3½ oz) parsley,
  finely chopped
Salt and pepper

Juice of 1 lemon
500 g (1 lb) butter, softened
100 medium snails, starved,
  washed and removed
  from shells (see opposite)

Pre-heat the oven to gas mark 7, 220°C (425°F).

Mix the garlic, shallots, parsley, salt and pepper and lemon juice. Push a small amount of butter to the bottom of each clean empty snail shell, then add the snails and seal with more butter.

Put on a snail dish and pop into the oven. As soon as the butter is bubbling, remove and serve immediately. (From Burgundy.)

Escargots à l'Alsacienne
Alsace Snails

———

SERVES 6

12 dozen fresh snails, starved, washed and removed from shells (see page 68)

For the stock:

1 bottle Riesling   1 onion, stuck with a clove
2 carrots

For the snail butter:

325 g (11 oz) butter   2 shallots, chopped
3 cloves garlic, chopped   Salt and pepper

First make the stock. Put all the ingredients in a large saucepan with 2 litres (3½ pints) water and bring to the boil. Simmer for 45 minutes, removing any scum that accumulates.

Pre-heat the oven to gas mark 7, 220°C (425°F).

Meanwhile, crush all the snail butter ingredients together in a pestle and mortar.

Take each carefully dried snail shell and put a small amount of stock in the bottom, then some of the butter, followed by the animal itself which will help to push the stock and butter right to the bottom of the shell. Seal the shell with more butter.

Just before serving, place the snails on a snail platter and pop into the oven, until the butter bubbles. (From Alsace.)

Civet d'Escargots
Snail Stew

SERVES 4

3 onions, finely chopped
6 cloves garlic, finely
  chopped
150 g (5 oz) lean bacon,
  finely chopped
100 g (3½ oz) raw ham,
  finely chopped
2 small red peppers, de-
  seeded and finely chopped
4 dozen large prepared
  snails (see page 68)
100 g (3½ oz) lard
75 g (3 oz) flour
2 bottles red wine
Stock
2 tablespoons tomato purée
1 bouquet garni
Salt and pepper
350 g (12 oz) mushrooms,
  sliced
50 g (2 oz) butter
50 g (2 oz) shelled walnuts,
  crushed
2 tablespoons cherry eau de
  vie
1 tablespoon vinegar
1 small handful parsley,
  chopped

In a large saucepan fry the onions, garlic, bacon, ham and peppers with the snails in the lard until the onions are transparent. Dust with the flour and stir carefully. Add the wine and enough stock to cover. Add the tomato purée, bouquet garni, salt and pepper. Cover and simmer for 1½ hours.

Sauté the mushrooms in some of the butter and add to the mixture. Mix the crushed walnuts with the rest of the butter. Remove the stew from the heat and add the cherry eau de vie, the walnut butter, the vinegar and the chopped parsley. Serve immediately.

Makes a change from tinned snails in garlic butter, what? (From Languedoc.)

ESCARGOTS FRANÇOISE DU PRÉ
Snails Françoise du Pré in Ramekins

SERVES 6

3 shallots, finely chopped
125 g (4 oz) butter
6 dozen snails, starved,
    washed and removed
    from shells (see page 68)
625 g (1¼ lb) ceps,
    chanterelles or field
    mushrooms, sliced

50 ml (2 fl oz) Marc de
    Bourgogne or brandy
450 ml (15 fl oz) double
    cream
Salt and pepper
1 sprig tarragon, finely
    chopped
1 tablespoon mustard

Fry the shallots in the butter until transparent, add the snails and the mushrooms and warm through. Chuck in the brandy and flame.

Add the cream and reduce for 10 minutes. Add the salt, pepper and tarragon. Add the mustard at the last minute and stir in well. Serve in warmed ramekins. (From Burgundy.)

GÂTEAU DE POIREAUX
Leek Pie

For a light weekend lunch after a round of grotesque business meals, a meatless dish can be a delight. Even I, a confirmed carnivore, enjoy this kind of pie, especially with some chilled light red wine.

SERVES 6

1 kg (2 lb) young leeks, halved lengthways and each half cut into 4	*Salt and pepper*
	1 egg yolk
	1 small glass milk
100 g (3½ oz) butter	

For the pastry:

300 g (10 oz) flour, sifted	*Salt and pepper*
150 g (5 oz) butter, cut into small pieces	

To make the pastry, combine the flour, butter, salt and pepper in a bowl. Add enough water to make a firm dough. Mix well and divide into two balls, a larger one for the bottom of the pie and a smaller one for the top. Allow to rest for 30 minutes in the refrigerator before using.

Pre-heat the oven to gas mark 6, 200°C (400°F).

Meanwhile, blanch the leeks for 5 minutes and drain well. Melt the butter in a pan and add the leeks. Season with salt and pepper and cook gently until all the water from the leeks has evaporated. Allow to cool.

Roll out the pastry and line the bottom of a pie dish with the larger piece. Cover with the leeks and the pastry lid. Pinch the edges together and cut a small round hole in the top. Bake in the oven for 40 minutes.

While the pie is cooking, beat the egg yolk into the milk in a pan over a low heat and whisk furiously so that it thickens like custard and does not congeal like runny scrambled egg. Season with salt and pepper.

Just before serving the pie, pour the thickened sauce through the hole in the lid. (From Charente.)

PETITS PÂTÉS DE PÉZENAS
Lamb Pies

SERVES 4

For the pastry:

400 g (14 oz) flour
Pinch of salt

200 g (7 oz) lard, cut in
   small pieces
1 egg, beaten

For the filling:

200 g (7 oz) lean mutton,
   finely minced
100 g (3½ oz) mutton fat
   from around the kidneys,
   finely minced

15 g (½ oz) brown sugar
Finely grated rind of
   ½ lemon
Salt and pepper
1 egg yolk, beaten

Sift the flour into a large bowl, make a well in the centre and add the salt, lard and egg. Mix well and slowly add enough water to make a firm dough. Allow to rest for 1 hour in the refrigerator.

Pre-heat the oven to gas mark 6, 200°C (400°F).

Mix the mutton, fat, sugar, lemon rind, salt and pepper together. Prepare a greased baking sheet on which to assemble the pies.

Roll out the pastry to 6 mm (¼ in.) thick. Cut into 16 × 6 cm (2½ in.) rounds.

Roll out the pastry trimmings again and cut into 4-cm (1½-in.)-wide strips. Shape the strips into rectangles large enough to fit exactly on eight of the pastry rounds to build up the sides. Seal the edges carefully and fill with the meat mixture. Place another round on top and carefully seal. Make a little hole in the lid and paint the whole thing with beaten egg yolk. (The finished product should look like a small pork pie.)

Bake in the oven. Eat hot. (From Languedoc.)

PÂTÉ DE FOIE GRAS À L'ALSACIENNE
Alsace Goose Liver Terrine

SERVES 4 TO 8

2 × 500 g (1 lb) goose
   livers, de-veined and
   skinned
50 ml (2 fl oz) Madeira or
   port

Salt and finely ground
   white pepper
100 g (3½ oz) fat streaky
   bacon, thinly sliced
65 g (2½ oz) truffles, cut in
   1 cm (½ in.) cubes

Mash together the goose livers, Madeira, salt and white pepper until you have a smooth, firm paste. Put in a bowl, cover with greaseproof paper and refrigerate for 12 hours.

Pre-heat the oven to gas mark 3, 160°C (325°F).

Line a terrine with the streaky bacon. Heap the chilled foie gras into it. Make a lengthways incision down the middle about half as deep as the foie gras and push in the cubes of truffle. Close the incision and smooth the surface. Put the lid on the terrine, sealed with flour and a little water. Cook for 45 minutes in a *bain-marie*, in the oven.

Allow to cool and refrigerate until ready to serve. (From Alsace.)

TERRINE DE CANARD
Whole Duck Terrine

This is a really difficult dish which is well worth the trouble because it will impress your friends like nobody's business!

Here a couple of my most important cookery principles really do come into play – planning and good shopping. First you must find a butcher who has free-range ducks. Then you must smile nicely and ask him to take the bones and flesh out, leaving the skin completely intact. You are going to use the skin to surround the whole terrine.

If you try skinning the duck yourself, you'll find it's not all that difficult. Cut off the wing tips with a sharp knife. Cut a slit from the head to the tail along the back and gradually ease the skin from the flesh with your fingers and a small sharp knife. Pull the skin from the legs and wings as if pulling off a sweater.

SERVES 10

1 × 2.25 kg (5 lb) duck, prepared as above	300 g (10 oz) fatty smoked bacon, finely minced
1 large glass brandy	300 g (10 oz) belly of pork, coarsely minced
50 ml (2 fl oz) oil	
25 g (1 oz) carrots, chopped	1 egg
25 g (1 oz) onions, chopped	1 tablespoon green peppercorns
1 bouquet garni	
1 sprig thyme	20 g (¾ oz) shelled pistachio nuts
1 bayleaf	
1 clove garlic, crushed	1 truffle, chopped (optional)
Salt and pepper	Butter

First cut the two breast fillets of the duck into pieces about 2.5 cm (1 in.) long. Marinate the pieces in brandy with the liver for 2 hours. Mince the rest of the duck flesh finely.

Meanwhile, brown the duck bones in a little oil. Add the carrots and onions. When they start to brown, add about 1 litre (2 pints) cold water, the bouquet garni, sprig of thyme, bayleaf and the garlic and simmer for 1 hour. Strain through a fine sieve and then reduce until you have just over 150 ml (5 fl oz) left. Add the strained marinade, season with salt and pepper and put in the refrigerator.

Next fry the marinated fillets and liver of the duck in the remaining oil. Allow to cool and chop into 6 mm (¼ in.) cubes.

Pre-heat the oven to gas mark 2, 150°C (300°F).

In a mixing bowl combine the minced duck meat with the bacon and belly of pork. Beat in the egg and add the stock, salt and pepper and the green peppercorns. Mix in the pistachio nuts and truffle (if you can afford it!) and finally add in little pieces of the cooked fillets and liver.

Cut your duck skin in such a way as to line a buttered 1.4 to 1.75 litre (2½ to 3 pint) terrine completely, with flaps hanging over the side. These will be used to close over the whole dish. Add the minced mixture and close over the flaps of skin. Cover and bake for about 2 hours. Allow to cool, put some weights on top to press down tightly, and refrigerate.

To serve, tip the dish carefully out of the terrine and serve whole, so your guests are really impressed by what looks like a rectangular duck!

Pâté de Campagne
Country Terrine

The simple French country terrine, if made at home with fresh ingredients and served chilled with a few gherkins, some olives and some sweet summer tomatoes, is one of the finest hors d'oeuvres there is. Recipes vary from area to area, but they are all roughly based on pork, veal and pig's liver, and they tend to be quite fatty and crumbly, which is nice. Here is a typical version.

SERVES 4 TO 8

500 g (1 lb) belly of pork, finely chopped not *minced*

250 g (8 oz) pig's liver, *minced*

350 g (12 oz) veal, *minced*

125 g (4 oz) sheet of pork fat or slice of speck (cured pork fat), half cut into 1-cm (½-in.)-thick strips and half cut into little cubes

2 cloves garlic, crushed

6 black peppercorns, crushed

4 juniper berries, crushed

Pinch of ground mace

Salt and pepper

1 large glass dry white wine

1 generous splash brandy

Pre-heat the oven to gas mark 3, 160°C (325°F).

Mix everything except the strips of fat together and leave to stand for a couple of hours in a cool place.

Tip the lot into a terrine and lay the strips of fat over the top. Put the terrine in a *bain-marie* and cook in the oven for about 1½ hours. Leave to cool for 24 hours before eating.

TERRINE DE LÉGUMES AUX TROIS COULEURS
Three-coloured Vegetable Terrine

You can use any vegetables you like in this recipe – broccoli, chicory, lettuce, celery, and so on. You can cook them in small individual moulds or ramekins instead of a terrine, and serve as a vegetable garnish with a main course.

SERVES 10

500 g (1 lb) spinach
500 g (1 lb) cauliflower
500 g (1 lb) carrots
6 eggs
300 ml (10 fl oz) double cream,
whipped until thick

15 g (½ oz) salt
½ teaspoon white pepper
½ teaspoon nutmeg

Pre-heat the oven to gas mark 2, 150°C (300°F).

Cook each of the vegetables in boiling salted water separately. Strain them, squeeze out all the liquid and liquidise separately.

Beat 2 eggs into each vegetable and fold a third of the whipped cream into each. Season with salt, pepper and nutmeg.

Butter a terrine and put in the vegetables in alternate layers. Cook in a *bain-marie* for 1 hour. Allow to cool. Serve chilled or hot, as you like.

OEUFS EN MEURETTE
Eggs in Wine Sauce

SERVES 4 TO 6

2 slices bacon per person,
  cubed
50 g (2 oz) butter
2 tablespoons oil
1 clove garlic, chopped
1 onion, chopped

1 bouquet garni
1 litre (2 pints) red wine
2 eggs per person
Slices bread
Pork or goose fat

Fry the bacon in the butter and oil in a pan. Add the garlic, onion and bouquet garni. Add the wine and boil for 15 to 20 minutes.

Remove the bacon and strain the sauce. Return the sauce to the pan and add the bacon. Poach the eggs in the sauce.

Serve the eggs on slices of bread fried in pork or goose fat. Cover with the sauce and bacon cubes. (From Burgundy.)

TARTE ALSACIENNE
AUX OIGNONS
Onion Tart

SERVES 6 TO 8

For the pastry:

300 g (10 oz) wheat flour
150 g (5 oz) butter, cut in
  small pieces

Pinch of salt
1 egg, beaten

For the filling:

300 g (10 oz) fromage blanc* (minimum 60 per cent fat content)

Salt and pepper

2 pinches of nutmeg

100 g (3½ oz) lean smoked bacon, finely diced

300 g (10 oz) onions, finely chopped

Butter for frying

4 egg yolks, beaten

4 egg whites, beaten until stiff

First make the pastry. Sift the flour into a bowl, make a well in the middle and add the butter, salt and egg. Mix with your fingertips until the mixture forms a ball. Knead on a floured board until the dough is completely smooth. Roll into a ball, cover with a floured teatowel and allow to rest at room temperature for a couple of hours.

Pre-heat the oven to gas mark 5, 190°C (375°F).

Then roll out the pastry and use it to line a well-buttered quiche or flan dish. Prick the bottom all over with a fork and bake blind for 20 minutes in the oven.

Pre-heat the oven to gas mark 7, 220°C (425°F).

Mix the fromage blanc with a little salt, pepper and nutmeg. (Remember that the smoked bacon is already quite salty.) Beat until smooth.

Fry the bacon and onions in butter until the onions are transparent. Drain off the butter. Add the bacon and onions to the fromage blanc.

Add the egg yolks and delicately fold in the egg whites. Pour into the cooked pastry shell and bake in the oven for 30 to 45 minutes. The tart should be a chestnut brown all over. Turn out of the dish and serve hot. (From Alsace.)

*Fromage blanc is fresh cream cheese, sometimes known as fromage frais.

JAMBON AUX FIGUES FRAÎCHES
Ham and Fresh Figs

———

SERVES 4

16 very ripe fresh figs　　　*400 g (14 oz) raw (Parma)
ham, very thinly sliced*

Chill the figs overnight. Cut each one into four without cutting all the way through. Arrange on a serving dish with the ham slices. (From Languedoc.)

ABRICOTS FARCIS
Apricots Stuffed with Creamed Goat's Cheese

———

SERVES 4

125 g (4 oz) goat's cheese　　*1 teaspoon mint, finely
4 tablespoons double cream*　　*chopped
1 teaspoon chives, finely*　　　*8 ripe apricots, cut in half
chopped*　　　　　　　　　　*and stoned*

Blend the cheese and cream together into a smooth, soft paste. Stir in the chives and mint and use the mixture to stuff the apricot halves.

GOUGÈRE BOURGUIGNONNE
Savoury Profiterole Ring

SERVES 4 TO 6

450–600 ml (15 fl oz–1 pint) milk	*8 eggs*
135 g (4½ oz) butter	*135 g (4½ oz) Gruyère cheese, finely grated, plus extra to sprinkle*
7 g (¼ oz) salt	
Pinch of pepper	*2 tablespoons cream*
250 g (8 oz) flour	*Beaten egg to glaze*

Pre-heat the oven to gas mark 3, 160°C (325°F).

Put the milk, butter and salt and pepper in a heavy-bottomed saucepan. Bring to the boil and immediately take off the heat. Add the flour and beat well with a wooden spoon. Return to a low heat and keep beating until the batter comes away easily from the sides of the pan in a sort of glossy ball.

Remove from the heat and beat in the eggs 2 at a time, the cheese and the cream.

On a buttered pie plate or baking sheet, dollop the dough in egg-size mounds, one against the other, in a circle. Brush with beaten egg and sprinkle with grated cheese. Bake in the oven until the crusts are golden and the insides moist. Serve warm. (From Burgundy.)

SALADE PROVENÇALE
Provençal Salad

———

SERVES 4

2 pale green, crisp frisée

3–4 crunchy white endives,
 leaves left on

6 whole salted anchovies,
 rinsed and dried

4 free-range eggs, hard-
 boiled and halved

1 kg (2 lb) tomatoes, some
 green, some ripe, quartered

1 handful black olives

1 wine glass best-quality
 olive oil

2 or 3 cloves garlic, finely
 crushed

Black pepper

Sea salt

Dash or two of wine vinegar

Gently combine all the ingredients with your fingers in a
large salad bowl, adding the eggs last. Fluff the heavy ingredients to the top of the salad. (From Provence.)

SALADE PÉRIGOURDINE
Périgord Salad

———

SERVES 4 TO 6

2 really crisp, crunchy
 lettuces (not the limp
 imported things)

Walnut oil

Cooked or preserved goose
 giblets (if you don't fancy
 this, you can use little
 pieces of bacon)

50 g (2 oz) bread, cut into
 1 cm (½ in.) squares

125 g (4 oz) shelled walnuts

Wine vinegar

Put the lettuce into a salad bowl in readiness. Meanwhile, pour some oil into a frying pan and fry the giblets or bacon for 2 or 3 minutes. Add the bread cubes, fry until crunchy and golden, and then add the walnuts.

Turn up the heat, taking care not to burn anything, and add a dash of vinegar to the pan. Stir it all around for a second or two and pour this hot mixture over the lettuce. (From Périgord.)

SALADE DE TOMATES À LA FAÇON DE MME MONIQUE CONIL
Tomato and Cheese Salad

This will only work brilliantly if you really do use best-quality ingredients – it will be grim if you use corn oil and Cheddar cheese, for example.

Quantities are up to you, but let's say for 6 people:

1 kg (2 lb) tomatoes, some very ripe, some a little green, thinly sliced
1 tablespoon caster sugar
Sea salt and black pepper
1 wine glass olive oil

A couple of dashes white wine vinegar
4 tablespoons fresh basil, chopped
175 g (6 oz) mozzarella cheese, cut into 6 mm (¼ in.) cubes

Put all the ingredients into a large salad bowl, mix carefully so that you don't damage the tomatoes, and refrigerate for at least 1 hour. Toss gently again before serving.

Salade Niçoise

SERVES 4 TO 5

Hearts of 2–3 real lettuce: crisp leaves that are curled tightly together in a monochrome of green (not Chinese leaves, icebergs)

1 handful lightly cooked runner or French beans from your garden

8 ripe tomatoes, sliced

2 green tomatoes, sliced

½ teaspoon ground sea salt

5–6 tablespoons olive oil

8 free-range eggs, hard-boiled and halved

150 ml (5 fl oz) glistening black olives (if packed in brine, drain, dry and marinate in olive oil)

275 g (9 oz) tinned tuna fish in olive oil

125 g (4 oz) tinned anchovy fillets in olive oil

1 tin sardines in olive oil

Wash and thoroughly dry the lettuce and put into a large salad bowl. Add the beans, tomatoes, sea salt and olive oil. With your fingers, gently turn the salad until everything is coated with oil and salt.

Add all the other ingredients and, again with your fingers, carefully mix them together. As you lift your fingers from the bowl, bring the eggs and olives to the top as if you were fluffing up your hair after a shower. (From Provence.)

Asperges à l'Alsacienne
Alsace White Asparagus

SERVES 6

*2 kg (4 lb) white asparagus, ends removed, peeled and tied in
bunches*

For the butter sauce:

150 g (5 oz) butter	*Pinch of fresh thyme*
Juice of ½ lemon	*Salt and pepper*

For the vinaigrette:

125 ml (4 fl oz) nut oil	*Salt and pepper*
50 ml (2 fl oz) vinegar	*1 shallot, finely chopped*
mixed with 1 teaspoon	
clear honey	

Plunge the asparagus bundles into simmering salted water for
20 minutes. When cooked, remove, strain and lay in rows on
a platter.

Meanwhile prepare the 2 sauces.

To make the butter sauce, melt the butter over a low heat
until it foams, then gently beat in the lemon juice, thyme, salt
and pepper. Whisk until frothy and serve immediately.

To make the vinaigrette, mix together the oil, the honey
vinegar, salt, pepper and shallot. Beat vigorously and serve
immediately poured over the warm asparagus. (From
Alsace.)

LA PATRANQUE
Auvergne Rarebit

You'll be surprised how good this is – and very filling. Have a tomato salad with it, and a few iced beers, as a great lunch!

SERVES 4

4 thick slices coarse white country bread, cut into chunks
Milk
50 g (2 oz) butter

4 thick slices Tomme de Cantal cheese, cut in slivers
5–6 cloves garlic, chopped
Salt

Moisten the chunks of bread in the milk.

In a large frying pan melt the butter and add the bread. When the bread starts to sizzle, add the cheese, garlic and salt. Squash it all together until you have a sort of sticky dough.

Allow to become golden on the bottom, then pop under a hot grill until golden on top. Serve immediately. (From Auvergne.)

FEUILLETÉ AUX ANCHOIS
Anchovies in Flaky Pastry

These are brilliant with an aperitif, or as hot hors d'oeuvres.

SERVES 4

8 anchovy fillets
4 black olives, stoned and
   halved

1 egg yolk, beaten

For the pastry:

125 g (4 oz) flour
Salt

150 g (5 oz) butter at room
   temperature

Sift the flour into a large bowl, make a well in the centre and add a pinch of salt and enough water to make a firm dough. Allow to rest for 15 minutes.

Roll out on a floured board into a large square. Cut up the butter and put in the middle and fold over the edges of the pastry so that the butter is completely enclosed. Roll out into a rectangle; if the butter appears, dust with flour. Fold into three. Turn the pastry and repeat the process six times with a 15-minute rest every two turns.

Pre-heat the oven to gas mark 7, 220°C (425°F).

Finally, roll the pastry out into a long rectangle 1 cm (½ in.) thick. Cut into eight equal rectangles. Put 2 anchovy fillets and 2 olive halves on four of the rectangles. Moisten the edges with water. Sandwich the other rectangles on top, pinching the edges together. Make a criss-cross pattern on each rectangle and paint with beaten egg yolk. Bake on an oiled baking sheet in the oven for 25 minutes or until golden brown. (From Languedoc.)

L'ANCHOÏADE
Anchovies on Toast

If you purée some stoned black olives into the following mixture, you have Tapenade – a pungent paste to spread on sticks of celery, or to stuff hard-boiled eggs with, or just to spread on to hot toasted country bread to nibble with an aperitif.

SERVES 6

2 × 50 g (2 oz) tins
   anchovies, drained and
   rinsed
Olive oil

1 teaspoon wine vinegar
6 slices good white country
   bread
Black pepper

Pre-heat the oven to gas mark 7, 220°C (425°F).

Mash the anchovies in a pestle and mortar with approximately 2 tablespoons olive oil. Add the vinegar and mix well. Spread the mixture on the bread and arrange on a baking sheet. Drizzle a little oil on each and add lots of black pepper.

Pop in the oven for 10 minutes and serve immediately with wedges of hard-boiled eggs and black olives. (From Provence.)

BOUDIN NOIR AUX POMMES
Black Pudding with Apples

————

Good French black pudding has a smooth fine filling with little nuggets of fat pushed into thin edible skins and bears no resemblance to those factory-manufactured monstrosities in plastic tubes that you find on the deli counters of supermarkets. In the Pays Basque, the *boudin noir* is brilliant. Many hotels and restaurants make their own – like Chez Pantchou in Biarritz, where they are very fatty and crunchy on the outside; or Hôtel Bonnet at St Pée sur Nivelle, where they are made with shredded pork and chillies as well as blood. Shop around for good black pudding, or bring some back from holiday.

SERVES 4

1 kg (2 lb) boudin noir (blood sausage), cut in 4
2 tablespoons oil

6–8 medium apples (Cox's will do), peeled, cored and roughly chopped

Fry the *boudin* in the oil until cooked through. Remove and keep warm. Add the apples to the pan and toss until golden brown and tender. Serve the *boudin* on a bed of apples.

CÈPES À LA SAVOYARDE
Ceps with Ham and Vegetables

Wild mushrooms and edible fungi abound in this country if you take the trouble to look. But buy a book on the subject first.

SERVES 4 TO 6

1 kg (2 lb) fresh ceps	*1 clove garlic, finely chopped*
2 tablespoons nut oil	
1 slice raw ham, finely chopped	*1 small handful parsley, chopped*
2 large onions, finely chopped	*75 g (3 oz) butter*
	Salt and pepper
	Breadcrumbs

Soak the ceps for a few minutes in water containing a little vinegar. Dry carefully before slicing them. Fry them in the oil until they are no longer watery.

In a separate pan, fry the ham, onions, garlic and parsley in the butter until the onions are translucent. Add the ceps and cook together for 5 minutes. Season with salt and pepper to taste. Arrange on a hot serving platter. Scatter enough fresh breadcrumbs into the pan to absorb the juices, heat through, add to the mushrooms and serve. (From Savoy.)

BEIGNETS DE VIANDE
Meat Fritters

This is a good way to use the remains of roast chicken, beef, lamb or pork, or any flesh you fancy or happen to have in the larder.

SERVES 4

400 g (14 oz) cooked meat, very finely chopped	*Salt and pepper*
	Oil for deep-frying

For the choux pastry:

300 ml (10 fl oz) white wine	*275 g (9 oz) flour*
50 g (2 oz) butter	*6 eggs*
Salt	

First prepare choux pastry by boiling 300 ml (10 fl oz) water with the wine, butter and a pinch of salt. Turn down the heat and stir in the flour until it forms a smooth ball. Pull the pan off the heat altogether and beat in the eggs, one by one. Leave to rest for about 20 minutes.

In the meantime, season the meat with salt and pepper. Heat some oil in a pan. Mix the meat and pastry together, roll into mouth-sized balls and deep-fry until they swell up and turn golden.

Serve with tartare sauce (simply mayonnaise with chopped capers, gherkins and parsley added to it). Now all you need to do is prepare a simple salad of good crisp lettuce, and open the wine.

OEUFS À LA GENEVOISE
Cheese Custard

SERVES 6

6 egg yolks
450 ml (15 fl oz) chicken
   stock or milk
Nutmeg

Pepper
300 g (10 oz) Gruyère
   cheese, cut in fine slices

Pre-heat the oven to gas mark 6, 200°C (400°F).

Mix the egg yolks with the stock or milk. Add the nutmeg and pepper. Butter an ovenproof dish and line it with the Gruyère. Pour on the egg mixture and cover. Bake in the oven for 20 minutes. It should have the consistency of a thick custard. (From Savoy.)

BEIGNETS DE CHAMPIGNONS
Mushroom Fritters with Beer Batter

SERVES 4

300 g (10 fl oz) mushrooms
Lemon juice

Butter
Oil for deep-frying

For the batter:

50 g (2 oz) butter, melted
250 g (8 oz) flour
3 eggs, beaten
Salt and pepper

300 ml (10 fl oz) lager or
   light beer
300 ml (10 fl oz) milk,
   warmed

First make the batter by mixing the butter, flour, eggs, a

pinch of salt and pepper. Then whisk in, little by little, the lager or beer and finally stir in the warm milk, until you have a smooth batter.

Wash and dry the mushrooms and marinate them in lemon juice for 2 or 3 minutes. Then fry them gently in butter for 4 or 5 minutes.

Heat the oil, dip the mushrooms into the batter and deep-fry until they are crisp and golden.

As with the meat fritters, serve with a freshly made salad.

NOUILLES FRAÎCHES À LA CRÈME
Noodles in a Creamy Cheese Sauce

Noodles – as required
Equal quantities of
  Béchamel Sauce (see
  page 16) and single
  cream, mixed together

Parmesan cheese, grated
Black pepper

Cook the noodles in the usual way and strain them. Return to the saucepan and cover with the *Béchamel Sauce* and cream mixture. Stir in some grated Parmesan cheese and re-heat gently. Season well with black pepper.

PÂTES FRAÎCHES AU PESTO
Pasta with Olive Oil and Basil

Try and use fresh spaghetti for this superbly simple dish. So
simple, but so good. But don't you dare use dried basil. And
don't be tempted to use any mushrooms or peppers or anything else at all!

SERVES 6

1 kg (2 lb) spaghetti	150 ml (5 fl oz) olive oil
Salt	Black pepper
1 heaped saucer fresh basil leaves, chopped	Parmesan cheese, grated

Cook the spaghetti *al dente* in masses of boiling salted water.
Strain and run under the hot tap to remove any starch or
stickiness.

Meanwhile, have ready a large mixing bowl into which you
have put the basil and the olive oil. Add the spaghetti and mix
thoroughly with at least 15 twists of your black pepper mill.
Sprinkle to taste with Parmesan cheese and eat at once with
lashings of red wine. (From Provence.)

PIPERADE

This is not scrambled eggs with peppers and tomatoes, it's a
sauté of vegetables into which eggs are beaten, and the Basque people are very particular about it. They argue amongst
themselves as to whether you should use the hot pimentos
from Espellette or simple red or green peppers. The best
compromise is to use red and green peppers and then spice up
the whole thing with a pinch of sweet paprika, because your
chances of buying the *piment d'espellette* in this country are
pretty remote. Anyway:

SERVES 4

Oil and butter for frying
2 red peppers, de-seeded
   and chopped
1 green pepper, de-seeded
   and chopped
4 ripe tomatoes, peeled, de-
   seeded and chopped
½ fresh red chilli (piment
   d'espellette) or a pinch of
   paprika
1 clove garlic, finely
   chopped

Thyme
1 bayleaf
Parsley
Salt and pepper
1 teaspoon caster sugar (the
   secret ingredient given to
   me by Mimi in Biarritz)
6 eggs
4 slices Bayonne or any
   cured ham (e.g., Parma),
   or good bacon

In your favourite pan heat some oil and butter and cook all
the vegetables, spices and seasonings with the sugar until
they become mushy. Beat the eggs with a little water and stir
them in as for scrambled eggs. Meanwhile, fry the slices of
Bayonne ham and serve as an accompaniment to the
Piperade. (From Basque Country.)

My favourite pizza

MAKES 4 SMALL PIZZAS

For the dough:

7 g (¼ oz) sugar

160 ml (5½ fl oz) tepid milk

25 g (1 oz) yeast

15 g (½ oz) fat

500 g (1 lb) flour, sifted

7 g (¼ oz) salt

For the topping:

Tomatoes, peeled, de-seeded
and finely chopped

Tinned anchovy fillets

Capers

Oregano

Gruyère cheese, grated

Dissolve the sugar in the milk and 150 ml (5 fl oz) water and mix in the yeast. Leave for 10 minutes in a warm place. Rub the fat into the dry ingredients and stir in the yeast mixture. Cover and leave to prove at room temperature for 45 minutes.

Knead and leave for a further 15 minutes. This will make 1 kg (2 lb) dough.

Pre-heat the oven to gas mark 6, 200°C (400°F).

Roll the dough into very thin rounds when required. Place each on a well-greased plate and prick all over. Leave to prove for 20 minutes before cooking.

Over each round of dough spread some chopped tomatoes (or use Puréed Tomatoes – see page 26), 4 anchovy fillets and half a dozen capers. Sprinkle on a pinch of oregano and cover liberally with grated Gruyère cheese. Bake in the oven for approximately 20 minutes. (From Provence.)

QUICHE LORRAINE

The poor Quiche Lorraine, once aptly (and sadly) described by Elizabeth David as a culinary dustbin, is blazoned on blackboards in art centres and wine bars throughout the land. And the resulting soggy pastry case containing congealed custard dotted with bits of ham, tinned asparagus and sliced mushrooms is a belly-chilling travesty.

This is how it should be done. These are the only ingredients you are allowed to use!

SERVES 4 TO 6

250 g (8 oz) shortcrust pastry
4 eggs, beaten
450 ml (15 fl oz) double cream
Salt and pepper

25–50 g (1–2 oz) smoked bacon, diced and lightly fried
2 teaspoons butter, cut into small pieces

Pre-heat the oven to gas mark 6, 200°C (400°F).

Line a well-buttered 20 cm (8 in.) pie dish with the pastry. Prick the bottom all over with a fork.

Beat the eggs and cream together and add salt and pepper. Sprinkle the bacon into the pie shell and pour in the eggs and cream. Dot with the pieces of butter. Bake in the oven for approximately 25 minutes or until set. (From Lorraine.)

TARTE FLAMBÉE
Cheese and Bacon Pastry

SERVES 4 TO 6

For the bread dough:

350 g (12 oz) plain flour,
   sifted
1 egg

15 g (½ oz) salt
20 g (¾ oz) yeast

For the topping:

150 g (5 oz) smoked bacon,
   finely diced
250 g (8 oz) onions, finely
   chopped
20 g (¾ oz) butter
1 tablespoon nut oil

250 g (8 oz) fromage blanc
   (see note on page 81)
Salt and pepper
1 teaspoon thyme leaves

Prepare the dough. Put the flour in a bowl and make a well in the centre. Add the egg, salt, yeast and enough warm water to make a firm but not too sticky dough. Knead until the dough is completely smooth.

Roll into a large ball, cover with a floured tea towel, and leave for 1 hour in a warm place.

Pre-heat the oven to gas mark 6, 200°C (400°F).

Meanwhile, fry the bacon and onions in the butter and oil until the onions are translucent. Mix the fromage blanc with the salt, pepper and thyme.

Roll out the dough until 6 mm (¼ in.) thick, place on an oiled baking sheet and pop into the oven for 5 minutes. Remove and turn up the oven to gas mark 10, 250°C (500°F). Scatter the tart base with the onions and bacon, followed by dollops of the fromage blanc mixture. Return the tart to the oven for about 15 minutes, until the edges of the dough look like burned bread.

Alternatively, for a more simply made topping, just grate some cheese and onion, mix with some small cubes of fatty smoked bacon, sprinkle over the rolled-out dough and bake. You could chop some parsley into soured cream and spread this over the cooked tart. (From Alsace.)

RACLETTES

(Or how to put large lumps of cheese in front of a wood fire and have a brilliant meal.)

Traditionally, a raclette – there is no sensible translation – was cooked in front of a wood fire with the aid of a long metal fork. The idea was to put one edge of a large block of hard cheese next to the fire, and as it heated up and melted, you scraped it on to a plate, runny and soft and hot, and ate it with jacket potatoes, gherkins and pickled onions.

But today you can buy a little electric device which supports the cheese and heats it without fuss or mess. You can buy such a thing from the Swiss Centre, 10 Wardour Street, London W1.

You can use any hardish cheese, from Gruyère to Reblochon, or even Cheddar. You can, perhaps, make some simple sauces to go with the Raclettes besides the potatoes, and perhaps also serve a slice of grilled ham or bacon. (From Savoy/Alsace.)

FONDUE AUX HERBES
Fondue with Fresh Herbs

———

Fondues are great fun and simple to prepare. If you have an open fire, you can cook in front of the hearth, and drink lots of well-iced vodka or schnapps. You need thick, small glasses and the alcohol must be almost frozen solid.

SERVES 4

1 clove garlic, crushed
300 g (10 oz) Emmenthal cheese, finely diced
250 g (8 oz) Gruyère cheese, finely diced
300 ml (10 fl oz) white wine
1 teaspoon lemon juice
3 teaspoons cornflour
25 ml (1 fl oz) kirsch
2 tablespoons fresh herbs (parsley, chives, chervil), finely chopped
Black pepper
Cubes of fresh bread

Rub the garlic around the fondue dish. Pop in the cheese, wine, lemon juice and the cornflour mixed with the kirsch, and bubble it up gently, whisking all the while, until it's all amalgamated into a smooth creamy fondue. Now stir in the fine fresh herbs and season with freshly ground pepper. Serve with the cubes of bread. (From Savoy.)

FONDUE AU ROQUEFORT
Fondue with Roquefort

———

If you are lucky enough to live near a baker like Margaret Vaughan of The Settle in Frome, you could buy onion bread or pork fat bread to dip into this little delight.

SERVES 4

50 g (2 oz) butter
300 ml (10 fl oz) white wine
25 ml (1 fl oz) Cognac
400 g (14 oz) Roquefort or
   other good blue cheese,
   finely diced

300 g (10 oz) Brie, rind
   removed, finely diced
Pinch of celery salt
Pinch of grated nutmeg
Black pepper
Cubes of fresh bread

Melt the butter in the fondue pot, add the wine and Cognac and bring to the boil. Reduce the heat and whisk in the cheeses in little pieces, until it is all mixed smoothly together. Season with celery salt, nutmeg and pepper. Serve with the bread cubes for dipping.

FONDUE NORMANDE
Normandy Fondue

SERVES 4

1 clove garlic, crushed
300 ml (10 fl oz)
   unsweetened apple juice
625 g (1¼ lb) hard French
   or Swiss cheese (e.g.,
   Emmenthal or Comté),
   grated

2 teaspoons cornflour
6 teaspoons lemon juice
2 teaspoons sweet paprika
1–2 pinches of grated
   nutmeg
Cubes of fresh bread

Rub the garlic around the fondue pot, add the apple juice and bring it to the boil. Pop in the cheese and the cornflour mixed with the lemon juice. Reduce the heat. Whisk from time to time until it's all gooey and good. Season with paprika and nutmeg and serve with the cubes of bread. (From Normandy.)

FONDUE SAVOYARDE
Savoy Fondue

SERVES 6

1 clove garlic
500 g (1 lb) Beaufort or
    Comté cheese, rind
    removed, cut in cubes
500 g (1 lb) Emmenthal,
    rind removed, cut in
    cubes

125 g (4 oz) Vacherin, rind
    removed, cut in cubes
6 glasses dry white wine
Nutmeg
Pepper
75 ml (3 fl oz) kirsch
White bread, cut in large
    bite-size chunks

Rub the garlic clove all over the inside of the fondue pot. Put in the cheeses and wine, nutmeg, pepper and kirsch. Cook over a low heat until the cheese has melted and the fondue is smooth. Serve with the chunks of bread for dipping. (From Savoy.)

Crêpes (Pancakes)

The only secret that people who make good, thin, regular-sized pancakes have is the frying pan. It's well worth buying a special heavy metal pan with an interior base diameter of not more than 15 cm (6 in.), which you use exclusively for pancakes; or buy a specialist pan from places like Kitchens of Bristol.

Before you use a new pan for the first time, wash it thoroughly with non-scratch detergent, then dry it, fill it with coarse salt and put it on a low heat until the edges of the salt begin to brown. Throw away the salt, wipe out the pan and fill it with fat or oil of any kind. Heat the pan gently until the fat begins to smoulder and smoke. Tip out the fat and wipe dry with a cloth.

Now you are ready to cook the first round of pancakes – which, because you will have put too much oil into the pan, you will have to throw away. It doesn't matter – it's all part of running in the pan. The pan should be well oiled, but not so well oiled that the oil can run around the pan.

Savoury pancakes make excellent lunches or light suppers, and the trick is to make a load of them, pack them into bundles for your anticipated need, and freeze them. Of course, *you* will always prepare yours freshly: quite right, too. So here are two basic and trustworthy recipes for sweet and savoury pancake batter.

PÂTE SALÉE
Savoury Batter

---

250 g (8 oz) flour, sifted	*6 teaspoons melted butter or*
4 eggs, beaten	*oil*
½ teaspoon salt	*500 ml (17 fl oz) milk*

Put the flour in a mixing bowl, make a hole in the middle and stir in the beaten eggs, salt and butter or oil. Now whisk in the milk, little by little, until you have a smooth paste. You should rest the batter for 1 hour before using it.

PÂTE SUCRÉE
Sweet Batter

———

3 eggs
40 g (1½ oz) caster sugar
250 g (8 oz) flour, sifted
Pinch of salt

2 teaspoons melted butter or
   oil
500 ml (17 fl oz) milk
2 teaspoons rum or Cognac

Beat the eggs in a mixing bowl and add the sugar, flour, salt
and butter or oil. Then, whisking all the while, add the milk,
little by little, and beat until smooth (or use a food processor). Leave for 1 hour before cooking, which is when you
add the alcohol, by the way.

You can fill savoury pancakes with practically anything, and a
few suggestions are given below. If you are using pre-frozen
pancakes for a hot dish, be sure to defrost them gently before
re-heating in a pan with just a little melted butter. In the first
recipe, however, the pancakes are served cold.

CRÊPES FARCIES DE
FROMAGE BLANC
Pancakes Stuffed with Cream Cheese

———

MAKES 12 PANCAKES

300 ml (10 fl oz) fromage
   blanc
125 ml (4 fl oz) double
   cream

1 teaspoon each of chopped
   chives, parsley, chervil
   and onion
Salt and pepper

Combine the fromage blanc with the cream and mix in the herbs. Season with salt and pepper and spread over the pancakes. Roll them into tubes and serve with a salad of perhaps celery, nuts and lettuce.

GALETTES DE SARRAZIN
Buckwheat Pancakes

MAKES 10 PANCAKES

500 g (1 lb) buckwheat flour, sifted	*100 g (3½ oz) butter, melted*
2 eggs, beaten	*2 pinches of salt*
300 ml (10 fl oz) dry cider	*175 g (6 oz) lard*

Put the flour in a large bowl and make a well in the centre. Add the eggs. With a wooden spoon keep stirring while you add alternate amounts of cider and water until you have a smooth pancake batter. Add the butter and salt. Allow to rest for a couple of hours at room temperature.

In a flat heavy frying pan or crêpe pan, melt enough lard to stop the pancakes from sticking. Pour in enough batter to make an average-size pancake. Smooth the batter out with the back of a spoon to make sure that it is as thin as possible. Turn the pancake over and butter the cooked side. Cover half of it with cheese, ham or cooked onions, or a mixture of all three. Fold the pancake in half and butter it again. Turn over once more and cook for a further minute. Proceed as before with the rest of the batter. Remember to oil the pan between each pancake.

Keep the pancakes warm and serve in a large stack with plenty of cider to drink. (From Brittany.)

CRÊPES AUX ENDIVES
Pancakes Stuffed with Chicory

MAKES 6 PANCAKES

6 heads chicory
6 thin slices ham (preferably
  a cured ham like
  Bayonne)

Béchamel Sauce (see page
  16)
100 g (3½ oz) cheese,
  grated

Wrap each chicory head in a slice of ham, then wrap in a pancake. Add the cheese to the *Béchamel Sauce* and pour over the pancakes. Brown under the grill.

CRÊPES AU FOIE
Pancakes Stuffed with Liver

MAKES 12 PANCAKES

125 g (4 oz) chicken livers,
  chopped
350 g (12 oz) lamb's liver,
  chopped
2 shallots, finely chopped
50 g (2 oz) butter

Pepper
2 hard-boiled eggs, finely
  chopped
Tomato Sauce (see page 20)

Cook the livers with the shallots in butter. Season with pepper and stir in the chopped hard-boiled eggs. Spread a little liver stuffing on to each pancake, roll into tubes and cover with the *Tomato Sauce*. Dab on a few knobs of butter and flash under the grill for a few minutes.

Omelettes

There are two principal styles of omelette, the light fluffy one to be cooked and consumed at once, and the thick country one, usually eaten cold.

The art of omelette cooking is an acquired skill, and practice is more useful than advice. The perfect omelette should be golden on the outside, fluffed up and creamy inside.

For a plain omelette, 2 eggs per person are enough (try to obtain free-range eggs: they make all the difference) and they should not be whisked too much. I add a tablespoon or dash of water to this, a pinch of salt and a grind of pepper. Be sure to have a small heavy-bottomed pan, 15 to 20 cm (6 to 8 in.) in diameter, exclusively for omelettes.

Make sure that the pan is very hot, then melt a small knob of butter into it – ensure that the whole surface is covered before adding the beaten egg mixture. Wiggle the pan so that the mixture covers the base and, as it begins to seal or cook around the edges, lift the omelette away from the pan with a spatula or fork, twisting the pan at the same time so the uncooked mixture runs underneath. After a moment or two, tip the pan and fold the omelette in half. Now add another little knob of butter to the hot pan, so that it runs under the omelette, tip out on to a hot plate and serve at once. It is better to cook and serve one perfect omelette at a time, even though the other guests are kept waiting, than it is to keep them warm until all are prepared.

For a filled omelette add the stuffing of your choice after the mixture has started to firm up and before you fold it over.

A tablespoon of finely chopped fresh herbs – chives, parsley and chervil – added to a light creamy omelette is delicious. But you can add almost anything you like.

OMELETTE À LA LANGUEDOCIENNE
Languedoc Omelette

SERVES 4

75 g (3 oz) garlic sausage, peeled and thinly sliced

75 g (3 oz) goose, chicken or duck fat

30 g (1¼ oz) bread, cut into croutons and rubbed with garlic

50 g (2 oz) cooked chicken, duck or goose

2 cloves garlic, minced

Thyme and parsley, finely chopped

Salt and pepper

8 eggs, beaten

In a large frying pan fry the sausage in the fat until warmed through. Remove and keep warm. In the same fat, fry the croutons. When they are done, add the chicken, duck or goose. Beat everything else together with the eggs. Cook quickly, stirring, until the omelette sets. Turn out on to a serving platter and serve immediately. (From Languedoc.)

OMELETTE NORMANDE
Normandy Omelette

SERVES 2

4 eggs, separated

75 g (3 oz) butter

1 tablespoon double cream

Salt and pepper

Beat the egg whites until they form soft peaks.

In a frying pan melt 50 g (2 oz) of the butter and add the egg yolks. Stir as they begin to set. When they are still a little runny, add the cream, salt and pepper and the beaten egg whites. Allow to set without turning. Melt the remaining butter in a separate pan.

Fold the omelette in half and serve on a warm platter with the melted butter drizzled over.

You could add mushrooms, herbs or ham to this mixture before folding. (From Normandy.)

OMELETTE À LA PROVENÇALE
Provençal Omelette

This is the kind of heavy omelette that tastes as good cold as hot, so it's ideal for picnics or a light lunch.

You want a good heavy iron pan about 15 to 20 cm (6 to 8 in.) in diameter, reserved exclusively for dishes like this. If you ever get lucky on the race course at Isle sur la Sorgue, you might meet a friend of mine who makes this kind of thick omelette, but instead of vegetables he fills it with about 175 g (6 oz) sliced fresh truffle. Which I once ate with him in the hot Provençal sun as Croix de Guerre won the three-thirty.

Which in turn reminds me of the most expensive plate of potatoes that I ever ate in my life. It was in Périgord at the Vieux Logis at Trémolat. Tired of playing gastronomic superstars, I rejected the exotic *soufflé*, *Confit de Canard*, *Cèpes Poêlés* and *Ragoût de Poisson Parfumé au Saffron* that glided between the American-filled tables under polished silver domes held by white-coated English-speaking Belgian waiters, and demanded something simple. Like a plate of *Pommes Sarladaise aux Truffes* – which is, quite simply, slivers of par-boiled potato fried in goose fat in a heavy-lidded pan till they are golden, at which point a handful of sliced truffles are chucked in (the lid is important as it keeps the aroma of truffle from escaping, thus permeating the potatoes which, now I come to think of it, also had little batons (lardons) of home-cured bacon tossed into them). The resulting black and gold concoction was put on to a large white plate and then under the ubiquitous silver dome. For this privilege I was charged eighteen of our English pounds, which I in no way begrudged!

To return to the omelètte.

SERVES 4

1 large onion, finely chopped	*Olive oil*
2 tomatoes, skinned, de-	*Salt and pepper*
* seeded and chopped*	*Fresh thyme*
2 courgettes, thinly sliced	*6 free-range eggs, beaten*
1 red pepper, de-seeded and	
* finely chopped*	

Fry the vegetables in the oil until they are translucent, season with salt, pepper and thyme and put to one side.

Make sure the pan is clean, add more oil, put it back on the heat and add half the beaten eggs. Once this begins to firm up, pour in the vegetable mixture and cover with the remaining beaten eggs. Let it cook for about 5 minutes, slide on to a plate, flip back into the pan, uncooked side down, and cook for about another 5 minutes. Eat hot or cold. (From Provence.)

OMELETTE SAVOYARDE
Savoy Omelette

SERVES 4

150 g (5 oz) lean bacon,
  diced

Butter or lard

1 potato, peeled and finely
  chopped

1 leek, finely chopped

8 eggs

2 tablespoons double cream

Salt and pepper

75 g (3 oz) Gruyère cheese,
  cut in small cubes

Parsley, chopped

Blanch the bacon in boiling water. Drain and dry before frying in an omelette pan with a little butter or lard until it has browned. Remove the bacon and add the potato and leek to the fat.

Beat the eggs with the cream, salt and pepper in a large bowl. Put more butter in the pan and return the bacon. When the fat is hot, pour on the eggs. Add the cheese and parsley. Serve the omelette flat and moist. (From Savoy.)

OMELETTE AUX TRUFFES
Truffle Omelette

SERVES 2

1 fresh or preserved truffle
50 ml (2 fl oz) Cognac
4 eggs

50 ml (2 fl oz) double cream
Salt and pepper
1 tablespoon goose fat

If using a fresh truffle carefully brush clean and wash it. Slice finely and steep for 1 hour in the Cognac. Add 50 ml (2 fl oz) water and bring to the boil. Allow to cool before using. Reserve the cooking liquid.

If using a preserved truffle, simply marinate it for 1 hour in the Cognac. Reserve the marinade.

Separate 1 of the eggs and beat the white until stiff. Beat the yolk with the rest of the eggs, together with the cream, salt, pepper and 1 tablespoon truffle cooking liquid or marinade. At the last minute, carefully fold in the egg white and truffle slices, reserving a few for decoration. Melt the goose fat in a shallow frying pan. When it begins to smoke, pour in the eggs. Cook over a high heat. When done, fold in half and slide on to a platter.

Mind you, my friends, Mme Moulin, a Périgord landlady of my acquaintance, would not agree with this recipe – she wouldn't put truffles into an omelette for a start. She'd rather have ceps and make the omelette really thick and heavy. In fact, when I cooked her a light fluffy cep one, she scolded me unmercifully!! (From Périgord.)

OMELETTE À LA PAYSANNE
Provençal Omelette Cake

The idea here is to make a dozen very thin omelettes about 15 cm (6 in.) in diameter, which are flavoured and therefore coloured with tomato, olives and spinach, so that you make, say, four green ones, four red ones and four black ones. You lay these on top of each other and end up with a multi-coloured cold omelette cake. It is not a dish easy to find any more, but once it was a popular lunch for farmers to eat in the fields. What you do is beat up a load of eggs ready to make omelettes. You'll need two tablespoons each of puréed black olives (don't forget to take the stones out), smooth fresh tomato sauce and puréed cooked spinach. Divide the omelette mixture into three portions and stir the olives into the first, tomato into the second and spinach into the third. Now simply cook the omelettes so that they are flat, round and firm. When cold, pile them into a cake. (From Provence.)

VEGETABLES

Visit any local market in any French town or market from Rennes to Besançon or Béziers to La Rochelle, and you cannot fail to spot the one thing that really separates them from us. The French care about fresh vegetables. Watch a French house-wife as she makes her way slowly along the loaded stalls, stopping to examine the glowing red and orange orbs of tomatoes, not worrying about the misshapen, lumpy ones, searching for the peak of ripeness and flavour, or gently squeezing the raffia-tied bundles of fat white and purple asparagus, like Easter candles, or picking over the creamy heads of cauliflowers, rejecting all but the perfect one. What you are seeing is a true artist at work, patiently assembling all the materials of her craft, just as the painter squeezes the oil colours onto his palette ready to create a masterpiece.

ASPERGES AUX MORILLES
Asparagus with Morels and Shallots

SERVES 4

1.5 kg (3 lb) asparagus
50 g (2 oz) butter
Salt and pepper
200 g (7 oz) fresh morel
  mushrooms

2 shallots, finely chopped
Juice of 1 lemon
Parsley

Peel and blanch the asparagus in boiling water for about 7 minutes. Drain and fry in butter for a few minutes. Place on a platter and season with salt and pepper.

Next fry the morels in a little butter, season and put to one side. Add the rest of the butter to the pan and fry the chopped shallots until they become transparent. Add the morels to the shallots and pour in the lemon juice. Cover the asparagus with the sauce. Serve hot, garnished with parsley. (From Provence.)

MORILLES
Morels

SERVES 3

400 g (14 oz) fresh morels
75 g (3 oz) butter
1 tablespoon flour
150 ml (5 fl oz) chicken
  stock

Salt and pepper
3 slices white bread
2 eggs
2 tablespoons double cream
Juice of 1 lemon

Fry the morels in one-third of the butter. Dust with the flour and add the chicken stock, salt and pepper. Simmer for 5 minutes.

Fry the bread in the rest of the butter and arrange on a serving platter. Keep warm.

Beat the eggs with the cream and lemon juice and pour on to the morels. Stir in well. When the eggs have just set, pour the mixture on to the fried bread and serve. (From Savoy.)

CÈPES À LA SARLADAISE
Ceps Cooked with Potatoes and Garlic

SERVES 3 TO 4

750 g (1½ lb) old potatoes,
  peeled and sliced
4 tablespoons goose or duck
  fat
1 slice smoked bacon, finely
  diced

750 g (1½ lb) ceps, chopped
3 large cloves garlic, minced
1 small handful parsley,
  chopped
Salt and pepper
1 bouquet garni

Rinse the potato slices in hot water to prevent them from
sticking together. Melt the goose fat in a frying pan. Fry the
bacon and add the potatoes. Brown lightly and add the ceps.
Cover and cook gently for a few minutes.

Add the garlic, parsley, salt, pepper and bouquet garni.
Cook gently for a further 15 minutes. Serve with roast meat
or game. (From Périgord.)

It must be the peasant in me, but I really enjoy potatoes in all
forms – boiled, roasted, mashed. And when puréed with
cream and eggs and butter till almost a thick soup they are
brilliant with a simple grilled chop and its fat and juices
poured over the purée: a real personal favourite. But here are
some others.

POMMES DE TERRE FARCIES
Stuffed Potatoes

SERVES 4

8 medium potatoes, peeled
100 g (3½ oz) streaky
bacon, cut in tiny pieces
1 onion, finely chopped
4 cloves garlic, finely
chopped
3–4 sprigs parsley, finely
chopped

Salt and pepper
1 egg
3 tablespoons flour
3–4 tablespoons milk
3 tablespoons oil
1 tablespoon butter

Pre-heat the oven to gas mark 3, 160°C (325°F).

Cut a round, lengthways, off the top of each potato: this will be the lid. Carefully dig the potatoes out with a sharp spoon. Remove as much flesh as possible without damaging the potato 'shell'. Keep the bits.

Mix the bacon, onion, garlic, parsley and salt and pepper together with the egg. Add the flour little by little, mixing well. Add the milk until you have a firm dough.

Stuff the potatoes with the dough and put their lids on.

Heat the oil and butter together in a large pan. Over a high heat add the potatoes, lid-side down. Allow to brown. Reduce the heat, turn the potatoes over and add the reserved potato bits. Salt lightly. Transfer to an ovenproof dish and bake in the oven for 45 minutes. (From Auvergne.)

Pommes de Terre à l'Auvergnoise
Oven Baked Potatoes with Bacon

———

Originally this dish was cooked in a baker's oven and took on the delicious fragrance of freshly baked bread. If you know a friendly baker, it's well worth trying.

SERVES 4

1 kg (2 lb) potatoes, peeled and thinly sliced
3–4 cloves garlic, chopped
1 bayleaf, quartered
Salt and pepper

100 g (3½ oz) streaky bacon, cut into small pieces
4 thin slices good bacon

Pre-heat the oven to gas mark 6, 200°C (400°F).

Butter an earthenware baking dish. Layer the potato slices into the dish, scattering the garlic, bayleaf, salt and pepper among them.

Fry the streaky bacon until crispy. Add it and its fat to the potatoes, plus enough boiling water nearly to cover. Place the slices of bacon on top.

Bake in the oven for 45 minutes to 1 hour, until the potatoes are tender and the bacon browned. (From Auvergne.)

GRATIN SAVOYARDE
Potato and Cheese Bake

SERVES 6

1 clove garlic
75 g (3 oz) butter
1 kg (2 lb) potatoes, peeled and thinly sliced
Salt and pepper
125 g (4 oz) Gruyère cheese, grated

2 onions, finely chopped
Parsley, finely chopped
1 kg (2 lb) ceps or other wild mushrooms, chopped
250 ml (8 fl oz) double cream

Pre-heat the oven to gas mark 4, 180°C (350°F).

Rub a gratin dish all over with the garlic and butter it liberally. Put one layer of potatoes, a little salt, pepper, Gruyère, onion and parsely in the dish. Then add a layer of ceps, onion, parsley and Gruyère. Continue the layers, finishing with a layer of potatoes and cheese. Dot with butter and pour over the double cream. Bake in the oven for 1¾ hours. (From Savoy.)

TOURTE AUX POMMES DE TERRE
Potato Pie

SERVES 6

For the pastry:

350 g (12 oz) flour, sifted
½ teaspoon salt

175 g (6 oz) butter, cut in
pieces

For the filling:

6 medium potatoes, peeled
and thinly sliced
Salt and pepper

75 g (3 oz) butter, cut in
pieces
1 egg yolk, beaten
6 tablespoons double cream

Combine the pastry ingredients and add a little water gradually until you have a soft dough. Don't handle the pastry any more than is necessary. Form into a ball and leave in the refrigerator for at least 1 hour.

Pre-heat the oven to gas mark 6, 200°C (400°F).

Roll out two-thirds of the pastry on a floured surface and line a pie dish with it, making sure that it comes well up the sides. Layer in the potatoes, salt, pepper and butter. Roll out the rest of the pastry and cover the pie, making sure that the edges are carefully pinched together. Cut a hole in the middle of the pastry cover for the cooking steam to escape. Paint the pie with beaten egg yolk.

Bake the pie in the oven for 45 minutes to 1 hour, until the potatoes are tender and the pastry is brown. Unmould the pie, carefully cut away the lid and pour on the cream. Replace the lid and serve immediately. (From Auvergne.)

POMMES DE TERRE À LA SAVOYARDE
Savoy Potato Pie

SERVES 4 TO 6

1 kg (2 lb) potatoes, peeled
75 g (3 oz) chervil, finely
*   chopped*
450 ml (15 fl oz) hot milk

50 g (2 oz) butter
6 eggs, beaten
Salt and pepper
Nutmeg

Pre-heat the oven to gas mark 6, 200°C (400°F).

Boil the potatoes until tender and mash them. Add the chervil, milk and butter. Slowly stir in the eggs. Season with salt and pepper and nutmeg to taste. Butter an ovenproof dish and pour in the potato mixture. Pop in the oven for 25 minutes, or until golden brown. Serve as a main dish with a salad. (From Savoy.)

LA TRUFFADE
Puréed Potatoes with Garlic and Tomme de Cantal Cheese

SERVES 4

75 g (3 oz) butter
7–8 medium potatoes, boiled
*   in their skins, peeled and*
*   mashed*

Salt and pepper
4–8 cloves garlic, crushed
300 g (10 oz) Tomme de
*   Cantal cheese, grated*

Melt the butter in a large saucepan, add the potatoes, salt and pepper, garlic and cheese. Mix well over a low heat until the cheese goes 'stringy'. Serve immediately. This dish is delicious on its own or with pink-grilled spring lamb chops. Remember to pour the meat fat and juices over the potatoes. (From Auvergne.)

POMMES DE TERRE AUX PRUNEAUX ET RAISINS
Potatoes with Prunes and Raisins

Some of you, in passing the deep-freeze chests of your local supermarket, may have seen little packets of a potato preparation called rosti. Some of you might have been to northern Europe or Alsace and had genuine rosti, which, as you know, is grated potato fried with bits of bacon in a pan until it is crispy on the outside and rather like a very thick omelette. Well, this remarkable Savoy dish is a kind of a rosti, except that it's cooked with soaked and stoned prunes and raisins. It could be served as a sort of pudding, although you would not want very much to eat before it. It could be served as a kind of sweet-and-sour vegetable dish to go with a little roast leg of pork, or perhaps with a roast game bird like pheasant or partridge, or even a rabbit stew. The recipe I give here requires quite a lot of preparation and then is baked in a *bain-marie* in the oven for a long time – that is the traditional way. But I have decided to change it the Floyd way.

Follow my instructions below for preparing the mixture, but instead of baking it in the oven in a *bain-marie*, tip it into a heavy frying pan and fry on both sides for at least 15 minutes, taking care not to burn it, until the last few moments, when you brown it on both sides by tipping it over as you might a pancake. The result of all of this, for those of you old enough or poor enough to remember, is the equivalent of the great British Bubble and Squeak, except that it is made from prunes, raisins and grated potatoes, not mashed-up potato and Brussels sprouts. It's super.

SERVES 4

3 large potatoes, peeled and
   grated, well rinsed,
   drained and dried
500 g (1 lb) prunes, stoned,
   soaked and drained
250 g (8 oz) raisins, soaked
   and drained

Dash of eau de vie
2 tablespoons flour
1 tablespoon sugar
500 g (1 lb) bacon, diced

Pre-heat the oven to gas mark 5, 190°C (375°F).

Mix all the ingredients together, except the bacon which you fry and then add to the mixture. Put the whole lot in a baking dish, press it in really hard, pop it into a *bain-marie* and cook in the oven for a couple of hours, until it becomes a kind of cake. This is the traditional way of preparing it; but, as I have said in the introduction, you could fry it. (From Savoy.)

PÂTÉ DE CHOU
Cabbage Pie

This is really a kind of Yorkshire pudding stuffed with cabbage. It will go very well with boiled ham or pork dishes. And, believe it or not, it is great cold with homemade *Tomato Ketchup* (see page 26).

SERVES 6

1 medium cabbage, tough core and outer leaves removed, quartered	1 small handful parsley, chopped
125 g (4 oz) streaky bacon, cut into small pieces	2 eggs, beaten
2 shallots, minced	200 g (7 oz) flour
2 cloves garlic, minced	300 ml (10 fl oz) milk
	Salt and pepper
	2 tablespoons oil

Cook the cabbage in boiling water until tender. Drain well and chop.

Pre-heat the oven to gas mark 6–7, 200–220°C (400–425°F).

Meanwhile, combine the bacon, shallots, garlic, parsley and eggs. Slowly add the flour and enough milk to produce a sort of thick pancake batter. Add salt and pepper.

Put the oil into a pie dish and pop into the oven. When the oil is smoking, pour in half the batter and cover with the cooked cabbage. Pour on the rest of the batter and return to the oven to bake for 45 minutes or until golden brown. Turn out and serve immediately, or keep until the next day when you can re-heat it in a pan with some butter and it will taste even better. (From Auvergne.)

CHOU ROUGE
Red Cabbage

SERVES 2 AS A MAIN COURSE,
OR 4 TO 6 AS AN ACCOMPANIMENT

1 red cabbage, coarse
* leaves and core removed,*
* finely chopped*
2 onions, chopped
125 g (4 oz) smoked bacon,
* diced*
1 tablespoon lard

300 ml (10 fl oz) red wine
300 ml (10 fl oz) chicken
* stock*
Salt and pepper
1 bayleaf
1 large apple, peeled, cored
* and chopped*

Blanch the cabbage in boiling water for 10 minutes and drain.

Pre-heat the oven to gas mark 5, 190°C (375°F).

In a casserole sweat the onions, bacon and lard. Add the cabbage, wine, stock, a little salt, lots of pepper, the bayleaf and the apple.

Cover and seal, and bake in the oven for about 2 hours. (From Lorraine.)

CHOU FARCI
Stuffed Cabbage Leaves

SERVES 4 TO 6

1 firm cabbage
500 g (1 lb) sausagemeat
1 thick slice stale white bread, soaked in milk
2 cloves garlic, finely chopped

1 handful parsley, chopped
Salt and pepper
3 tablespoons tomato purée
Butter
Gruyère cheese, grated

Blanch the cabbage in boiling salted water for 15 minutes, drain well, reserving the cooking water, and allow to cool.

Cook the sausagemeat in a little of the cabbage water for 15 minutes. Mix with the bread, garlic, parsley, salt and pepper. Remove some of the cabbage leaves and trim off any tough pieces.

Pre-heat the oven to gas mark 5, 190°C (375°F).

Place 1 tablespoon of sausagemeat in each leaf and roll into a ball. Continue until all the stuffing is used up. Pack the cabbage balls into an ovenproof dish and pour over the tomato purée, thinned with a little water. Dot with butter and grated Gruyère. Pop into the oven for 25 minutes.

This method can also be used for courgettes, aubergines and tomatoes. The aubergines and courgettes should be blanched and halved before you scoop out the middles and stuff them. Use olive oil instead of tomato purée. (From Provence.)

TOMATES À LA PROVENÇALE
Braised Tomatoes

SERVES 6

*12 tomatoes, halved and de-
  seeded*
2 tablespoons olive oil
4 cloves garlic, minced
*1 small handful parsley,
  finely chopped*

Fresh breadcrumbs
1 tablespoon thyme
Salt and pepper

Pre-heat the oven to gas mark 6, 200°C (400°F).

Fry the tomatoes briefly on both sides in some oil. Arrange them, cut-side up, in a roasting tin. Sprinkle each one with a mixture of the garlic, parsley, breadcrumbs, thyme, salt and pepper. Bake in the oven for 10 minutes. Serve hot with roast meat. (From Provence.)

POIVRONS FARCIS
Stuffed Peppers

You won't be in the Pays Basque long before you realise that they've got quite a thing about peppers and pimentos. (And squid, which I have to admit I'm not all that keen on.)

So here, then, is a super little snack from the region.

SERVES 4

4 red or green peppers	2 eggs, beaten
1 onion, finely chopped	300 ml (10 fl oz) chicken or
Olive oil	meat stock
100 g (3½ oz) spicy	50 g (2 oz) fresh
sausage, diced	breadcrumbs
200 g (7 oz) pork, finely	
minced, or sausagemeat	

Pre-heat the oven to gas mark 6, 200°C (400°F).

First put the peppers whole into the oven for about 10 minutes, until they just begin to brown. Take them out and peel off the skin carefully. Cut off the bottom and pull out the pith and pips. Turn down the oven to gas mark 5, 190°C (375°F).

Meanwhile, fry the onion in olive oil until soft, add the diced sausage and minced pork or sausagemeat and fry for 5 minutes or so. Take off the heat and beat in the eggs. Stuff the peppers with this preparation, moisten each one with a little stock. Top off with breadcrumbs and a little dash of olive oil and bake in the oven for about 1 hour.

This has just reminded me of a brilliant summer starter. Put red and green peppers into the oven as I've described above, for about 20 minutes, and prepare them in the same way. Allow them to cool and then cut into strips, soak in olive oil, add fresh black pepper, sea salt and a dash of wine vinegar and chill for an hour or two. Serve as a starter with fresh bread. It's truly delicious. (From Basque Country.)

HARICOTS BLANCS À LA CHARENTAISE
Stewed Haricot Beans

SERVES 6

*1 kg (2 lb) fresh haricot
  beans, shelled*
2 tablespoons oil
*5 little onions, peeled and
  left whole*
1 branch thyme
*1 tomato, peeled and
  chopped*

2 cloves garlic
Pepper
2 tablespoons butter
2 branches parsley, chopped
Salt
1 tablespoon double cream

In a large pan, toss the haricots in the oil over a low heat. Add the onions and thyme. Cook for 15 minutes, stirring well. Add the tomato and garlic and cover with boiling water. Add plenty of pepper, but no salt until the last minute as it will make the beans tough.

Simmer for 45 minutes. Five minutes before serving add the butter, parsley and salt. At the last minute stir in the cream. (From Charente.)

GRATIN DE BLETTE
Swiss Chard in White Sauce

SERVES 4 TO 6

*1.5 kg (3 lb) Swiss chard,
  white ribs only*
50 g (2 oz) butter
2 tablespoons flour

2 glasses milk
Gruyère cheese, grated
Salt and pepper

Blanch the chard in boiling salted water for 30 minutes.
Pre-heat the oven to gas mark 6, 200°C (400°F).

Make a white sauce with the rest of the ingredients.
Arrange the drained chard in an ovenproof dish and cover
with the white sauce and a thick layer of cheese. Pop in the
oven until brown and bubbling, or put under the grill. (From
Provence.)

RATATOUILLE

SERVES 8 TO 10

1 aubergine	10 tomatoes
1 courgette	Olive oil
Salt	1 clove garlic, chopped
1 red pepper	Parsley, finely chopped
1 green pepper	Pepper
2 onions	Thyme, chopped

The vitally important thing about ratatouille is that each
vegetable is cooked separately. So cut all the vegetables into
equal-sized pieces – fork-sized, perhaps.

Prepare the aubergine and courgette first. Sprinkle with
salt and leave to 'sweat'. Then dry with kitchen paper.

In a large frying pan cook each vegetable in olive oil (also
very important), one after the other, until they are tender,
then put to one side with all the juices from the pan. During
this process, if necessary, top up the oil from time to time.
Now put the lot into a saucepan, add the garlic, parsley, salt,
pepper and thyme and all the left-over oil and cook for 10 to
15 minutes just to mix them all up. Leave to cool, refrigerate
and eat cold. (From Provence.)

BEIGNETS DE COURGETTES
Courgette Fritters with Tomato Sauce

SERVES 4

For the fritters:

1 kg (2 lb) large courgettes (or marrow), peeled, de-seeded and cut in large chunks

2 eggs, beaten
Salt and pepper
150 g (5 oz) flour
Oil for deep-frying

For the sauce:

750 g (1½ lb) tomatoes, roughly chopped
2 cloves garlic, chopped

4 sprigs fresh thyme
Salt and pepper

Boil the courgettes for 20 to 30 minutes, until tender but still in one piece. Drain and mash, and leave in a sieve until completely drained.

Meanwhile make the sauce. Cook the tomatoes, garlic and thyme together over a low heat until most of the liquid has evaporated. Push through a fine sieve. Add salt and pepper and re-heat when ready to serve.

In a bowl combine the courgettes, eggs, salt and pepper. Add the flour a little at a time. Mix well.

Heat the oil until hot but not smoking. Cook spoonfuls of courgette batter in batches. Fry until golden. Remove and drain on kitchen paper. Keep warm while you fry the rest of the fritters. Serve immediately as a starter with the tomato sauce to dip in, or as an accompaniment to roast veal or pork – but not with gravy, of course. (From Auvergne.)

Choux de Bruxelles aux MARRONS
Brussels Sprouts Cooked with Chestnuts

SERVES 4

500 g (1 lb) chestnuts (or use preserved – see page 28)

1 litre (2 pints) chicken stock

1 kg (2 lb) even-sized Brussels sprouts

Salt and pepper

250 g (8 oz) streaky bacon, cut into batons

50 g (2 oz) butter

If you are using fresh chestnuts, cut a small gash in the side of each chestnut and blanch for 1 minute in boiling water. Peel off the skins (the outer and softer inner skins) and cook for 20 minutes in the chicken stock.

Cook the Brussels sprouts in boiling salted water and strain. Fry the bacon batons in butter and add the sprouts. Next add the chestnuts, salt and pepper and simmer for about 5 minutes before serving.

You see, you could have a meal of, say, simply fried fillets of fish with melted butter and lemon juice, followed by this splendid sprout dish, finishing off with some good cheese and fruit – lots of wine, of course. A varied and nutritous meal without too much fuss. (From Alsace.)

FISH

Big cranes dip into the hold of this rusted streaked white ship. Huge articulated trucks with hungry high-sided trailers are lined up against clanking conveyor belts and chutes ready for loading. In the first truck the driver sleeps, despite the noise. Men wearing thick gloves, chattering loudly, wait for a signal from the load master. Fork-lift truck drivers rev their engines as the big cranes winch a clutch of dull torpedoes high into the breezy spring morning and lower them with a crash into the hoppers. But these torpedoes are not the weapons of war. They are fish, some 8 feet long. Here in Concarneau in Brittany the *Reefer Progress* is discharging 3000 tonnes of frozen tuna from the Ivory Coast.

From the window of the Relais La Coquille I watch the frantic activity of the port as I sit and sip Muscadet. Fishing boats alongside are being repainted; others on the hard, freshly built, are ready to slip, and in the big sheds the jigs and hoists are busy building yet more. In the kitchen of La Coquille, Jean-François is inspecting the morning's delivery of fish; big pollock, plump soles, bright red mullet, wriggling shrimps, squirming langoustines – pale pink and flipping like big grasshoppers – baskets of scallops, boxes of winkles, clams and oysters like precious coins recovered from some long sunk wreck, lovingly packed in seaweed. Apprentices are chopping, filleting and busying themselves around the big kitchen. A fisherman in rubber boots is loading crayfish and lobsters into the big tank in the dining room. A young lad struggles to tip a basket of live prawns into a vat of boiling water bigger than he is. It is eight in the morning and all over France kitchens like this one are starting another day.

Over on the quay the first truck is loaded with tuna. Big dorsal fins are silhouetted above the high sides of the trailer as it pulls away. One or two fish have fallen between the loading chute and the trailer. One of the gang kicks them to one side – perks for the boys, by arrangement, of course. The market place is crowded and men and women alike jostle around the fish stalls buying the day's lunch. A fillet of whiting here, a kilo or two of soft-shelled crabs here. With every purchase the merchant offers a lemon and a sprig of parsley. I squeeze in and buy a large slice of tuna – 'From the Ivory Coast?' I enquire. 'No. From here,' says the man proudly. I will make a salad of tuna fish and rice for some friends tonight.

In a shed behind the Restaurant Mons, Courtain is tasting soup from a 100-litre pot simmering gently on a huge gas ring. Two workers in the corner, in rubber aprons and boots, are filleting a mountain of fish, while another drags in a hand-cart full of crayfish. The foreman pours cognac and spices into one of the six huge pots. No one speaks. The only sounds are the hiss of gas, the bubbling of the pots and the rhythmic chopping of leeks being carefully cut. Every pot of this wonderful fish soup is made to an old family recipe. Only fresh fish and vegetables are used, the soup is puréed by hand – a machine, though quicker, crushes too finely and wrecks the flavour. I taste the soup and Monsieur Courtain pours me a slug of fine cognac into an empty soup tin.

'They, the banks, want me to expand. I won't. We make all we can sell and any other way we wouldn't be able to maintain the quality. And you know, what is money? If you are not happy and proud of your work, it counts for nothing,' he says. 'And anyway, if I expanded I'd have to employ more people, then I'd have to put preservatives and colouring into the soup. And worse still I'd have to put pepper into the cognac so that the staff wouldn't drink it all!'

And he pours me another large one. Fine cognac. And pepper free.

'Let us drink,' he says, 'to our wives. May they never be widows.'

The recipes that follow are a selection of personal favourites. You do not have to be a genius to cook them – you just need a little common sense.

Fish is good for you. It is healthy. It is also very splendid to eat. There are so many varieties and so many ways to cook it that it's a travesty that here in Britain we don't take full advantage of the riches of our shores. This is in part the fault of the authorities in this country, like the Ministry of Ag. and Fish., and more importantly the White Fish Authority, who seem unable to get their act together, and in part due to an inherent British apathy and squeamishness towards fish. All too often I hear that people don't eat fish because of the bones, or because of some half-remembered experience of steamed fish at school, or even because of whale meat during the war. The French have not got anything special over us – they are not freaks, they just enjoy fish. So too, I hope, will you when you come to try some of the delights that are to come. These are not the esoteric creations of a race of master chefs, they are simply the intelligent preparation of the good things in life as executed by ordinary chefs, cooks and house-wives all over France. So please may I bore you for a moment or two with a little lecture.

Firstly, wherever possible, buy fresh fish. Check that the flesh is firm and the eyes bright. Look inside the gills – they should be pink. Fish does not smell of fish, fresh fish smells of the sea.

Plan your meals carefully and make friends with your fishmonger. For some of the dishes in this book you may need to order your fish in advance. If you don't like filleting and gutting ask the fishmonger to prepare the beast for you.

Fish should not be overcooked. Never boil fish, always cook it gently. If you are grilling fish, make sure that the grill is really hot before starting to cook. Where possible, remove the skin from poached fish before you serve it. The skin on most grilled fish is a useful protection to the flesh and should be left on.

Remember, a simple fillet of some so-called 'humble fish' gently fried in foaming butter and served with a squeeze of fresh lemon juice is vastly superior to any extravagant concoction of frozen prawns and shrimps cooked in wine and cream. And don't over-complicate the accompaniment. Nothing goes better with fish than simple boiled potatoes, whether they be succulent new Jersey Royals or plain boiled winter ones.

A last point. If you are still not interested and want to continue frying bits of fish in batter, then at least use the best batter possible: a mixture of plain flour and water whisked to a thickish paste with a good dash of vinegar added to it.

The French are passionate about fish stews, made with both sea and freshwater fish, and don't worry about bones and bits. Of all kinds of fish stew, Bouillabaisse is probably the best-known and most abused (often served from frozen pre-prepared packs). Here are a few authentic regional versions.

Bouillabaisse

SERVES 6 TO 8

2 large onions, finely
    chopped
1 leek, finely chopped
4 cloves garlic, crushed
5 ripe tomatoes, chopped
25 ml (1 fl oz) olive oil
1 sprig thyme
1 sprig fennel
1 tablespoon grated orange
    rind

2.25 kg (5 lb) mixed fish
    (which can include John
    Dory, bass, gurnard,
    wrasse, dogfish, small
    soft-shelled crabs, saith,
    weever fish)
Salt and pepper
2 sachets saffron
1 quantity Rouille (see page
    23)
1 quantity Aïoli (see page
    23)
1 kg (2 lb) boiled potatoes

In a large pan, fry the onions, leek, garlic and tomatoes in the olive oil until golden. Then add the thyme, fennel and orange rind, mix in well and cook for a further 5 minutes.

Bring 2.3 litres (4 pints) water to the boil – it must be boiling furiously in readiness for the next phase so that it will liaise and thicken the resulting soup, which is essential for this dish. Add the boiling water to the olive oil and vegetables over a high heat, whisking vigorously for 1 to 2 minutes, until the sauce thickens noticeably. You could perhaps add another slurp of olive oil at this time and keep boiling until you have the right consistency.

Now add the fish – if they are unequal in size, start with the biggest first so that they all cook evenly. Season with salt and pepper, add the saffron and simmer until cooked – say, 10 or 15 minutes.

Lift the fish carefully from the sauce and remove the skin and bones. Arrange it in an attractive shallow dish, and moisten with a cupful or two of the strained sauce. Strain the remainder of the sauce into a tureen and serve as a soup garnished with *Rouille* and *Aïoli*. Then eat the fish with boiled potatoes and more *Aïoli*. (From Provence.)

LA CHAUDRÉE
Fish Stew

SERVES 6

18 cloves garlic, whole	Sprigs thyme
100 g (3½ oz) butter	1 leek, chopped
750g (1½ lb) squid, beaks, heads and ink sacks removed, cut in chunks	750g (1½ lb) eels, cleaned and cut in chunks
1 tablespoon flour	6 small skate wings
500 ml (17 fl oz) white wine	1 large sole, cut in chunks, or 6 small ones
1 handful parsley, chopped	Salt and pepper
1 bayleaf	

Fry the garlic cloves in 50 g (2 oz) of the butter, taking great care that they don't burn but turn a nice gold colour. Add the squid and sauté for 5 minutes before stirring in the flour and adding the wine. Top up with boiling water until the squid are completely covered. Add some of the parsley, the bayleaf, several sprigs of thyme and the leek.

Simmer for 15 minutes before adding the eels, and for a further 15 minutes before adding the skate and sole. Cook for 5 more minutes. Add the rest of the butter and parsley, and season with salt and pepper. (From Charente.)

COTRIADE
Brittany Fish Stew

SERVES 6 TO 8

200 g (7 oz) butter
3 large onions, 1 stuck with
   2 cloves, the other 2 chopped
2 kg (4 lb) potatoes, peeled

1 bouquet garni (thyme,
   bayleaf, parsley)
Salt and pepper
Croutons

For the fish:

1.5 kg (3 lb) conger eel, cut
   in 2.5 cm (1 in.) slices
500 g (1 lb) bass, gutted,
   washed and cut in 8 cm
   (3 in.) chunks
1.5 kg (3 lb) wrasse, gutted,
   cut in 3

500 g (1 lb) mackerel,
   gutted, washed and cut in
   3
500 g (1 lb) whiting, gutted,
   washed and cut in 3
500 g (1 lb) sardines, gutted
   and washed

Melt the butter in a large saucepan and add the chopped onions. Add the whole onion, potatoes, bouquet garni and chunks of eel. Cover with water, add salt and plenty of pepper. Bring to the boil and cook for 15 minutes.

Add the bass, wrasse and mackerel and cook for a further 5 minutes. Finally add the whiting and sardines and cook for another 5 minutes.

Remove from the pan all the fish and potatoes (except for 3 potatoes, 2 chunks of conger eel, a piece of mackerel, a piece of whiting and 3 sardines) and keep warm.

Strain the bouillon and keep warm over a low heat. Discard the bouquet garni but save everything else in the sieve and put it into a mortar. Crush everything together. Put this back into the bouillon and sieve again, so it is transformed into a thickened sauce.

Serve the fish and potatoes with some of this sauce, the rest with the croutons as a soup to start with. (From Brittany.)

BOURRIDE

SERVES 4

2 live lobsters
4 fillets thick white fish
　(bass, monkfish, turbot,
　brill, and so on)

200 ml (7 fl oz) double
　cream
300 ml (10 fl oz) Aïoli (see
　page 23)

For the stock:

Fish head and bones
2 slices lemon
2 leeks, chopped

1 carrot, sliced
1 bayleaf

Put all the stock ingredients into a pan with 1 litre (2 pints) water, simmer for 20 minutes, then strain. Into the strained stock place the lobsters, bring to the boil with a lid on the pan, reduce the heat and simmer for 20 minutes.

Remove the lobsters and keep warm while you poach the fillets of fish in the same stock for, say, 15 minutes, depending on their thickness. Cut the lobsters in half and arrange on a large serving dish with the fish fillets. Keep warm.

Now reduce the remaining stock to about a third of its original volume and, over a low heat, stir in the cream. Carefully whisk half of the *Aïoli* into the sauce, stirring over a low heat until the sauce takes on the colour and consistency of custard. Pour over the fish and serve at once, with the other half of the *Aïoli* handed separately. (From Provence.)

BLANQUETTE DE LA MER
Poached Fish with Vegetables

Here is a superb recipe that my friend Jean-François le Mettre cooks in his restaurant on the fish quay at Concarneau in Brittany. It's a great dish if you are poor since you can use quite ordinary fish like whiting, gurnard and mussels, or if you are rich you could use turbot, bass and lobsters. Anyway, the choice is yours, but this is Jean-François' particular favourite way of doing it:

Per person you need:

50 g (2 oz) white cabbage, very finely shredded	*2 scallops*
	Cream
1 carrot, finely sliced	*A knob of butter*
1 fillet of sole	*A little fresh root ginger, finely chopped*
1 fillet of red mullet	
1 fillet of pollock	*Salt and pepper*
3 or 4 mussels	*Finely chopped chives*
2 langoustines	

You will also need:

2.3 litres (4 pints) fish stock (see page 16)

Reserve about 1 litre (2 pints) of the stock to poach the fish in, then reduce the rest to one-fifth of its original volume and strain. Now blanch the cabbage and carrot in boiling water. Strain and place on a plate. Poach the fillets of fish, the mussels, langoustines and the scallops for 2 or 3 minutes in the reserved stock.

Strain them and arrange on a bed of chopped carrot and cabbage. Over a low heat beat into the concentrated fish stock a little fresh cream, some butter, a pinch of finely chopped ginger and some salt and pepper, until you have a smooth sauce. Pour this over the fish and serve at once, sprinkled with chopped chives. (From Brittany.)

CASSOLETTE DE ST JACQUES À LA NORMANDE
Normandy Casserole

SERVES 1

50 g (2 oz) butter
2 scallops, halved
1 shallot, minced
1 clove garlic, minced
1 teaspoon Calvados
12 clean mussels, steamed
  open, juices reserved

20 fresh shrimps, cooked
  and shelled
Pinch of paprika
Pinch of thyme
Salt and pepper
1 tablespoon double cream
1 slice lemon
1 slice bread, fried in butter

In a pan melt the butter and gently heat the scallops with the shallot and the garlic for 6 minutes.

Flame with the Calvados and add the mussel juices, the shrimps, paprika, thyme, salt and pepper. Reduce over a medium heat for 3 minutes.

Add the double cream and the mussels, and heat gently. Serve in earthenware ramekins with a slice of lemon and the fried bread. (From Normandy.)

MATELOTE AU RIESLING
Riesling Fish Stew

SERVES 8

500 g (1 lb) pike	*300 g (10 oz) tench*
500 g (1 lb) trout	*300 g (10 oz) eel*
300 g (10 oz) perch	

For the marinade:

1 onion stuck with a clove	*Pinch of nutmeg*
1 clove garlic, chopped	*Salt and pepper*
1 large carrot, sliced	*Riesling*
1 bouquet garni	

For the sauce:

300 g (10 oz) chanterelles or	*2 egg yolks*
field mushrooms, chopped	*25 g (1 oz) butter, cut in*
300 ml (10 fl oz) double	*small cubes*
cream	*Salt and pepper*

Scale, gut and wash the fish. Reserve the heads and bones.

Place the fish fillets in a large dish with the onion, garlic, carrot, bouquet garni, nutmeg and the salt and pepper. Pour on enough Riesling to cover. Allow to marinate for 12 hours, covered, in the refrigerator.

Pre-heat the oven to gas mark 7, 220°C (425°F).

Carefully remove the fish fillets from the marinade and place in a casserole. Put the marinade and the reserved fish heads and bones in a saucepan with an equal amount of water. Boil, uncovered, for 15 minutes. Strain and pour enough of this *court bouillon* over the fish to cover. Cover the casserole and pop in the oven for 20 minutes.

Meanwhile, blanch the mushrooms in boiling salted water for 15 minutes.

Remove the fish from the liquid and place on a serving platter. Keep warm. Strain the court bouillon again and boil, uncovered, for 10 minutes. Remove from the heat and whisk in the double cream and egg yolks until the sauce becomes thick and creamy. Add the cubes of butter and keep whisking until they melt. Add the mushrooms and the salt and pepper. Coat the fish with the sauce and serve immediately. (From Alsace.)

POCHOUSE
River Fish Stew

Shameful but true – the French angler is not interested in the sport – only the pot. Quelle horreur!

SERVES 12

2.25 kg (5 lb) river fish
(such as pike, eel, carp,
perch, tench)
2 onions, chopped
1 head garlic, chopped
1 small handful thyme
3 bayleaves

Salt and pepper
2 bottles white wine
(preferably Aligoté)
40 g (1½ oz) butter
25 g (1 oz) flour
Garlic croutons

Scale, gut, bone and wash the fish, and skin the eel if you have one. Cut into chunks.

In a large saucepan put the fish, onions, garlic, herbs, salt and pepper and cover with the wine. Bring to the boil and simmer for 20 to 30 minutes. Cream the butter and flour together to make a *beurre manié* and add this to the pan in small pieces. Stir until the sauce thickens.

Put the fish into heated serving bowls and pour the strained sauce over it. Serve with garlic croutons. (From Burgundy.)

MARMITE DIEPPOISE
Fish Stew in a Creamy Sauce

SERVES 6 TO 8

1 × 350 g (12 oz) sole, head removed and gutted

1 kg (2 lb) mixed red and grey mullet, heads removed and gutted, red mullet livers reserved

200 g (7 oz) whiting, finely chopped

2 carrots, chopped

1 onion stuck with a clove

2 cloves garlic

1 bouquet garni

1 litre (2 pints) cider

450 ml (15 fl oz) dry white wine (Muscadet or Gros Plant)

Salt and pepper

Pinch of cayenne

50 g (2 oz) butter

200 g (7 oz) mushrooms, finely chopped

2 shallots, finely chopped

1 leek, chopped

2 tablespoons flour

1 kg (2 lb) mussels, steamed open, removed from shells (keep a few whole and reserve the juices)

300 ml (10 fl oz) double cream

Juice of ½ lemon

75 ml (3 fl oz) Calvados

2 egg yolks

250 g (8 oz) peeled prawns

Croutons

A few whole prawns

To make the stock:

Put all the fish heads, the chopped whiting, the carrots,

onion, garlic and the bouquet garni in a large saucepan.
Cover with a mixture of cider and wine. Add salt and pepper
and cayenne. Simmer for 20 minutes. Carefully strain and
press out all the juice.

To make the sauce:

In another saucepan melt the butter. Add half the mushrooms, the shallots and the leek. Allow to sweat for 5 minutes
and add the flour, mix well and slowly pour in the stock.
Bring back to the boil and simmer for 10 minutes, stirring all
the time. Add the cooking juices from the mussels and strain.
The sauce should be quite thin.

To cook the fish:

Cut all the fish into large chunks. Add the fish and the mullet
livers to the sauce and simmer for 25 to 35 minutes. Beat the
cream with the lemon juice, Calvados, egg yolks and the rest
of the mushrooms. Stir into the fish, remove from the heat
and add the peeled prawns. Serve immediately with the
croutons. Decorate with the whole mussels and whole
prawns. (From Normandy.)

Soufflé de Bar au Coulis de LANGOUSTINE
Bass Soufflé with Prawn Sauce

This is a superb dish from my friend Claude Arnaud of Le
Saint-Hubert at Saint-Saturnin d'Apt.

SERVES 4

For the Soufflé:

300 g (10 oz) fillet of bass, chopped	*250 ml (8 fl oz) double cream*
Salt and pepper	*Pinch of cayenne pepper*
1 egg white	

For the prawn sauce:

75 ml (3 fl oz) oil	*1 teaspoon tomato purée*
1 kg (2 lb) langoustines	*3 tomatoes, crushed*
2 carrots, chopped	*1 bouquet garni*
½ onion, finely chopped	*Salt and pepper*
1 shallot, finely chopped	*450 ml (15 fl oz) double cream*
1 clove garlic, crushed	
75 ml (3 fl oz) Armagnac	*Tarragon*
300 ml (10 fl oz) white wine	

First prepare the sauce. Heat the oil in a flameproof casserole
dish. Add the langoustines and leave for 5 or 6 minutes.
Remove from the pan, shell them and set aside.

Put the carrots, onion, shallot and garlic into the casserole
and add the langoustine shells. Pour in the Armagnac and
flame. Leave covered for 3 or 4 minutes.

Add the wine to the casserole, along with the tomato purée,
the crushed tomatoes, bouquet garni, salt and pepper. Leave

to boil for 10 minutes. Next add the double cream and tarragon and leave to simmer for another 10 minutes. Finally, strain the sauce through a fine sieve. (There is too much sauce for four, but it's not worth making less, so freeze half for another occasion.)

Pre-heat the oven to gas mark 4, 180°C (350°F).

To make the soufflé, put the chopped fish, salt and pepper into a food processor for about 3 minutes. Add the egg white and mix again for 1 minute. Refrigerate this mixture for about 30 minutes. Return to the food processor, adding the cream, little by little. Finally add a pinch of cayenne pepper.

Bake in the oven in a *bain-marie* for 20 minutes. Serve immediately. Pour the sauce on a large dinner plate, place the soufflé on the sauce and surround with the langoustines. (From Provence.)

Bar au Sel
Bass in Sea Salt

SERVES 6

*1 small handful parsley,
   chopped*
*100 g (3½ oz) butter,
   softened*
3 cloves garlic, chopped
*1 teaspoon tarragon,
   chopped*
Salt and pepper

*1 × 1.5 kg (3 lb) bass,
   scaled, gutted and
   washed*
*2.75 kg (6 lb) coarse sea
   salt*
*Melted butter and lemon
   wedges to serve*

Pre-heat the oven to gas mark 7, 220°C (425°F).

Mix together the parsley, butter, garlic, tarragon, salt and pepper. If the fish has roe, add this too. Stuff the fish's belly with the mixture and sew up the opening.

In a large casserole put a 3 cm (1½ in.) layer of sea salt. Place the fish on its back on this, and cover with the rest of the salt, until no part of the fish is exposed. Bake in the oven for 35 minutes.

Remove from the oven very carefully (it will be very hot). Turn out on a wooden board. You might have to hit the bottom of the casserole in order to knock out the salt block. Carefully knock the salt from around the fish. Serve immediately with hot melted butter and lemon wedges. It will be delicious and not salty at all! (From Brittany.)

BOUILLINADE
Fish and Potato Bake

SERVES 4

1 tablespoon lard
Parsley, chopped
4 cloves garlic, chopped
Salt and pepper
Cayenne pepper
Saffron
625 g (1¼ lb) potatoes,
  peeled and sliced

1 kg (2 lb) mixed fish
  (gurnard, whiting,
  monkfish), scaled, gutted,
  washed and cut in chunks
Flour
2 tablespoons olive oil

Melt the lard in a large casserole. Add the parsley, garlic, salt, pepper, cayenne and saffron. Place alternate layers of potato and fish dusted with flour in the casserole, finishing with a layer of potatoes. Cover with cold water and bring to the boil. Add the olive oil. Cover and simmer for 20 minutes. (From Languedoc.)

CABILLAUD FAÇON BRIKATENIA
Cod with Bacon and Red Pepper Sauce

SERVES 6

1 large red pepper
150 ml (5 fl oz) double
  cream
Salt and pepper
300 ml (10 fl oz) fish stock
  (see page 16)
6 × 125–175 g (4–6 oz)
  fillets fresh cod
Butter for frying

50–75 g (2–3 oz) very fine
  fresh breadcrumbs
175–250 g (6–8 oz) piece
  smoked streaky bacon,
  de-rinded and cut into
  batons about 6 mm
  (¼ in.) thick and 2.5 cm
  (1 in.) long

First make the sauce. Blanch the red pepper whole in boiling water. Allow to cool, then cut and de-seed. Liquidise the red pepper with the cream and strain through a fine sieve. Warm gently in a pan, season with salt and pepper and add sufficient fish stock until the sauce is of a thin custard consistency (you need enough sauce to cover thinly six dinner plates; the sauce is under the fish, not over it). Keep warm.

Fry the cod fillets in butter on one side only, for about 2 minutes. Then sprinkle the breadcrumbs over each uncooked side, put a little knob of butter on each one and pop them – in the same pan – under a pre-heated grill, until the fish finishes cooking and the breadcrumbs are golden. At the same time, fry the pieces of bacon until they are a little crunchy.

Pour the sauce on to hot plates, place the fish on top and scatter over the cooked bacon pieces. Serve with boiled rice or plain boiled potatoes. (From Basque Country.)

BRANDADE DE MORUE
Purée of Salt Cod

———

I suppose that what tripe and brains are to the meat world –
that is, loathed and reviled here in Britain – salt cod, or tea
fish or toe rag, is to fish. This is a great pity for it tastes
supreme when well prepared. Anyway, I *love* it, which is
why I have included so many recipes for it!

SERVES 4

1 kg (2 lb) salt cod, soaked   *Juice of 1 lemon*
  overnight in repeated   *Nutmeg*
  changes of cold water   *Pepper*
450 ml (15 fl oz) olive oil   *Croutons*
450 ml (15 fl oz) hot milk

Put the cod in a saucepan of cold water, bring to the boil and
simmer for 10 minutes. Drain, cool and remove the skin and
bones and flake the flesh.

Add the fish to a quarter of the olive oil over a low heat.
Mash into a purée, slowly adding the rest of the olive oil until
the mixture resembles dough. Slowly mix in the hot milk
until the fish is the consistency of mashed potatoes. Stir in the
lemon juice, add some nutmeg and pepper to taste and serve
with croutons. (From Languedoc.)

Morue Fécampoise
Salt Cod in a Cream Sauce

SERVES 6

1 kg (2 lb) salt cod, soaked overnight in several changes of cold water
1 litre (2 pints) milk
Salt and pepper
1 litre (2 pints) dry cider
1 litre (2 pints) mussels, cooked, removed from their shells, juice reserved
2 onions, chopped
3 cloves garlic
4 carrots, sliced

1 bouquet garni (thyme, bayleaf, fennel)
6 potatoes
6 shallots, finely chopped
1 handful parsley, chopped
Butter for frying
1 glass Calvados
450 ml (15 fl oz) double cream
Pinch of thyme
1 slice lemon
10 black olives
Croutons

Marinate the fish in the milk with plenty of pepper for 1 hour.

Prepare a *court bouillon* with the cider, 300 ml (10 fl oz) water, the mussel juice, onions, 1 whole garlic clove, the carrots, bouquet garni and unpeeled potatoes. Bring to the boil and simmer for 20 minutes. Poach the cod in this *bouillon* for 20 minutes.

Now prepare the sauce. Sweat the shallots, 2 chopped garlic cloves and parsley in some butter. Remove from the heat and flame with the Calvados. Add a cup of the *court bouillon*, a very little salt and some pepper. Reduce by two-thirds and add the cream and thyme. Allow to thicken over a low flame, stirring frequently.

When the fish has cooked, drain it well and flake. Keep warm on a serving platter.

When the sauce has thickened, add the mussels. Cover the fish with the sauce. Place the lemon slice in the centre and surround with the olives, croutons and carrot slices from the *court bouillon*. Serve with boiled potatoes. (From Normandy.)

GRATIN DE MORUE
Gratin of Salt Cod

This is the sort of simple peasant dish that really builds you up on a cold winter's day and leaves you with an interesting aftertaste in the mouth. You need a good light red wine to wash it down with.

SERVES 4 TO 6

1 kg (2 lb) salt cod, soaked overnight in several changes of cold water
6 onions
1 bayleaf
1 sprig thyme

25 g (1 oz) butter
1 kg (2 lb) potatoes
Béchamel Sauce (see page 16)
100 g (3½ oz) Gruyère cheese, grated

Pre-heat the oven to gas mark 5, 190°C (375°F).

Poach the cod in fresh water with one of the onions, the bayleaf and thyme for 5 minutes or so. Strain and remove the bones. Chop the remaining onions finely and brown them in butter.

Cook the potatoes and cut into slices. Put the lot into a gratin dish and pour over the *Béchamel Sauce*. Sprinkle with the cheese and bake in the oven until golden.

Morue à l'Auvergnade
Salt Cod with Onions and Potatoes

Or, in other words, a superior fish cake!

SERVES 4

8 medium potatoes, peeled
  and finely sliced
Butter and oil for frying
3 large onions, finely
  chopped

750 g (1½ lb) salt cod,
  soaked overnight in
  several changes of cold
  water
Salt and pepper

For the court bouillon:

½ glass vinegar
1 onion, thinly sliced
1 carrot, chopped

1 sprig thyme, 2 bayleaves,
  1 sprig parsley
Pepper

Put all the *court bouillon* ingredients in a pan with 1.4 litres (2½ pints) water, bring to the boil and simmer for 20 minutes. Allow to cool.

In a large covered pan fry the potatoes in the butter and oil. Shake often so that they do not discolour.

In a separate pan sauté the onions until transparent.

Put the salt cod in the *court bouillon* and bring to the boil. Then reduce the heat so that the fish poaches very gently for 15 minutes. Remove the fish, take off the skin and bones and flake the flesh.

When the potatoes are cooked, crush them with a fork and add the onions and fish. Cover the pan and let the mixture sizzle for 10 minutes. Add pepper and some salt if necessary. And don't serve until the bottom has browned and is crunchy. (From Auvergne.)

CARPE À LA BOURGUIGNONNE
Carp in Wine Sauce

You can also cook pike in this way.

SERVES 8

*2.25 kg (5 lb) carp, gutted,
  scaled and cut in chunks*
*150 g (5 oz) lean bacon, cut
  in small pieces*
5 cloves garlic, chopped
1 onion, chopped
1 bouquet garni

Salt and pepper
990 ml (1¾ pints) red wine
*100 g (3½ oz) butter,
  softened*
1 tablespoon flour
Garlic croutons

In a large saucepan put the carp, bacon, garlic, onion, bouquet garni and salt and pepper. Barely cover with the wine and boil for 20 minutes. Reduce the heat. Make a *beurre manié* with the butter and flour mashed together. Add bit by bit to the fish stew and stir in well. This should thicken the sauce nicely. Cook for a further 30 minutes. Serve immediately scattered with garlic croutons. (From Burgundy.)

Filets de BROCHET ou PERCHE aux AMANDES
Fillets of Pike or Perch with Almonds

SERVES 6 TO 8

2 × 2 kg (4½ lb) pike or
perch, scaled, gutted and
filleted
300 ml (10 fl oz) Riesling
125 ml (4 fl oz) milk
Salt and pepper

150 g (5 oz) butter
3 tablespoons nut oil
300 g (10 oz) flaked
almonds
2 lemons

Marinate the fish fillets in the Riesling and milk for 30 minutes. Carefully pat dry with kitchen paper, and salt and pepper them.

In a large frying pan melt 100 g (3½ oz) of the butter with the oil until the mixture froths. Cook the fish fillets, skin-side up, for 5 minutes in the butter mixture. Turn the fillets and cook for a further 2 minutes. Do not allow the butter mixture to brown. Remove the fish, put on a well-buttered dish and keep warm.

Add the rest of the butter, the almonds and juice of 1 lemon to the pan. When the almonds have turned golden brown, pour the mixture on to the fish and garnish with the remaining lemon, cut into slices. (From Alsace.)

Filets de Perche au Chambertin
Fillets of Perch with Red Wine Sauce

You can make this with any fish, but perch is especially good prepared in this way. Believe it or not, I cooked this dish for eighteen of Burgundy's most noted chefs at the Hôtel de la Cloche at Dijon. They ate it happily under the glare of the French press and TV cameras, not to mention a BBC television crew (we were filming a programme at the time, so the filmers were being filmed too – quite bizarre).

Anyway, they ate it all, though one chef said he preferred his Gevrey-Chambertin in a glass! However, it's a good dish, so try it.

SERVES 6

1 fillet of perch per person   *Fish stock (see page 16)*

For the sauce:
125 g (4 oz) shallots, finely chopped   *½ bottle Gevrey-Chambertin*
      150 g (5 oz) butter

Poach the fillet in a little fish stock. Drain, reserving the stock.

To make the sauce, put the shallots and wine into a saucepan with 150 ml (5 fl oz) of the reserved fish stock and allow to reduce until there are about 5 tablespoons of liquid left. Over a low heat whisk in the butter, little by little, until you have a smooth red creamy sauce which you strain through a fine sieve and pour over the fish. (From Burgundy.)

BROCHET au FOUR
Roast Pike

SERVES 4 TO 6

*100 g (3½ oz) fresh
breadcrumbs*
150 ml (5 fl oz) single cream
*1 kg (2 lb) onions or
shallots, chopped*
1 head garlic, minced
*1 large handful sorrel,
chopped*
Butter
2 eggs, beaten
Salt and pepper

*1 × 1.5 kg (3 lb) pike,
scaled, gutted and
washed*
*1 small handful parsley,
chopped*
Thyme
Bayleaf
2 glasses wine
1 teaspoon cornflour
*150 ml (5 fl oz) double
cream*

Pre-heat the oven to gas mark 6, 200°C (400°F).

Soak the breadcrumbs in the single cream. Sweat 1 onion with the garlic and sorrel in some butter until the onion is tender. Transfer to a bowl and mix in the eggs, breadcrumbs and salt and pepper. Stuff the fish with this mixture and sew up the opening.

Butter a roasting tin big enough to hold the fish whole. Put in the remaining onions, all the herbs, the wine, salt and pepper. Put the pike on top of the onions and dot with butter. Roast in the oven for 35 minutes, basting frequently.

Remove the fish from the pan and arrange on a serving platter. Beat the cornflour and double cream together and add to the onions and juices in the pan. Stir over a low heat until the sauce has thickened, then pour over the fish. (From Lorraine.)

FILET DE DORADE EN PAPILLOTE CLAUDE ARNAUD
Bream Fillets in Envelopes

SERVES 4

2 courgettes, cut into thin rounds	Salt and pepper
	1 shallot, finely chopped
2 tomatoes, cut into thin rounds	4 bayleaves
	4 sprigs thyme
Butter	Parsley, chopped
50 ml (2 fl oz) olive oil	4 tablespoons fish stock (see
4 good fillets of bream	page 16)

You will also need 4 pieces of tin foil cut into rounds about 30 cm (12 in.) in diameter.

Pre-heat the oven to gas mark 9, 240°C (475°F).

Bake the courgettes and tomato rounds on a buttered oven dish for 10 minutes. Leave to cool. Now oil each piece of foil and place a fillet of bream on it. Season with salt and pepper.

Put a pinch of chopped shallot on each one, along with a bayleaf, sprig of thyme and a pinch of chopped parsley. On top of these lay alternate rounds of courgette and tomato. Moisten each one with a tablespoon of fish stock and place a small knob of butter on each.

Here comes the funny bit. Fold each round of tin foil to envelope the fish in the shape of a flat balloon. Seal it tightly but leave a little hole to blow into. Puff up the envelope like a balloon. Quickly seal the little hole and pop into the oven for about 7 minutes.

Serve in the 'balloons', which you cut open at the table. Savour the exquisite aroma before you tuck in. (From Provence.)

ST PIERRE À L'OSEILLE
John Dory in a Cream Sorrel Sauce

SERVES 6

1 glass dry white wine
1 glass cider
500 g (1 lb) sorrel, chopped
2 onions, chopped
2 shallots, minced
1 bouquet garni (thyme, bayleaf, parsley)
Salt and pepper

2.25 kg (5 lb) John Dory, gutted
30 g (1¼ oz) butter
150 ml (5 fl oz) double cream
Pinch of paprika
Garlic croutons

First make the court bouillon. In a large saucepan put the wine, cider, 1 glass water, a handful of sorrel, the onions, shallots and bouquet garni. Season with salt and pepper. Bring to the boil and simmer for 15 minutes before carefully straining.

Place the fish in a large frying pan and cover with the court bouillon. Bring to the boil and simmer for 20 minutes. When it is cooked, carefully fillet it and keep warm on a serving platter.

Now make the sauce. Sweat the remaining sorrel in the butter. When it has become a green purée, add half a cup of the court bouillon and the cream. Season with salt, pepper and paprika and reduce by a third before pouring over the fillets. Serve with the garlic croutons. (From Normandy.)

Alose à la SAVOYARDE
Shad cooked in Court Bouillon with Vegetables

SERVES 6

75 g (3 oz) butter
2 kg (4 lb) shad (or perch, or trout), scaled, gutted and washed

4 artichoke bottoms
12 small onions
150 g (5 oz) mushrooms
1 lemon, sliced

For the court bouillon:

1 large onion, quartered
1 small carrot
2 glasses dry white wine

1 bouquet garni (thyme, bayleaf, parsley)
Salt and pepper

First make the *court bouillon*. Put all the ingredients into a saucepan with 1 litre (2 pints) water. Bring to the boil and reduce for 30 minutes before straining.

Meanwhile, melt the butter in a flameproof casserole big enough to take the fish. When the butter starts to brown, put in the fish, artichokes, the little onions and mushrooms. Add the court bouillon and cover. Simmer for 1½ hours. Serve garnished with the lemon slices. (From Savoy.)

Rouget grillé
Grilled Red Mullet

---

2 red mullets per person,
  scaled, gutted and
  washed
Thyme

Fennel
Olive oil
Salt and pepper

Stuff the fish with the thyme and fennel.

Cook the fish under a very hot grill or, even better, over very hot coals. Baste constantly with olive oil. They will take approximately 10 minutes on each side, depending on their size. Sprinkle with salt and pepper before serving. (From Provence.)

Calmars au vin rouge
Squid Stewed in Wine

SERVES 4

750 g (1½ lb) squid,
  cleaned, ink sacks
  removed, cut in chunks
4 large onions, minced

2 heads garlic, minced
100 g (3½ oz) butter
1 litre (2 pints) red wine
Salt and pepper

Stew the squid, onions and garlic in the butter until all the squid's juices have evaporated. Cover with red wine. Add salt and pepper to taste. Simmer for 2 hours or until tender. Serve with boiled potatoes. (From Charente.)

CALMARS FARCIS
Stuffed Squid

SERVES 6

6 × 8–10 cm (3–4 in.) squid
Onions, finely chopped
150 g (5 oz) ham, diced
3 cloves garlic, chopped
3 shallots, finely chopped
Oil for frying
2 tablespoons dried
   breadcrumbs
1 egg

Salt and pepper
1 glass white wine
6 tomatoes, peeled and
   chopped
3 sprigs parsley, finely
   chopped
60 ml (2½ fl oz) double
   cream

Wash the squid, remove the skins and ink sacks. Cut off the wings and heads. Reserve the tentacles and wings and chop them finely. Discard the heads and beaks. In a pan fry the onions, ham, chopped squid, garlic and shallots in some oil until the onions are transparent.

Mix the breadcrumbs with the egg, salt and pepper and enough of the wine to moisten. Add to the ham and onion.

Stuff the squid bodies with the ham mixture and sew up the hole. In a flameproof casserole or deep frying pan brown them gently in some oil, add the rest of the wine and about 200 ml (7 fl oz) water. Add the tomatoes and parsley. Simmer for 45 minutes. Remove the squid and keep warm. Add the cream to the sauce and warm through. Pour over the squid and serve immediately. (From Charente.)

RAIE AU BEURRE NOIR
Skate in Brown Butter

SERVES 6

2 kg (4 lb) skate wings, skinned

For the court bouillon:

1 litre (2 pints) Muscadet or Gros Plant
1 carrot, sliced
1 large onion stuck with 2 cloves
2 cloves garlic
1 tomato, peeled and de-seeded
1 leek (white part only)
Salt and pepper

For the brown butter:

200 g (7 oz) butter
65 g (2½ oz) capers
150 ml (5 fl oz) vinegar

Put all the *court bouillon* ingredients into a pan with 3 litres (5 pints) water, bring to the boil and simmer for 10 minutes. Poach the skate in this liquid for 15 minutes. Remove and keep warm on a serving dish.

Melt the butter in a pan. As soon as it browns lightly, remove from the heat and add the capers, 50 ml (2 fl oz) of the *court bouillon* and vinegar. Reduce for a minute or two and pour over the skate. Serve with boiled potatoes. (From Brittany.)

GIGOT DE LOTTE
Roast Monkfish

SERVES 4 TO 6

1 kg (2 lb) monkfish tail, skinned
Salt and pepper
Lemon juice
1 tablespoon parsley, finely chopped
2 cloves garlic, very finely chopped

Knob of butter
8 small whole onions, sautéed in butter until golden
50 g (2 oz) smoked bacon, diced
1 glass dry white wine
150 ml (5 fl oz) double cream

Pre-heat the oven to gas mark 6, 200°C (400°F).

Run a knife lengthways through the fish and remove the single backbone. Season both fillets with salt and pepper and lemon juice and sprinkle all the parsley and all the garlic on top of one of the fillets. Place the other fillet on top and tie the fish back together in its original shape with several little pieces of string.

Butter a roasting tray and put the fish on it with the onions and bacon. Place in the oven for 30 minutes. Now add the wine to the roasting tray. Turn the fish over and cook for a further 15 minutes or so. Then remove the fish, onions and the bacon to a warm serving dish.

Over a low heat stir the cream into the juices in the roasting pan. Strain the sauce over the fish and serve.

The name 'Gigot de Lotte' implies that the whole thing looks a bit like a roast leg of lamb, so you serve the dish by carving it in slices. (From Brittany.)

LOTTE AUX PETITS LÉGUMES
Monkfish and Spring Vegetables

SERVES 6

1 kg (2 lb) monkfish, cut in
  large pieces
2 onions, chopped
750 g (1½ lb) celeriac,
  peeled and cut in bite-
  size chunks
12 new potatoes, peeled and
  grated
150 g (5 oz) small turnips,
  peeled and diced
150 g (5 oz) carrots, peeled
  and diced

200 g (7 oz) petits pois
150 g (5 oz) Swiss chard
  (white part only), finely
  chopped
100 g (3½ oz) smoked
  bacon, cut into chunks
150 g (5 oz) butter
Salt and pepper
25 ml (1 fl oz) double cream

For the fish stock:

300 ml (10 fl oz) Muscadet
Monkfish trimmings
300 g (10 oz) whiting or
  other white fish, gutted
150 g (5 oz) sardines or
  other oily fish, gutted
1 carrot, finely chopped
1 turnip, finely chopped
3 tomatoes, peeled, de-
  seeded and chopped

1 onion, finely chopped
1 clove garlic, finely
  chopped
1 clove
Salt and pepper
Pinch of cayenne
1 bouquet garni (parsley,
  thyme, bayleaf)

Put all the fish stock ingredients into a large saucepan with 1
litre (2 pints) water, bring to the boil and simmer for 30
minutes. Strain and reserve the liquid. Remove the bouquet

garni from the sieve. With a wooden spoon, force the remaining solids through the sieve and into the liquid, then reduce for a further 10 minutes.

Pre-heat the oven to gas mark 6, 200°C (400°F).

In another large pan gently fry the monkfish, vegetables and bacon in the butter until the onions are transparent. Season with salt and pepper and arrange them on an oven-proof dish.

Moisten the fish and vegetables with some of the stock and pop into the oven for 20 minutes or so.

When the fish is ready, whip the double cream with the rest of the stock. Heat through and pour it over the fish and vegetables just before serving. (From Brittany.)

SOLE À LA NORMANDE
Normandy Sole

SERVES 6

*500 g (1 lb) mussels, cooked,
  juice reserved*
*300 ml (10 fl oz) dry white
  wine (Muscadet or Gros
  Plant)*
450 ml (15 fl oz) dry cider
2 onions, chopped
1 carrot, peeled and sliced
*1 bouquet garni (thyme,
  bayleaf, parsley)*
Salt and pepper
*3 large sole, filleted, rolled
  up and held together with
  a toothpick*

12 prawns, cooked
1 shallot, minced
25 g (1 oz) butter
100 ml (3½ fl oz) Calvados
*450 ml (15 fl oz) double
  cream*
Pinch of thyme
*500 g (1 lb) mushrooms,
  finely chopped*
12 stuffed olives
1 lemon, cut into wedges

Pour the mussel juice into a deep frying pan. Add the wine,
the cider, onions, carrot and bouquet garni. Add pepper,
bring to the boil and simmer for 15 minutes. Add the rolled
sole fillets to the simmering court bouillon, making sure that
it covers the fish, and poach for 10 minutes. Add the mussels
and prawns just before the fillets are cooked.

Remove the fillets and arrange on a serving platter with the
prawns and mussels. Keep warm.

Now make the sauce. Sweat the shallot in the butter.
Remove from the heat, add the Calvados and flame. Add a
large glass of *court bouillon* and reduce by two-thirds. Add
the cream and thyme. Allow to thicken over a low heat and
add the mushrooms.

Rectify the seasoning and coat the fillets with the sauce. Decorate with the olives. Serve with lemon wedges. (From Normandy.)

GRATIN DE TRUITE
Trout in Cheese Sauce

SERVES 4

4 trout, gutted, skinned and boned	2 eggs
Butter	1 tablespoon double cream
Salt and pepper	135 g (4½ oz) Gruyère cheese, grated
1 glass dry white wine	

Pre-heat the oven to gas mark 6, 200°C (400°F).

Arrange the trout in a buttered flameproof gratin dish. Dot with butter, sprinkle with salt and pepper and add the wine. Heat on top of the stove until the wine is bubbling.

Beat the eggs and cream together and pour over the fish. Cover with grated cheese and bake in the oven for approximately 20 minutes until golden brown. (From Savoy.)

TRUITE AU BLEU
Blue Trout

Trout is readily available in Britain, so why not forget plain grilled, or fried in butter, and be a little adventurous with this recipe or one of the ones that follow?

Use only fresh fish for Blue Trout: there is no point in using frozen.

SERVES 6

6 freshly caught trout,
carefully gutted so as not
to remove the slime that
covers the body and
which makes the trout
'blue' when cooked

Lemon wedges

For the court bouillon:

2 carrots, chopped
1 large onion, halved and
stuck with a clove
1 clove garlic
2 leeks (white part only)

1 bouquet garni
2 glasses Riesling or
Sylvaner
½ glass wine vinegar
Salt and pepper

For the sauce:

200 g (7 oz) butter, cut in
small cubes
Juice of 1 lemon

Pinch of thyme
Salt and pepper
1 teaspoon double cream

Bring the *court bouillon* ingredients to the boil in 4.5 litres (8 pints) water and simmer for 20 minutes. Plunge in the trout and simmer for 8 to 10 minutes, depending on their size.

While the *court bouillon* is cooking, prepare the sauce. Melt the butter over a low heat until it starts to froth. Add the lemon juice, the thyme and the salt and pepper. Whisk until well amalgamated. Just before serving whisk in the cream.

Carefully drain the trout and place on a serving platter garnished with lemon wedges. Serve the sauce separately. (From Alsace.)

TRUITE AUX LARDONS
Trout with Bacon

SERVES 4

4 trout, gutted	75 g (3 oz) butter
Flour	100 g (3½ oz) streaky
Salt and pepper	bacon, cut in small pieces

Dust the trout with the flour and season with salt and pepper. Brown the trout in the butter in a large frying pan. Remove carefully when cooked and keep warm.

Add the bacon to the butter and fry until brown. Pour the bacon and the fat over the trout and serve immediately. (From Auvergne.)

TRUITE AU COURT BOUILLON
Poached Trout

SERVES 4

2 carrots, chopped
2 onions, chopped
2 shallots, chopped
2 cloves garlic, chopped
Parsley, thyme, bayleaf
450 ml (15 fl oz) dry white
   wine
Salt
Black peppercorns

4 trout, gutted
135 g (4½ oz) mushrooms,
   sliced
50 g (2 oz) butter
50 g (2 oz) flour
3 egg yolks
Juice of 1 lemon
Cayenne pepper

Put the carrots, 1 onion, the shallots, garlic and herbs in a large saucepan with 450 ml (15 fl oz) water and the wine. Add the salt and a few peppercorns. Simmer for 20 minutes, strain and cool.

Put the trout in the *court bouillon*, bring to the boil and simmer gently for 10 minutes. Remove the trout, skin them and take out the backbone. Keep warm.

Meanwhile, cook the other onion and the mushrooms in the butter until the onions are tender. Add the flour, stir in well and add 450 ml (15 fl oz) of the *court bouillon*. Simmer for 10 minutes.

In a bowl beat the egg yolks together with the lemon juice. Add a little of the mushroom sauce and stir well, add a little more and repeat until the egg yolk mixture is warm. Pour into the mushroom sauce and immediately remove from the heat. Season with cayenne pepper.

Cover the trout with the sauce and decorate with parsley. (From Languedoc.)

THON à la BASQUAISE
Tuna Fish with Peppers and Tomatoes

The port of St Jean de Luz in the Pays Basque is famous for
tuna fish, and if you are ever down that way in summer, the
early-morning market is well worth visiting. I like a slice of
fresh tuna simply charcoal-grilled with olive oil and garlic
and garnished with a bit of chilli sauce, or poached whole,
allowed to cool, flaked and tossed into a salade niçoise; but
way down yonder in St Jean de Luz and thereabouts, they
like to cook it with tomatoes and peppers. Here is the recipe:

SERVES 4

1 × 625 g (1¼ lb) slice tuna	1 small aubergine, finely diced
Olive oil	1 clove garlic, crushed
Salt and pepper	2 small fresh chillies, chopped
1 large onion, finely chopped	1 sprig thyme
4 green peppers, de-seeded and chopped	1 bayleaf
4 tomatoes, peeled, de-seeded and chopped	

First brown the tuna fish on both sides in olive oil and season
with salt and pepper. Put the fish to one side while you start to
fry the onion and peppers. When they are soft, add all the
other ingredients and stir them together.

Put the tuna back into this preparation and simmer for
about 20 minutes. Serve with boiled rice and salad. (From
Basque Country.)

MOUCLADE
Mussels in White Sauce

SERVES 4 TO 6

2.75 kg (6 lb) small mussels,
 well cleaned
2 glasses white wine
1 small onion, whole
8 cloves garlic, minced
1 clove
Nutmeg
1 handful parsley, chopped
1 bayleaf
Thyme

2 large onions, chopped
6 shallots, chopped
200 g (7 oz) butter
2 tablespoons flour
Salt and pepper
Pinch of saffron or curry
 powder
3 egg yolks
150 ml (5 fl oz) double
 cream

Put the mussels in a large saucepan with the wine, the small
whole onion, 2 cloves garlic, the clove, nutmeg, some
parsley, the bayleaf and thyme. Cook over a medium heat,
covered, shaking occasionally until all the mussels have
opened. Reserve the cooking liquid.

Remove the top shells of the mussels and discard. Keep
warm.

Gently cook the remaining garlic, chopped onions and
shallots in the butter until transparent. Add the flour, salt
and pepper. Stir well until the mixture is frothing.

Pour on the strained mussel cooking liquid cut with water,
otherwise it will be too salty. Add the saffron or curry powder
and simmer until thick and smooth.

Beat the egg yolks and cream together and whisk into the
sauce over a low heat. Pour over the mussels and sprinkle
with parsley.

ÉCREVISSES À LA BOURGUIGNONNE
Stewed Freshwater Crayfish

I like crayfish the Provençal way – simply fried in olive oil, then flamed in marc of Cognac and finally simmered for a few minutes with *Tomato Sauce* (see page 20) with a little fiery harissa or cayenne pepper added. This recipe and the one on page 181 are rather more refined.

SERVES 6

1 large carrot, finely
   chopped
3 shallots, minced
3 tablespoons goose fat
60 crayfish, gutted and
   washed, central tail piece
   removed
½ glass Cognac
Salt and pepper
1 litre (2 pints) white wine
   vinegar

1 bouquet garni (thyme,
   parsley, bayleaf)
1 clove garlic, minced
150 ml (5 fl oz) double
   cream
1 tablespoon truffle peelings
1 tablespoon parsley,
   chopped
1 slice smoked bacon, finely
   chopped

In a large frying pan fry the carrot and shallots in the goose fat. Add the crayfish and stir until uniformly red. Flame with the Cognac. Add salt and pepper and the wine vinegar. Add the bouquet garni and garlic. Boil for 10 minutes.

Lower the heat and stir in the cream, truffle peelings, parsley and bacon. Bring back to the boil and simmer for 20 minutes. Remove the bouquet garni. Adjust the seasoning and serve straight from the pan. (From Burgundy.)

CIVET DE LANGOUSTES
Crawfish in Red Wine

SERVES 4 TO 6

1.5 kg (3 lb) live crawfish
Fish trimmings (not oily fish) for the stock
Parsley, thyme, bayleaf
Salt and pepper
750 ml (1¼ pints) red wine (or, better still, a 'cooked wine' (vin cuit) like Banyuls)
2 carrots, finely chopped
2 onions, finely chopped

2 shallots, finely chopped
5 cloves garlic, crushed
2 tomatoes, peeled, de-seeded and chopped
150 g (5 oz) raw ham, chopped
Olive oil
1 glass eau de vie
Cayenne
Flour
Butter at room temperature

Split the crawfish down the middle and cut through the tail joints. Reserve the creamy bits from the head.

Prepare the stock with the fish trimmings, the small legs from the crawfish, the herbs, salt, pepper and 300 ml (10 fl oz) of the red wine. Cover with cold water, bring to the boil and simmer for 30 minutes.

Meanwhile, gently fry the carrots, onions, shallots, garlic, tomatoes and ham in oil for 5 minutes. Keep warm. Fry the crawfish pieces in oil until they become bright red. Add the eau de vie and flame. Add the rest of the wine, the stock, the vegetable and ham mixture and a pinch of cayenne. Simmer gently for approximately 25 minutes. Remove the crawfish and keep warm.

Mix the reserved creamy bits from the crawfish head with the flour and butter, until you have a smooth mixture. Add some of the sauce and stir well, add a little more and repeat before adding the mixture to the rest of the sauce. Stir well, check the seasoning and simmer for 1 minute. Pour over the crawfish, sprinkle with parsley and serve. (From Languedoc.)

ÉCREVISSES AU VIN BLANC
Freshwater Crayfish Cooked in White Wine

SERVES 3

2 carrots, finely chopped	2 sprigs tarragon
2 onions, finely chopped	Salt and pepper
2 shallots, finely chopped	36 live crayfish, well
50 g (2 oz) butter	washed
1 litre (2 pints) white wine	25 g (1 oz) flour
(preferably Aligoté)	1 tablespoon tomato purée
1 bouquet garni	3 tablespoons double cream

In a large saucepan gently fry the carrots, onions and shallots in 25 g (1 oz) butter. Add the wine, bouquet garni, tarragon and salt and pepper. Boil until it has reduced by a third.

Into this *court bouillon* throw the live crayfish. When they turn bright red, remove and keep warm. Reduce the court bouillon by half and sieve it. Make a *beurre manié* with the remaining butter and flour and add it, little by little, to the simmering *court bouillon*. Stir in well. Add the tomato purée and cream.

Arrange the crayfish on a large deep platter and pour the sauce over. Serve immediately, and eat with your fingers. (From Lorraine.)

HOMARD À L'ARMORICAINE
Lobster à l'Armoricaine

SERVES 6

2.75 kg (6 lb) live lobsters
50 ml (2 fl oz) nut oil
90 ml (3½ fl oz) Calvados
6 shallots, finely chopped
*2 cloves garlic, finely
  chopped*
*1 small handful parsley,
  finely chopped*

*6 ripe tomatoes, peeled, de-
  seeded and chopped*
*1 bouquet garni (thyme,
  bayleaf)*
300 ml (10 fl oz) Muscadet
Sea salt
Black pepper
50 g (2 oz) butter

With a sharp 30 cm (12 in.) cook's knife, kill the lobsters with a sharp lunge through the back of the head. Then cut them in half down the middle of the body. Cut the tail in chunks following the line of the joints. Reserve the coral. Break open the claws without crushing the meat. (See diagram overleaf.)

In a large saucepan heat the oil and toss the lobster chunks in it until they turn red. Pour off the excess oil.

De-glaze the pan with the Calvados and flame it. Add the shallots, garlic, parsley, tomatoes and bouquet garni. Pour on the wine and add the salt and pepper. Cover and simmer for 20 minutes over a low heat.

Remove the lobster and keep it warm in a deep serving dish. Reduce the liquid by half. Meanwhile mash the coral and butter together. Add the mixture bit by bit to the reduced sauce. Beat well until the sauce is thick and smooth. Strain over the lobsters and serve immediately. (From Brittany.)

HOMARD À LA CRÈME
Lobster and Mussels in a Cream Sauce

———

SERVES 6

2 live 750 g (1½ lb)
lobsters, prepared as
opposite
750 ml (1¼ pints) cider
1 litre (2 pints) dry white
wine
1.5 kg (3 lb) mussels, well
washed
5 shallots, minced

3 sprigs parsley, chopped
4 cloves garlic
Freshly ground black pepper
50 g (2 oz) butter
1 tablespoon nut oil
1 small glass Calvados
1 bouquet garni
450 ml (15 fl oz) double
cream

In a large saucepan bring half the cider and a quarter of the
wine to the boil. Throw in the mussels, shallots, parsley and
garlic. Add a generous amount of pepper. Cover and cook for
10 minutes, shaking occasionally.

Remove the mussels and reserve the juice. Take them out
of their shells, apart from a few pretty ones.

In a large pan melt the butter with the oil and toss the
lobster pieces in the mixture until they turn red. Remove
from the heat and flame with the Calvados. Return to the heat
and add the remaining cider, wine, strained mussel juices and
bouquet garni. Reduce by a third.

Add the pink matter from the head of the lobsters to the
double cream and beat well. Add to the lobster pieces. Throw
in the mussels and thicken the sauce, stirring frequently.

Remove the bouquet garni. Reassemble the lobster on the
serving platter and surround with the mussels. Decorate with
the mussels still in their shells and pour over the sauce.
(From Normandy.)

ASSIETTE DE FRUITS DE MER
Seafood Platter

This is a beautifully arranged platter of cooked and raw shellfish on a bed of seaweed and ice. The seafood that makes it up obviously can vary from season to season and from area to area.

Below is listed a nearly complete repertory of shellfish that you might find in Brittany.

MAKES A LARGE PLATTER FOR 6 PEOPLE

Raw shellfish:

Common oysters, marenne oysters, Portuguese oysters
Clams (pravies and palourdes)
Cockles, small mussels
Sea urchins
Amandes de mer

Cooked shellfish:

Winkles, grey shrimps, sword shrimps
Pink shrimps, scallops, cooked mussels
Dublin Bay prawns, common crabs, spider crabs
Lobsters and langoustes

For the court bouillon:

4.5 litres (1 gallon) sea water
750 ml (1¼ pints) Muscadet
125 ml (4 fl oz) cider vinegar
1 tablespoon sugar
1 large onion stuck with 2 cloves
Thyme, bayleaves, parsley and fennel
1 handful seaweed
Black pepper

FISH

Put all the *court bouillon* ingredients in a very large pan, bring to the boil and simmer for 30 minutes. It is then ready to cook any shellfish you have collected. They will need to be cooked separately for different lengths of time. Allow to cool before adding them to the platter. Serve with *Mayonnaise* or *Shallot Vinaigrette* (see pages 21 and 18). (From Brittany.)

Preparing Lobster

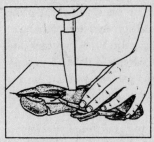

1 Use a sharp knife to kill the lobster

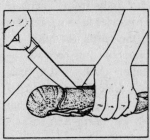

2 Cut in half lengthways

3 Remove the black or green thread

185

MEAT

Y ou crunch over the nut shells and cigarette ends that litter the floor of this cool bar where men unshaven and late home for lunch are demanding another one. Outside, in the shade of the plane trees that stand tight against the dark green waters of the river Sorgue the tourists sit beneath big umbrellas as they tuck into charcoal-grilled lamb chops with deep red tomatoes, crispy golden on the top with garlic and parsley, and into purple steaks running with juice that taints pink the crisp french-fried potatoes.

Here the two spurs of the river from north and west join to create the basin where boys fish and ducks swim. There are two bridges. One takes the heavy trucks laden with Cavaillon melon or Vaucluse asparagus to the north, the other – a pedestrian footway to the hotel opposite – is occupied by black-waistcoated waiters with sallow cheeks and no customers who wistfully gaze at the Café Bellevue – chez Pichelin – where I am standing with a pastis on this hot August day. Guy Pichelin whacks me on the back. 'Ça va general? Your table is ready.'

I choke on the pastis and hit him back. 'Good. What's to eat?'

'What do you want? Roast milk lamb with purée, pork chops with petits pois, steak frites, spaghetti and chicken, *pike quenelles* and crayfish sauce, *civet de porcelet*. You tell me, old cabbage. She's cooking good, but best is the civet.' Guy nods to the kitchen where his wife is not so much cooking as slaving in the cramped alcove that passes for a kitchen. She is dishing out portions of the civet – cubes of pork marinated in thick red Côtes du Rhône and root vegetables (which are afterwards puréed to thicken the sauce) and fresh herbs, then simmered for several hours. Each dish is served with a mountain of fresh pasta and a pale green salad of endives and frisé. Meanwhile chops and steaks sizzle on the charcoal grill, filling the place with the most tantalising aromas.

Earlier I had watched her choosing the day's meat at the butchers, with lips pursed and eyes narrowed as she poked, prodded and sniffed joints and chops, loins and legs with the intensity of a diamond dealer. It is a scene worthy of Rembrandt. Huge purple and cream carcasses hang high in the window from great meat hooks. Below, the white marble shelf is like a painter's palette with freshly squeezed blobs of oil paint: vermilion steaks, pink cutlets, burnt sienna calf's liver, maroon oxtails, ochre eggs piled high, brilliant white lard and sprigs of green parsley. A fine picture indeed – and you can eat it too!

The butcher and his wife saw, chop and fillet, knives flashing over the scrubbed wood tables, while pale apprentices struggle with whole pigs on their shoulders. I drew patterns in the sawdust with the polished toe of my shoe, waiting for a pig's head. I'm in no hurry, I love butchers' shops. The butcher asks who's next, and twenty customers surge forward crying 'me'. An old man in carpet slippers wants a thin escalope of veal, another some neat beef rib bones for a pot au feu. Next follows a prolonged discussion about the merits of lamb from the salt marshes of Brittany with a lady in a leather skirt and high heels. Her brilliant red lips threaten unmentionable retribution on the plump butcher if the leg she had selected, in its coat of creamy white fat, is not absolutely superb. My turn comes at last. But, horror of horrors, the ears are missing from this noble head which I intend to roast for lunch tomorrow in the baker's wood-fired oven, after the baking is finished. 'Ah,' the butcher says, 'you didn't ask for the ears.' I am astounded – the ears when roasted are crispy and delicious. But he explains that a family of Spanish gypsies have a standing order for all his pig's ears and in future I must specify that I want them left on!

'So, have you decided?' Guy is back for the order and I'm still smarting about the pig's ears.

'Yeah, the *civet de porcelet*.'

'With noodles or gratin of chicory?'

'Chicory, and a bottle of Vin Sobre.' Which I think is a very amusing name for this little 'Côtes du Rhône Villages', wine that does anything but make you sober.

BROCHETTES D'AGNEAU
Marinated Grilled Lamb Kebabs

SERVES 6 TO 8

750 g–1 kg (1½–2 lb) leg of lamb or boned lean shoulder

For the marinade:

Juice of 1 lemon
2 cloves garlic, crushed
1 onion, finely grated

1 teaspoon dried oregano
3 tablespoons olive oil
Salt and pepper

Trim the fat off the lamb. Cut the meat into 2.5 cm (1 in.) cubes and put into a bowl. Mix the marinade ingredients together and pour over the meat, ensuring that all the pieces are coated. Leave for at least 1 hour.

Thread the meat on to skewers and cook for 7 to 10 minutes (more if you like your lamb well done). Turn the skewers frequently, basting with the marinade.

Serve with rice and warm pitta bread.

GIGOT D'AGNEAU AUX HARICOTS
Roast Leg of Lamb with Haricot Beans

SERVES 6 TO 8

1 kg (2 lb) dried haricot
  beans, soaked for 12
  hours
Salt and pepper
1 bouquet garni (parsley,
  thyme, bayleaf)
2 shallots
2 large onions, halved
1 large ripe tomato, peeled

3 cloves garlic
2 kg (4 lb) leg of lamb
8 small potatoes, peeled
185 g (6½ oz) butter
Thyme
50 ml (2 fl oz) Calvados
1 small bunch parsley,
  finely chopped

Put the soaked beans in a large saucepan with plenty of salted cold water and the bouquet garni. Bring to the boil and simmer for 2¼ hours, adding more water if necessary. Then add 1 whole shallot, the onions, tomato, 2 cloves garlic and pepper. Simmer for a further 15 minutes.

When the beans have been cooking for about 1½ hours, cut the remaining clove of garlic in four and push the pieces into the leg of lamb with a sharp knife.

Pre-heat the oven to gas mark 4, 180°C (350°F).

Put the lamb and potatoes in a roasting pan. Melt 100 g (3½ oz) of the butter and pour over. Sprinkle with the thyme and salt and pepper.

Pop the joint into the oven and roast for 45 minutes, turning occasionally.

Meanwhile, drain the beans and keep warm. Chop the remaining shallot and fry in a small saucepan in the remaining butter, add the cooked shallot, onions and tomato from the beans. Discard the bouquet garni. With a fork crush everything together in the saucepan until you have a smoothish sauce. Pour over the beans.

Arrange the lamb on a serving platter and surround with the beans and potatoes. Flame with Calvados. Scatter with chopped parsley and serve immediately. (From Brittany.)

VEAU à LA PROVENÇALE
Provençal Veal

This is a typical truck driver's lunch, often served with rice or a risotto in ordinary restaurants throughout Provence: not the sort of dish for dinner in a 'posh' restaurant.

SERVES 4 TO 6

2 cloves garlic, chopped
1 kg (2 lb) shoulder of veal, cubed
Olive oil
1 kg (2 lb) tomatoes, peeled, de-seeded and chopped

Salt and black pepper
1 sprig rosemary, chopped
75 g (3 oz) good-quality black olives, stoned

Fry the garlic and veal in the oil until the meat is well browned. Add the tomatoes, a little salt and lots of black pepper. Cover and simmer for 1½ hours over a low heat. The sauce should be thick, but if it looks a little dry, add water. Ten minutes before serving sprinkle with the rosemary and stir in the olives. (From Provence.)

Escalope de Veau à la Moutarde
Veal Escalope with Dijon Mustard

SERVES 4

Butter

4 thin veal escalopes

Salt and pepper

1 glass Marc de Bourgogne,
   or Armagnac, or Cognac

150 ml (5 fl oz) double
   cream

1 tablespoon mild Dijon
   mustard

Chicken stock (optional)

Melt some butter in a pan and, as it begins to turn nutty brown, fry the escalopes for 2 minutes on each side. Season with salt and pepper, pour in the alcohol and flame. This will create quite a bit of juice in the pan, so take the meat out at once, so that it does not boil in the liquid, and keep warm. Turn down the heat. Now stir the cream briskly into the juices and add the mustard. If at this stage the sauce is too thick, add 1 tablespoon chicken stock or even water to thin it down.

Stir in a knob of butter, season with salt and pepper and strain over the meat. Serve with boiled rice and a crunchy green salad. (From Burgundy.)

ESCALOPE DE VEAU AUX CHAMPIGNONS
Veal Escalope with Mushrooms

SERVES 6

6 × 150 g (5 oz) veal
  escalopes
300 ml (10 fl oz) milk
Salt and pepper
40 g (1½ oz) butter
2 tablespoons oil
500 g (1 lb) mushrooms,
  minced

1 clove garlic, chopped
25 g (1 oz) onion, chopped
1 sprig parsley, chopped
Juice of ½ lemon
300 ml (10 fl oz) cider
1 bouquet garni (thyme,
  bayleaf, parsley)
6 tablespoons double cream

Marinate the veal in the milk with salt and pepper for 1 hour. Melt 25 g (1 oz) of the butter with 1 tablespoon oil in a frying pan. Add the mushrooms and a little salt. Cover and cook until the mushrooms have released their juices, then add the garlic, onion, parsley, lemon juice and pepper. Allow to simmer gently while you cook the meat.

Melt the rest of the butter and 1 tablespoon oil in a pan. Fry the escalopes over a medium heat until lightly browned. Remove and keep warm on a serving platter. De-glaze the pan with the cider and add the bouquet garni. Reduce the mixture by two-thirds.

Remove the bouquet garni and stir in the cream. Allow to thicken. Cover the escalopes with half the sauce and mix the rest with the mushrooms before pouring over the meat. (From Normandy.)

TOURTE LORRAINE
Meat Pie

SERVES 4 TO 8

500 g (1 lb) pork shoulder, boned and cut in small chunks

500 g (1 lb) veal shoulder, boned and cut in small chunks

1 litre (2 pints) dry white wine

2 shallots, chopped

1 onion, chopped

1 clove garlic, crushed

1 small handful chives, chopped

1 sprig thyme

1 small bunch parsley, chopped

Salt and pepper

300 g (10 oz) puff pastry

3 eggs

75 ml (3 fl oz) double cream

Marinate the meat overnight in the wine with the shallots, onions, garlic, herbs and salt and pepper.

Pre-heat the oven to gas mark 4, 180°C (350°F).

Line a cake tin with enough pastry to hang over the sides. Drain the meat, onions and herbs (reserving the marinade liquid), and spread over the pastry. Fold the edges over and cover with a pastry lid. Seal the edges carefully. Paint with egg yolk and cut a small hole in the top. Cook for 1 hour.

Beat together the cream, eggs and 2 tablespoons marinade liquid, and pour through the hole in the top of the pie. Turn the oven off and return the pie to the oven for 20 minutes or so.

Smashing with mountains of fresh young spinach oozing in butter and freshly ground black pepper! (From Lorraine.)

CIVET À LA SAUCE COFFE
Marinated Pork

SERVES 4

1.5 kg (3 lb) pork shoulder, cut in bite-size chunks
50 g (2 oz) butter
50 g (2 oz) lard
1 glass red wine

150 ml (5 fl oz) fresh pig's blood
75 ml (3 fl oz) double cream
Salt and pepper

For the marinade:

2 onions, chopped
2 cloves
1 bouquet garni (thyme and bayleaf)

450 ml (15 fl oz) dry white wine

Combine all the marinade ingredients and marinate the meat for at least 12 hours. Drain and fry in the butter and lard in a large casserole until brown. Add the red wine, a glass of the marinade and enough water to cover the meat. Cook for 1¾ hours, adding more marinade if necessary.

Stir in the blood and cream over a low heat. Adjust the seasoning, and serve. (From Savoy.)

Merguez
Spicy Sausages

The people who cook *Ox Heart Brochettes* (see page 273) usually offer barbecued merguez as well. These are chipolata-sized spicy meat sausages. You simply push them whole on to a skewer and grill over a wood fire, turning from time to time. They are quite easy to make if your food processor has a sausage-stuffing attachment.

Order some sausage casings in advance from your butcher along with some very fatty meat (lamb or beef). You will also need some harissa, a chilli paste available in tubes from oriental stores.

*500 g (1 lb) meat, freshly
  minced*
1 teaspoon harissa
*½ teaspoon herbes de
  Provence*
*50 g (2 oz) fresh
  breadcrumbs*
*1 generous tablespoon
  tomato purée*
Salt and pepper

Mix all the ingredients together thoroughly and push into the sausage casings. Tie them off at about 7.5 cm (3 in.) intervals. Dead easy. (From Provence.)

ENTRECÔTE SAUCE PÉRIGOURDINE
Sirloin Steak with Truffle Sauce

---

200 g (7 oz) sirloin steak per person

Lard for frying

For the sauce:

Butter

2 heaped tablespoons flour

75 ml (3 fl oz) Madeira

Cognac

1 small shallot, finely chopped

50 g (2 oz) preserved truffles, chopped, juices reserved

Pinch of thyme

Salt and pepper

First make the sauce. Melt the butter in a heavy-bottomed pan. Add the flour and fry until pale brown. Pour in the Madeira, 150 ml (5 fl oz) water and a dash of Cognac. Add the shallot, truffles and thyme. Simmer gently and reduce to a thick sauce, and add salt and pepper. Whisk in a nut of butter to finish the sauce.

Fry the steaks in the lard over a very hot flame and pour the sauce over.

Please, please, serve the steaks rare, so that when you cut the meat the juices will run into the truffle sauce and enrich it wonderfully. (From Périgord.)

POT AU FEU
Simmered Beef Stew

The classic French stew has got to be the pot au feu. In this, quite ordinary cuts of meat are simmered very gently for a long time with vegetables. Because the cooking process is so slow (you must hardly let a bubble rise to the top of the pan during cooking), you get a beautifully clear, rich broth to drink first. You then, as with *Provençal beef stew* on page 201, eat the pieces of meat and the vegetables with sea salt and fresh mustard.

Please don't try to make this dish if you are in a hurry, because it does take a long time to cook. And it's well worth it. If there's still some left, you can re-heat the soup the next day and serve the left-over meat and vegetables cold, chopped up into small bits and dressed with a vinaigrette with a few gherkins and hard-boiled eggs.

SERVES 4 TO 6, ACCORDING TO APPETITE

*1.5 kg (3 lb) pot au feu meat
(shin of beef, or flank with
the bone still in)
6 carrots
6 small turnips
6 leeks
2 onions, stuck with cloves
2 cloves garlic*

*2 bayleaves
1 sprig thyme
1 sprig parsley
Salt and pepper
1 sprig celery leaves
2 marrow bones
6 medium potatoes*

In a large flameproof casserole, bring about 3 litres (5 pints) water to the boil. Pop in the meat, leave to boil for about 3 or 4 minutes until any scum comes up, remove the scum, turn down the heat and leave to simmer for at least 1 hour. Add all the vegetables, herbs and seasoning and cook for a further 1½ hours. Put in the marrow bones and potatoes. Once the potatoes are cooked, the whole dish is cooked. Don't forget to give your guests special implements for getting the marrow out of the bones.

FILET DE BŒUF
Fillet of Beef

SERVES 6

1.5 kg (3 lb) beef fillet
150 g (5 oz) streaky bacon, cut in slivers
1 clove garlic, cut in slivers
3 truffles, cut in slivers
1 piece caul, big enough to wrap the fillet in
6 small potatoes, peeled
6 small sausages

6 artichoke bottoms, cut in chunks
Butter for frying
½ tablespoon flour
1 shallot, chopped
1 tablespoon concentrated tomato purée
Salt and pepper

Pre-heat the oven to gas mark 6, 200°C (400°F).

Lard the fillet with the bacon, garlic and truffles before wrapping it in the caul and tying with string. Put in an oiled roasting tin with the potatoes and roast for 30 minutes in the oven, basting frequently. Add the sausages after 20 minutes.

Meanwhile, fry the artichoke bottoms in a little butter, dust with the flour and add a little water. Add the shallot, tomato purée, salt and pepper. Allow to simmer, covered, for 15 minutes.

Serve the beef surrounded with the potatoes, sausages and artichokes. (From Savoy.)

ALOUETTES SANS TÊTES
Stuffed Beef Olives

SERVES 6

*300 g (10 oz) lean pork,
  minced*
*1 small handful parsley,
  chopped*
3 cloves garlic, minced
Salt and pepper
*1 kg (2 lb) stewing beef, cut
  into slices, beaten as thin
  as possible*

2 tablespoons oil
*750 g (1½ lb) tomatoes,
  peeled, de-seeded and
  chopped*
2 tablespoons Cognac
2 tablespoons flour
1 glass red wine
Thyme

Mix the pork, parsley, 1 clove of garlic, salt and pepper together and distribute it evenly between the pieces of beef. Roll up and tie together with string or hold with a toothpick.

In a large saucepan or deep frying pan fry the rest of the garlic in the oil with half the tomatoes. Add the meat parcels and carefully brown. Flame with the Cognac and sprinkle with flour. Add the wine, remaining tomatoes, thyme, salt and pepper, and stir. Cover and cook gently for 2 hours. (From Provence.)

DAUBE À LA PROVENÇALE
Provençal Beef Stew

This excellent beef stew from Provence benefits from slow cooking, in an earthenware pot with a good tight-fitting lid.

SERVES 6

2 kg (4 lb) good stewing beef, cut in chunks	2 cloves garlic, chopped
250 g (8 oz) smoked streaky bacon, finely diced	2 tablespoons Cognac
	3 tablespoons flour
Oil	1 glass good red wine
	2 tablespoons wine vinegar

For the marinade:

4 glasses good red wine	1 bayleaf
2 tablespoons vinegar	1 small handful parsley, chopped
2 tablespoons garlic, finely chopped	Sea salt and black pepper
1 sprig thyme	1 large onion, chopped
3 cloves	

Combine the meat with all the marinade ingredients and leave overnight.

Fry the bacon in some of the oil with the garlic. Drain the meat, reserving the marinade, add to the bacon and brown all over. Pour over the warmed Cognac and flame. Sprinkle on the flour and stir well. Pour on the marinade, wine and vinegar. Stir well and cover. Simmer gently for 3 hours, adding water if necessary. The sauce should be rich and thick, and spicy; the meat very tender.

Often this dish is served with plain boiled noodles sprinkled with grated cheese and black pepper. (From Provence.)

KIG HA FARZ
Brittany Beef Stew

This is the Brittany version of the pot au feu. The way in which this dish differs from the other pots au feu in this book is by the addition of a huge dumpling made from buckwheat flour (*kig* = meat, *farz* = dumpling).

Prepare a pot au feu as in the following Cévennes recipe and, while that is starting to cook, make the dumpling, for which you need:

SERVES 4 TO 6

500 g (1 lb) buckwheat flour	135 g (4½ oz) butter,
1 cupful stock from the pot	melted
au feu	A good pinch of salt
4 eggs, beaten	2 tablespoons sugar
450 ml (15 fl oz) milk	200 g (7 oz) dried sultanas

Mix all the ingredients until you have a sort of thick Yorkshire pudding batter and leave to stand until the pot au feu has cooked for about 1 hour. You will need a pudding bag, about 20 × 30 cm (8 × 12 in.), made of linen. Pour the mixture into this bag, screw it up really tight and tie it off with string (the way your grandmother did when she made steamed puddings).

Now put the bag in with the rest of the pot au feu and leave to simmer for about another hour. At the end of this time lift out the dumpling, place it on the kitchen table and beat it with a rolling pin until it breaks up into little pieces and crumbles rather like fresh breadcrumbs. Spread this mixture on to a large serving platter. Place all the other ingredients of the pot au feu on the top and moisten with a little broth. Use the rest of the broth as a soup to start with, and then tuck into this mammoth body-building meal with lots of coarse sea salt and strong, fresh mustard. It's quite amazing!

I cooked this with my mate Jacques Yves at his restaurant in St Malo. Although an expert himself, he thought it best to invite his father to supervise the cooking – it was superb, because father insisted on adding half a dozen smoked sausages to the ingredients. (From Brittany.)

POT AU FEU À LA CÉVENNOISE
Beef Stew with Cabbage

This is really another version of the pot au feu, but with the delightful inclusion of cabbage.

1 kg (2 lb) short ribs of beef	*1 onion, chopped*
Salt and pepper	*75 g (3 oz) smoked streaky*
1 cabbage, chopped	*bacon*
12 carrots, chopped	*1 clove*
2 leeks, chopped	*1 bouquet garni*
8 potatoes, chopped	

Put the meat into a large flameproof casserole and cover with about 1.4 litres (2½ pints) salted water. Bring to the boil and simmer for 45 minutes. Scrape off any scum which may accumulate. Add all the vegetables, the bacon, clove, bouquet garni and seasoning and simmer for at least 1¾ hours.

To serve, strain off most of the juice, which can be used as a light soup. Eat the meat and vegetable dish separately afterwards with lots of coarse sea salt and freshly made mustard. (From Cévennes.)

BŒUF À LA BOURGUIGNONNE
Beef Bourguignon

This splendid stew has been raped and pillaged by pub and wine bar cooks the length and breadth of this fair land of ours – they add peppers and other unmentionable ingredients to what must be a simple, slow-cooked dish with no deviation from this recipe.

SERVES 6 TO 8

1.5 kg (3 lb) well-hung beef shin, shoulder and neck, cut in bite-size chunks

5 onions, roughly chopped

5 carrots, roughly chopped

5 shallots, roughtly chopped

3 cloves garlic, chopped

6 sprigs thyme

2 bayleaves

1 handful parsley, roughly chopped

2 bottles red Burgundy

6 thick slices streaky bacon, cubed

1 large glass brandy

150 ml (5 fl oz) Madeira

1 small calf's foot (optional, but preferable!)

250 g (8 oz) mushrooms, finely chopped

Butter

200 g (7 oz) baby onions, peeled

Salt and pepper

Marinate the beef, onions, carrots, shallots, garlic and herbs in the wine overnight. Remove the meat and reserve the marinade.

In a large heavy-bottomed saucepan, fry the bacon and then add the meat and brown. Add the brandy and flame. Add the Madeira and barely cover with the reserved marinade which you have sieved, discarding the vegetables. Add the calf's foot. Cover and simmer on a low flame for 3 hours. Top up with the marinade if it seems to be drying out.

Fry the mushrooms in a little butter and add to the meat. Toss in the baby onions. When the onions are tender, add the salt and pepper. Serve very hot. (From Burgundy.)

DAUBE À LA LANGUEDOCIENNE
Beef Stew with Haricots

The subtle and rich flavours of this stew depend upon the three-part and unhurried cooking process (and, of course, good ingredients). So don't try short cuts – they don't work. As my old granny used to say, 'More haste, less speed!'

SERVES 6 TO 8

1 kg (2 lb) beef neck, cut in chunks and rubbed with garlic

100 g (3½ oz) lard

100 g (3½ oz) streaky bacon

100 g (3½ oz) pork skin, blanched and cut into strips

3 onions, chopped

100 g (3½ oz) carrots, chopped

100 g (3½ oz) leeks (white part only), chopped

4 cloves garlic, minced

50 g (2 oz) dried ceps, soaked for 15 minutes

350 g (12 oz) tomatoes, peeled, de-seeded and chopped

2 bouquets garnis

Salt and pepper

1 bottle red wine (Corbières)

350 g (12 oz) dried haricot beans, soaked overnight

1 clove

250 g (8 oz) smoked pork sausage

1 small glass Armagnac

Parsley, chopped

Pre-heat the oven to gas mark 4, 180°C (350°F).

In a large lidded flameproof casserole brown the beef in some lard, then add the bacon, pork skin, 2 of the onions, carrots, leeks, garlic, ceps, tomatoes, 1 bouquet garni, salt and pepper. Cover with red wine. Put on the lid, pop in the oven, and allow to simmer for at least 3 hours.

Meanwhile, cook the haricots for 1½ hours with the other bouquet garni, the remaining onion and clove. Add salt half-way through the cooking time. Simmer gently and make sure the beans do not break up. When cooked, strain and put to one side.

After 3 hours' cooking time, cut the sausage in pieces and fry in the remaining lard until brown. Add it to the stew along with the beans. Skim off any fat, add the Armagnac and mix well. Return to the oven for a further 30 minutes. Remove the bouquet garni, correct the seasoning and scatter with chopped parsley before serving. (From Languedoc.)

POTÉE DE CAMPAGNE
Country Lamb Stew

The French are really good at very simple but tasty and rich stews, often called potées. Here is one made with lamb: brilliant to take in a large heat preserver to Cheltenham races on Gold Cup day.

SERVES 4 TO 6

1.5 kg (3 lb) shoulder of mutton, cut into 5 cm (2 in.) cubes
50 g (2 oz) lard
500 g (1 lb) carrots, thinly sliced
4 onions, thinly sliced
2 teaspoons flour

1 glass white wine
2 sticks celery, cut into 5 cm (2 in.) pieces
500 g (1 lb) small turnips, thinly sliced
1 bouquet garni
Salt and pepper

Brown the mutton in a pan with the lard. Add the carrots and onions and, when golden, sprinkle in the flour. Let it take colour and add the white wine and a drop of water. Pop in the celery and the turnips. Add the bouquet garni and salt and pepper, and simmer gently for about 2 hours over a gentle heat. Check from time to time and add more water if necessary.

Potée à la Lorrainaise
Lorraine Stew

———

Sadly, you will seldom find this robust dish in a restaurant. So, if you can't be bothered to cook it yourself, make friends with some French farmers and get invited home!

SERVES 4 TO 6

2 onions, chopped
4 leeks, chopped
1 tablespoon lard
500 g (1 lb) ham hock
1 green cabbage, coarse
  leaves removed
4 large carrots, chopped
2 small turnips, chopped
75 g (3 oz) haricot beans,
  soaked overnight
2 cloves
1 bayleaf

1 sprig savory
4 cloves garlic, crushed
250 g (8 oz) smoked lean
  bacon
4 smoked pure pork
  sausages
200 g (7 oz) green beans
200 g (7 oz) broad beans
200 g (7 oz) peas
6 medium potatoes
Salt and black pepper

Fry the onions and leeks in lard in a large flameproof casserole. Lay the ham on top and cover with water. Cover and cook gently for 1 hour. Then add the cabbage, carrots, turnips, haricots, cloves, bayleaf, savory, garlic and bacon. Cook for a further 1½ hours before adding the sausages, green beans, broad beans, peas and potatoes. Add a little salt and lots of black pepper. Cook for another 30 minutes.

Slice the vegetables and meat and serve together. Serve the liquid separately as a soup with croutons. (From Lorraine.)

CASSOULET

This is one of the great country dishes of France – rich, filling and delicious, and fatty. It's great for a winter party of at least eight people.

SERVES 8

1 kg (2 lb) belly of pork, rind removed and reserved, cut into large cubes
Salt and pepper
6 pieces preserved goose or duck (see page 33 for how to make your own) and its fat
750 g (1½ lb) dried white haricot beans, soaked in water overnight

10 cloves garlic
1 bayleaf, thyme and 1 pinch of powdered cloves
4 tomatoes, peeled, de-seeded and chopped
1 tablespoon tomato purée
4 lightly cured top-quality pork sausages
750 g (1½ lb) Toulouse (or similar) smoked sausage

First, fry the cubes of pork, seasoned with salt and pepper, in some goose fat until they are golden. Add the haricot beans, garlic, herbs, powdered cloves, pork rind, tomatoes and tomato purée. Cover the lot with fresh water and simmer gently for about 1½ hours.

Part-cook the sausages in some goose fat. Put to one side with the preserved goose pieces, until the beans are cooked. Transfer the bean preparation to a greased earthenware casserole, place the goose and sausages on top and cook in the oven for a further 20 minutes, until the goose has heated through, the sausages are cooked and you have a steaming plate of golden excellence. (From Languedoc.)

BAKEOFE

The Alsace cooks enthuse about this dish; and rightly so, for it is very good – but, then, so is a real Lancashire hotpot. And this is a kind of Alsatian Lancashire hotpot.

SERVES AN ARMY

750 g (1½ lb) beef brisket, cubed

750 g (1½ lb) lamb shoulder, boned and cubed

750 g (1½ lb) pork shoulder, boned and cubed

2.75 kg (6 lb) potatoes, peeled and cut in 6 mm (¼ in.) slices

500 g (1 lb) onions, chopped

Thyme

Salt and pepper

For the marinade:

250 g (8 oz) smoked bacon, cubed

1 litre (2 pints) Riesling

1 carrot, sliced

1 large onion, chopped

1 clove garlic, chopped

4 bayleaves, parsley and tarragon

Salt and pepper

2 cloves

Combine all the marinade ingredients, pour over the meats and marinate in the refrigerator for 24 hours, turning occasionally.

Pre-heat the oven to gas mark 4, 180°C (350°F).

Oil a vast earthenware casserole. Line the bottom with a quarter of the potatoes and onions. Scatter with all the smoked bacon from the marinade, some thyme, salt and pepper. Cover with the pork. Add another layer of potatoes and onions. Cover with the lamb. Add a third layer of potatoes and onions. Cover with the beef. Finish with another layer of potatoes and onions. Strain the marinade and pour the liquid over the meat and potatoes. Cover the casserole and seal with a mixture of flour and water. Cook for 3 hours in the oven. Then call in the troops. (From Alsace.)

SAUTÉ DE CHEVREAU
Kid Stew

SERVES 4

1 kg (2 lb) breast of kid (or lamb), cut in bite-size chunks

75 g (3 oz) lean bacon, cut in small pieces

1 onion, chopped

300 g (10 oz) butter

Stock

1 tablespoon vinegar

1 tablespoon fine breadcrumbs

1 tablespoon flour

Salt and pepper

2 sprigs thyme, marjoram and 1 bayleaf

1 small handful parsley, chopped

In a large casserole sauté the kid, bacon and onion in the butter.

When the meat is browned, pour in 2 cups of stock and the vinegar. Sprinkle on the breadcrumbs and flour. Stir well until the sauce is thick and smooth. Add salt and pepper and the herbs.

Cover and cook for 45 minutes over a low heat. If the sauce reduces too much, add more stock. Sprinkle the parsley over the finished dish.

This is delicious served with sauté potatoes and chopped spinach thickened with sour cream. (From Auvergne.)

POULTRY

The church clock in Nuits St Georges strikes twelve and the streets empty. Shopkeepers cover their wares and pull the blinds. Old men, fat purple faces under flat berets, shuffle and waddle like plump bull frogs from their places in the sun. The manager of the bank bounces onto the pavement, pecks left and right across the square, throws his leather jerkin over his shoulders, checks the door of the bank and scuttles for a restaurant.

I am sitting, sipping a kir, waiting for Pierre. Inside the bar the school kids are rolling coins into the juke box which is very loud in the autumnal lunchtime. An orange JCB with big black wheels, like a huge praying mantis, jerks noisily into the square, roaring flat out for a well-deserved aperitif, and judders to a halt. A sixteen-wheeled wine tanker from Morocco backs into the shade – I hope it is arriving to take wine from this golden coast rather than to supplement its fine burgundies with heavy North African wine. Unthinkable, of course.

A plaque on the wall opposite says that you pay for parking here, except between 12 and 2 p.m., which means that lunch can be eaten untroubled by such concerns! Though it would take a lot more than a parking ticket to interrupt the sacred ritual of the French lunch – especially here in Burgundy where fine steaks, charred mauve and black on the outside, are cut through like butter into the deep pink interior of charolais beef oozing with parsley butter; or are set like islands in marrow-enriched shallot and Gevrey-Chambertin sauce garnished with a crisp dark green sprig of fresh strong watercress. Here in Burgundy, where in winter plump, free-range ducks are gently simmered with baby turnips and carrots till the sauce is almost black, and in spring a duckling is roasted so fast in a very hot oven that the flesh is still a little pink and the juices that ooze out are rapidly reduced with a glass or two of good red wine and strained over the delicate breasts, while the legs are popped under the grill to finish cooking and then are eaten as a second course with some stewed peas and artichoke hearts – here in Burgundy you don't let anything get in the way of lunch.

I look at my watch. It's 12.14: Pierre is late for lunch and my tummy is rumbling. Yesterday he arrived breathless in the bar babbling excitedly about a new restaurant he had discovered, where, he said, making a ring of his thumb and first finger and kissing it briefly, the coq au vin is '*épatant*' not to mention divine and we must go. The chef, he said, was so particular that not only did he rinse the birds himself, he even cured the bacon for the dish himself. He also killed the beast so as to be sure of having fresh blood to thicken the sauce. In all, Pierre said, it was poetry of the '*tripes*' (stomach), and more than worth the twenty or so kilometres drive – which is why I was becoming anxious, for if he didn't arrive soon we would lose our place and the coq au vin would sell out. *Quelle horreur!*

A blue Renault bounces into the square and Pierre leaps out while the battered machine is still coasting to a halt against the pavement.

'Sorry I'm late. Car broke down. Had to borrow Frédérique's,' he gestured a thumb in the direction of the Renault. 'But hop in. Time's passing. *Allez!*'

We speed down a long straight road through the vineyards, thick with fruit and now empty of workers who are munching their lunch round the long trestle tables set up in the barns by the vignerons to cope with the annual invasion of pickers. Pierre is steering with an elbow, of course, his hands busy lighting a Gauloise. I wish he wouldn't as we swerve past a dog asleep in the centre of the road. Angrily he changes down and accelerates. The little engine is screaming and the body rattling as he winds it up to maximum revs. Then the engine cuts. '*Merde*.' He grabs the choke and pumps the throttle – but in vain. The car has died and we bound jerkily into the grass verge.

Maybe a lead is disconnected or something. I open the bonnet and start fumbling around. 'It could be the distributor. . . .' I look over my shoulder for Pierre who has disappeared. I see him standing, arms akimbo, in the middle of the road flagging down a passing car, which stops with a screech alongside.

'What's the problem?' asks the driver, getting out to peer under the bonnet.

'The problem?' says Pierre. 'The problem is we're late for . . . Oh, you mean the car. ***** the car. Can you give us a lift? We'll worry about the heap of *merde* later.'

You can't argue with Pierre. We abandon the car, bonnet propped open and unlocked. Pierre says to the man 'Step on it, *mon choux*. I'm hungry.'

I light a cigarette and shrink into the back seat. Nothing stands in the way of a good coq au vin.

POULET À LA NORMANDE
Braised Chicken with Apples

This is the kind of dish you should find in Somerset or Devon. After all, there's no shortage of apples, cider or good cream in that part of the world – just a shortage of will.

SERVES 6

6 poussins, or 3 young chickens
12 apples, peeled and cored
250 g (8 oz) butter

300 ml (10 fl oz) Calvados
450 ml (15 fl oz) dry cider
Salt and pepper
3 tablespoons double cream

In a large flameproof casserole brown the chickens and apples in 100 g (3½ oz) of the butter. Remove from the heat and flame with the Calvados. Pour in the cider and add salt and pepper. Simmer for 20 minutes for poussin, 35 minutes for larger birds, turning occasionally.

When the apples are tender, remove them and keep warm on a serving platter. Joint the cooked chickens and add to the apples.

Meanwhile, prepare the sauce. Reduce the cooking liquid over a high heat by three quarters. Whisk in the remaining butter, cut into cubes. Adjust the seasoning and add more Calvados if desired. Stir in the cream and cover the chicken and apples with the sauce. (From Normandy.)

Sauté de POULET à la BIÈRE
Chicken in Beer

Remember: the better the beer, the better the dish. At the very last minute before finishing the sauce, whisk in 2 tablespoons Guinness – it transforms the taste dramatically.

SERVES 6

1 × 1.5 kg (3 lb) corn-fed chicken, quartered
125 g (4 oz) butter
Oil
4 shallots, finely chopped
200 g (7 oz) mushrooms, sliced
350 ml (12 fl oz) pale ale or lager
1 small glass Marc d'Alsace (gin will do)
Salt and pepper
300 ml (10 fl oz) cream
2 tablespoons Guinness
Fresh parsley, finely chopped

Sauté the chicken pieces in 50 g (2 oz) of the butter and a little oil. Add the shallots and the mushrooms and continue to cook. When they are well browned, pour over the beer and the Marc d'Alsace. Season with salt and pepper and simmer on a gentle heat for about 1 hour, or until the chicken is tender.

Shortly before serving, arrange the chicken pieces in a deep dish and keep hot. On a high heat reduce the sauce by half, add the cream to thicken the sauce, and the rest of the butter, whisking all the while. Whisk in the Guinness. Pour the sauce over the chicken and sprinkle with the parsley. Serve with fresh pasta.

POULET AU CIDRE
Chicken in Cider

SERVES 4

1 plump corn-fed chicken
Salt and pepper
50 g (2 oz) butter
2 shallots, finely chopped
1 large carrot, finely chopped
4 apples, peeled and cored

Enough dried raisins and shelled walnuts to stuff the cored apples
Caster sugar
150 ml (5 fl oz) cider
2 tablespoons double cream
1 glass Calvados

Pre-heat the oven to gas mark 6, 200°C (400°F).

Season the chicken inside and out with salt and pepper. Melt the butter in a roasting pan. Add the shallots and carrot to the pan and roast the chicken, breast down on top of them, in the oven for 30 minutes. Turn the chicken on to its back and add the four stuffed apples, each one sprinkled with a little caster sugar and a knob of butter. Add the cider, season, and return to the oven for approximately 45 minutes.

Now take the chicken out of the oven. Place on a serving dish and keep warm, along with the four apples. Over a low heat, stir the cream into the juices from the roasting pan and strain into a serving jug.

Slightly warm the Calvados, pour it over the chicken and flame it. As the flames die down, pour over the sauce. (From Brittany.)

Coq au Pineau
Chicken in Wine Sauce

If possible use Pineau de Charente, a slightly sweet aperitif wine, for this recipe.

SERVES 6

2.25 kg (5 lb) capon, jointed

For the marinade:

450 ml (15 fl oz) white wine	*Pinch of allspice*
3 shallots, chopped	*Salt and pepper*
1 bouquet garni	

For the sauce:

50 g (2 oz) butter	*450 ml (15 fl oz) chicken*
300 g (10 oz) mushrooms,	*stock*
chopped	*25 g (1 oz) flour*
Juice of ½ lemon	*150 ml (5 fl oz) double*
200 g (7 oz) bacon, chopped	*cream*

Combine all the marinade ingredients, pour over the chicken and marinate overnight.

Drain the chicken, reserving the marinade, and brown in the butter in a large flameproof casserole.

Toss the mushrooms in the lemon juice. Add the bacon and mushrooms to the chicken and cook for 5 minutes. Add the chicken stock and simmer, covered, for 45 minutes.

Strain the marinade and add to the chicken. Simmer for a further 1 hour.

Mix the flour with some of the chicken juices and add to the chicken. Stir in well and cook for a further 15 minutes. Just before serving add the cream. (From Charente.)

Poulet au RIVESALTES
Chicken in Rivesaltes or Dry Marsala

SERVES 4

8 small onions, peeled
Butter
1 small chicken, jointed
100 g (3½ oz) smoked
  bacon, diced
1 bottle Rivesaltes or dry
  Marsala, or any 'cooked'
  wine like Roussillon or
  Banyuls

600 ml (1 pint) chicken
  stock
1 tomato, peeled, de-seeded
  and chopped
1 bouquet garni
Salt and pepper
8 mushroom caps
25 black olives, stoned
Garlic croutons

Fry the onions until golden in some butter in a large flameproof casserole. Remove and reserve.

Fry the chicken and the bacon until the chicken is brown all over, add the wine and enough stock to cover. Add the tomato, the bouquet garni, salt and pepper. Simmer for 25 minutes and add the reserved onions.

Simmer for 20 more minutes, add the mushrooms and olives and cook for a further 15 minutes. Check the seasoning. Remove the bouquet garni and serve with garlic croutons. (From Languedoc.)

FRICASSÉE DE POULET
Chicken in Wine

SERVES 6

1 large capon, cut into 8
  pieces
2 tablespoons butter
2 tablespoons flour
1 glass white wine
850 ml (1½ pints) chicken
  stock

3–4 onions, finely chopped
1 clove garlic, crushed
1 bayleaf
Salt and pepper

Gently cook the chicken in the butter until firm, but not brown.

Dust with the flour and allow to become golden. Throw in the wine, stock, onions, garlic, bayleaf and salt and pepper. Cover and simmer for 1 hour. (From Lorraine.)

COUSCOUS AU POULET
Couscous with Chicken

This is absolutely my favourite chicken dish: a happy mix of Arab and French cooking; spicy and yet delicate. And hugely filling.

SERVES 4 TO 5

1 boiling fowl, jointed
Oil for frying
4 cloves garlic, chopped
Salt and pepper
2 tins chick peas, strained,
    or 300 g (10 oz) dried
    chick peas, soaked and
    pre-cooked
1 large onion, chopped
1 × 415 g (14 oz) tin
    tomatoes
3 courgettes, sliced

1 red pepper, chopped
1 aubergine, chopped
1 tablespoon very hot
    paprika or cayenne, or
    (best of all) harissa
1 teaspoon turmeric
1 teaspoon thyme
2 bayleaves
500 g (1 lb) couscous,
    cooked according to
    instructions on packet

Brown the chicken pieces in oil.

Season well with garlic, salt and pepper. Cover with all the other ingredients except for the coucous, add 300 ml (10 fl oz) water and cook in a covered flameproof casserole on top of the stove on a low heat for about 1 hour.

When the chicken is tender, strain off all the sauce.

Mix all the bits, including the chicken, with the couscous and re-heat by steaming over boiling water in a colander – the couscous must not touch the water or it will become mushy.

Serve at once with the re-heated sauce poured over it. Have a side dish of harissa to hand so that you can make each helping more spicy if desired. You could also add some spicy hot sausages, like *Merguez* (see page 196), in the last moments of cooking. Throw in a few pieces of beef and lamb with the chicken and you have a Couscous Royale.

POULET AUX ÉCREVISSES
Chicken with Prawns

This recipe was given me by my old chums at the Vieux Logis in Trémolat, Périgord.

SERVES 4

75 g (3 oz) butter
1 × 1 kg (2 lb) chicken, cut
  into 8 pieces
20 prawns
1 tablespoon oil
1 onion, chopped
1 carrot, chopped
1 clove garlic, crushed
300 ml (10 fl oz) dry white
  wine

200 ml (7 fl oz) chicken
  stock
400 ml (14 fl oz) beef stock
1 tomato, de-seeded and
  chopped
1 bouquet garni
Salt and pepper
Tarragon leaves to garnish

Pre-heat the oven to gas mark 2, 150°C (300°F).

Heat 50 g (2 oz) butter in a large frying pan and fry the chicken pieces until golden brown. Remove and keep warm in a flameproof casserole in the oven.

Shell the prawns by taking the segment in the middle of each prawn's tail between two fingers, turning slightly and pulling to remove the intestine.

In a saucepan heat the oil until smoking and add the shelled prawns. When they have turned red, add the onion, carrot and garlic, stir well and pour over the white wine. Let the sauce reduce and add the chicken and beef stock, the tomato and bouquet garni. Season to taste. Let the mixture come to the boil, then take out the prawns and place them on a plate.

Remove the chicken from the oven. Pour sauce over the chicken and simmer over a gentle heat.

When the chicken pieces are cooked, take them out of the casserole. Bring the remaining sauce to the boil and reduce it, then whizz in a liquidiser or food processor or pass through a fine sieve. Season the sauce and add a little butter.

Serve each piece of chicken in the centre of a plate surrounded by prawns and covered with the sauce, garnished with a few tarragon leaves. (From Périgord.)

POULET AUX CHAMPIGNONS
Chicken with Mushrooms

SERVES 4

150 g (5 oz) butter
1 onion, chopped
125 g (4 oz) raw mountain
  or Parma ham
750 g (1½ lb) chicken,
  jointed

Salt and pepper
150 g (5 oz) chanterelles
  (or any similar wild
  mushrooms), halved
Parsley, chopped

Melt half the butter in a casserole and add the onion and ham. Add the chicken pieces and brown over a high heat. Add the salt, pepper, chanterelles and the rest of the butter.

Allow to cook for 1½ hours over a low heat, turning occasionally. Add the parsley and cook for a further 45 minutes before serving. (From Savoy.)

POULET SAUCE BETTERAVE
Chicken Breast with Beetroot Sauce

As a kid my favourite stolen midnight snack was a beetroot sandwich (home-grown and preserved beetroot, of course). And baby beetroot, boiled in the skin, peeled and sautéed briefly in butter, makes a fabulous accompaniment to a joint of roast pork or chicken. So why not a beetroot sauce? It's really good. And it's also the dreaded Nouvelle Cuisine!!

SERVES 4

4 small chicken breasts, boned and skinned
Salt and pepper
Butter
1 shallot, finely chopped
1 glass dry white wine
1 medium beetroot, cooked and puréed with its own weight in butter
150 ml (5 fl oz) double cream
Fresh chervil and very thin (julienne) strips of cooked beetroot to garnish

Season the chicken and sauté gently in butter for about 4 minutes on each side. Keep warm and covered.

Boil the shallot in the wine until it's almost reduced to nothing. Now stir in the beetroot butter into the remaining wine and shallot until melted. Add the cream until you have a smooth consistency and a bright purple sauce. Remove from the heat and keep warm.

There should be a little juice from the chicken that has been resting: pour this into the sauce. Then slice each breast into thin scallops and reconstruct into its original shape. Pour a little sauce on to each plate, lay the chicken on top of the sauce and decorate with strips of beetroot and chervil.

Poulet basquaise
Basque Chicken

SERVES 4

1 plump chicken, jointed
Flour
Oil
Salt and pepper
100 g (3½ oz) onions, finely
   chopped
2 red peppers, de-seeded
   and sliced
2 green peppers, de-seeded
   and sliced

4 tomatoes, peeled, de-
   seeded and chopped
2 cloves garlic, crushed
1 sprig thyme
1 bayleaf
Good pinch of cayenne
   pepper
1 glass dry white wine
Chicken stock

Dredge the chicken pieces in flour and fry in oil for about 10 minutes until golden brown. Season with salt and pepper and remove from the pan.

Fry the onions and peppers until soft, return the chicken to the pan and add all the other ingredients except the chicken stock. Simmer gently, turning the chicken from time to time, for about 45 minutes or until all the vegetables have amalgamated to form a rich sauce. Add a little chicken stock if the sauce becomes too thick during cooking. Check the seasoning before serving. (From Basque Country.)

Coq au Riesling
Capon in Riesling

As with all the poultry dishes in this book you will only get authentic results with this one by using the proper ingredients. So do buy Alsace Riesling and buy a proper farmyard capon – your efforts will be well rewarded.

SERVES 6 TO 8

1 × 2.25 kg (5 lb) capon,
  cut into 8 pieces
1 sprig each thyme and
  tarragon
2 bayleaves
Salt and pepper
1 litre (2 pints) Riesling –
  from Alsace!!
100 g (3½ oz) butter
300 g (10 oz) shallots, finely
  chopped

50 ml (2 fl oz) Marc de
  Riesling (brandy made
  from the left-over grapes
  after the Riesling has
  been made)
250 g (8 oz) mushrooms
Juice of ½ lemon
250 ml (8 fl oz) thick double
  cream

Marinate the capon and half the herbs with salt and pepper in the Riesling for 24 hours in the refrigerator. Turn occasionally.

Drain the capon, reserving the marinade, and cook for 10 minutes in 65 g (2½ oz) of the butter in a large pan without letting it brown. Add the shallots and the rest of the herbs and cook for a further 5 minutes. Throw in the brandy and flame. Season with salt and pepper and add 750 ml (1¼ pints) of the reserved marinade. Cover and allow to simmer for 35 minutes. Meanwhile, cook the mushrooms in the rest of the butter and the lemon juice.

When the capon is done, remove it from the pan and keep warm on a serving dish. Reduce the juices left in the casserole by a third. Lower the heat, add the cream and cook for 10 minutes. Add the mushrooms and cook for a further 5 minutes, at this stage adding a drop or two of Riesling just to emphasise the flavour. Put the mushrooms around the capon. Strain the sauce and cover the meat with it. Serve with *Spätzle* (see page 248) or noodles. (From Alsace.)

POULET RÔTI À L'AIL
Chicken Roasted with Garlic

If you do this dish properly, you get a sweet stuffing of almost puréed creamy garlic and the contrasting crunchy caramelised taste of the whole cloves roasted in the pan. Just pick them up with your fingers and munch the cloves whole – they're truly delicious. What a way to feast on those beautiful violet-tinted bulbs. You'll never buy a little box of skinny garlic again – I hope.

SERVES 4

1 corn-fed chicken	1 bayleaf
Salt and pepper	1 sprig thyme
Juice of 1 lemon	Olive oil
1 kg (2 lb) plump cloves garlic, half in their skin, half peeled	1 glass dry white wine

Pre-heat the oven to gas mark 5, 190°C (375°F).

Rub the chicken inside and out with salt and pepper, and squeeze lemon juice inside and over the skin. Stuff the bird with 500 g (1 lb) peeled garlic, the bayleaf and the thyme.

Brown the chicken in olive oil in a frying pan, then transfer it to a roasting tin, breast down. Pop into the oven for about 30 minutes, or until the bird takes colour. Add the remaining unpeeled garlic and 1 to 2 tablespoons olive oil to the tin, turn the chicken on to its back, baste and continue roasting for approximately 1 hour. (Remember that it will take a little longer than usual because of the stuffing.)

When the bird is cooked, remove it and the roasted unpeeled garlic cloves on to a warm serving dish. Add a glass of dry white wine to the juices in the roasting tin. Bubble this for a moment or two, season with salt and pepper and strain over the dish.

COQ AU VIN
Cockerel in Red Wine

Burgundy is supposed to be famous for Coq au Vin, but these days it's really hard to find an authentic one. In restaurants they vary from insipid chicken stewed in uncooked wine to mountainous piles of exaggerated culinary chauvinism. Here's how to do it properly, or rather it's a Floyd-adapted version of that of the redoubtable Mme LeClerc of the Hôtel du Terroit at Gevrey-Chambertin; where, by the way, she makes her 'kirs' with double crème de cassis and red Gevrey-Chambertin. They are amazing!!

SERVES 4 TO 5

2 kg (4 lb) free-range capon,
  jointed
150 g (5 oz) green streaky
  bacon, cut in cubes
20 small onions
125 g (4 oz) butter
½ glass brandy
1 litre (2 pints) red
  Burgundy

1 bouquet garni
2 cloves garlic
Salt and pepper
1 tablespoon sugar
200 g (7 oz) small
  mushrooms
1 tablespoon flour
Garlic croutons

Fry the chicken, bacon and onions in about 65 g (2½ oz) of the butter in a large pan. When they have started to brown, chuck in the brandy and flame. Pour on the red wine and add the bouquet garni, garlic, salt and pepper.

Bring to the boil, add the sugar, cover and simmer for approximately 3 hours or until the chicken is done. At the end of the cooking time heat the mushrooms in some butter.

Remove the chicken from the pan when it is done and keep warm. Discard the garlic and bouquet garni. Add the mushrooms to the sauce and simmer for 5 minutes.

Make a *beurre manié* with the remaining butter and the flour, and add it to the sauce little by little. Stir well until the sauce has thickened. Arrange the chicken pieces on a deep platter. Pour the sauce over and garnish with the garlic croutons. (From Burgundy.)

CANARD À LA ROUENNAISE
Duck in a Creamy Sauce

SERVES 6

1 × 2 kg (4 lb) duck	2 pinches dried rosemary
2 tablespoons vinegar	1 shallot, finely minced
175 g (6 oz) butter	1 new carrot, finely chopped
½ ripe tomato, peeled, de-seeded and chopped	100 ml (3½ fl oz) Calvados
2 onions, chopped	1 bouquet garni (thyme, bayleaf, rosemary and parsley)
2 cloves garlic	
1-cm (½-in.)-thick slice bacon, diced	1 glass cider
Salt and pepper	450 ml (15 fl oz) double cream

Pre-heat the oven to gas mark 6, 200°C (400°F).

Gut the duck, reserving the blood. Mix the blood with 2 tablespoons vinegar. Reserve the liver, heart and gizzard and chop finely.

Rub the inside of the duck with 50 g (2 oz) butter. Mix together the tomato, 1 of the onions, 1 (chopped) clove garlic, some of the bacon, salt and pepper and stuff the duck with the mixture. Sew up the opening. Pour over 25 g (1 oz) melted butter. Sprinkle with salt, pepper and rosemary. Pop in the oven, and roast for 40 minutes, breast down.

Now make the sauce. Melt the remaining butter and add the remaining onion and garlic, the shallot, carrot and the rest of the bacon. Add the chopped innards and cook over a low heat for a few minutes. Flame with the Calvados off the heat and add the bouquet garni and cider. Cover and simmer for 25 minutes. Strain well and keep warm.

When the duck is ready, pour the cooking juices into the

sauce. Keep warm. Add the cream and beat in the blood. Warm through and serve the sauce separately. (From Normandy.)

CANARD AU CHOU
Duck with White Cabbage

SERVES 4 TO 6

2 small white cabbages	*Salt and pepper*
500 g (1 lb) smoked bacon	*50 ml (2 fl oz) white wine*
4 teaspoons lard or goose/	*1 × 2.25 kg (5 lb) duck*
duck fat	

Pre-heat the oven to gas mark 5, 190°C (375°F).

Cut the 2 cabbages into quarters and cut out the stalk. Blanch in boiling water for about 20 minutes. Strain and rinse under cold water and put to one side.

Cut the bacon in little batons and blanch in boiling water for about 5 minutes. Dry them and then fry in the fat in a large pan. Add the cabbage, salt and pepper, wine and 50 ml (2 fl oz) water. Cover and cook for 1 hour.

Meanwhile, roast the duck in the oven, and, when it is golden, joint and season with salt and pepper. Put on top of the cabbage. Squeeze some juice from under the cabbage and pour over the duck. Cook for another 45 minutes.

CANARD À L'ALBIGEOISE
Braised Duck

It's incredible that most duck served in Britain is roasted to death and smothered in marmalade. Here are some brilliant alternatives.

SERVES 4 TO 6

3 leeks, chopped	*Flour*
Lettuce leaves, chopped	*1 large duck*
Spinach, chopped	*1 celery stalk, chopped*
3 carrots, chopped	*Pinch of sugar*
1 large onion stuck with a clove	*Saffron*
	Cayenne pepper
125 g (4 oz) streaky bacon, diced	*1 sprig fresh thyme*
	Salt and pepper
Knob of lard	*Marmalade*
14 baby onions	*4 pieces white toast*

Put the leeks, lettuce, spinach, carrots and large onion in a saucepan. Cover with cold water and simmer for 30 minutes. Strain and reserve the liquid.

In a large saucepan fry the bacon in the lard, add the whole baby onions and cook until golden. Sprinkle with flour and stir well. Add the duck and brown all over. Pour on the vegetable stock. Add the celery, sugar, saffron, cayenne and thyme. Simmer for 45 minutes, covered.

Remove the duck, cut into four pieces and keep warm.

Strain the sauce and reduce. Season with salt and pepper.

Thinly spread the marmalade on the toast, top with the duck portions and cover with the sauce. Serve immediately. (From Languedoc.)

CANARD AUX PETITS POIS
Duckling with Green Peas

SERVES 6

*1 × 2 kg (4 lb) duckling, liver,
heart and gizzard reserved*
Salt and pepper
1 sprig of thyme
1 bayleaf
125 g (4 oz) butter
3 tablespoons nut oil
*150 g (5 oz) smoked bacon,
diced*

10 small onions
1 carrot, sliced
*1 kg (2 lb) fresh peas,
shelled*
300 ml (10 fl oz) Muscadet
6 lettuce leaves
*1 bouquet garni (thyme,
bayleaf, tarragon)*
1 teaspoon sugar

Salt and pepper the duckling inside and out, pop the sprig of thyme, bayleaf and 25 g (1 oz) of butter into its belly and sew up the opening.

In a large heavy-bottomed saucepan brown the duckling all over in the oil and remaining butter. Remove and keep warm.

In the same saucepan gently fry the bacon, whole onions, carrot, liver, heart, gizzard and peas until the onions are translucent. Add a little salt and lots of black pepper, pour on the Muscadet and throw in the lettuce leaves, bouquet garni and sugar. Replace the duckling and bring to the boil. Simmer for 40 minutes, uncovered, basting the duckling occasionally with the juices.

Remove the duckling when it is cooked. Reduce the remaining liquid until it has nearly all gone, continually stirring the vegetables so that they don't stick.

Remove the bouquet garni and arrange the vegetables around the duckling. (From Brittany.)

Tourte de Canard
à la Bourguignonne
Duck Pie

SERVES 8

*1 × 2.25 kg (5 lb) duck,
boned and jointed, liver
reserved*

*250 g (8 oz) fat pork, cut in
bite-size chunks*

*250 g (8 oz) bacon, cut in
bite-size chunks*

*625 g (1¼ lb) lean pork, cut
in bite-size chunks*

250 g (8 oz) chicken livers

1 egg yolk

*Enough aspic to make up 1
litre (2 pints) liquid*

For the marinade:

1 bottle white wine

3 teaspoons salt

1 teaspoon pepper

2 teaspoons allspice

300 ml (10 fl oz) port

50 ml (2 fl oz) Cognac

6 shallots

Thyme and bayleaves

For the pastry:

750 g (1½ lb) flour, sifted

20 g (1 oz) salt

*400 g (14 oz) lard, cut in
pieces*

3 eggs, beaten

Combine all the marinade ingredients. Divide between the
meats and duck, adding the duck liver to the chicken livers,
and marinate each separately for 48 hours in the refrigerator.
Then drain, reserving the marinade.

Make the pastry. Mix the flour, salt and lard with your
fingertips. Add the eggs and enough water to make a firm
dough. Roll into a ball and refrigerate until ready to use.

Pre-heat the oven to gas mark 4, 180°C (350°F).

Divide the dough in two and line a deep baking dish with half of it. Put in one layer of drained meat and then one layer of drained duck. Repeat until the dish is nearly full. Close with a pastry lid, pinching the edges together well. Cut a small hole in the top. Decorate with the pastry trimmings and brush with egg yolk. Bake in the oven for 2½ hours. Leave to cool.

Then boil the strained marinade, add the aspic and allow to cool until it begins to thicken. Pour into the hole in the top of the pie. Refrigerate and serve when the aspic is firm.

OK, it's quite a lot of work. But it would make a splendid dish for, say, a Christmas Eve supper, along with a crisp winter salad, fine wines and about eight friends. (From Burgundy.)

FOIE GRAS CHAUD POÊLÉ AUX BLANCS DE POIREAUX
Fried Duck's Liver with Leeks in a Sherry Sauce

Another recipe from the Vieux Logis in Trémolat, Périgord.

SERVES 4

1 × 500 g (1 lb) duck's liver	*90 ml (3½ fl oz) oil*
2 large leeks	*200 ml (7 fl oz) sherry*
75 g (3 oz) butter	*90 ml (3½ fl oz) chicken*
Salt and freshly milled	*stock*
black pepper	*400 ml (14 fl oz) beef stock*

Cut the liver into eight equal slices. Place them on a board and remove all the blood vessels with a sharp knife, starting from the top and working through to the bottom of each slice.

Clean the leeks and cut each one into five julienne strips. Melt some of the butter in a saucepan and soften the leeks gently without letting them colour. Season to taste.

Season both sides of each slice of liver. Heat the oil in a frying pan, add the liver slices and brown them for 1 minute on each side. Remove and drain on kitchen paper.

Pour off the excess oil from the frying pan. Add the sherry and let the sauce reduce. Then add the chicken stock and beef stock and reduce again. Add the remaining butter and check the seasoning. Whizz in a liquidiser or food processor or pass through a fine sieve.

Serve the liver on a bed of leeks in the middle of each plate. Pour over the sauce. (From Périgord.)

COL D'OIE FARCI
Stuffed Goose Neck

Ah, these French, they don't waste a thing. All that's left from a well-butchered goose is the oinck! (or quack!)

SERVES 4 TO 6

1 goose neck (from chest to head)

75 ml (3 fl oz) Armagnac

350 g (12 oz) veal-and-pork sausagemeat

A few foie gras left-overs that you happen to have lurking in the fridge

15 g (½ oz) truffle, finely sliced

Salt and pepper

Pinch of thyme

Nutmeg

Goose fat or pure lard (see Preserved Goose, page 33)

Peel off the neck skin and marinate the neck in Armagnac for a few hours. Meanwhile, mix the sausagemeat, foie gras pieces, truffle, salt, pepper, thyme, nutmeg and 1 tablespoon Armagnac. Allow to rest in the refrigerator for an hour or so.

Stuff the neck as tightly as possible with the mixture. Tie each end as you would a sausage. Cook in a saucepan full of goose fat. The neck is cooked when it floats to the surface. Chill the goose neck, cover with melted goose fat and allow to cool. (From Périgord.)

OIE FARCIE AUX MARRONS
Goose Stuffed with Chestnuts

Goose is probably my favourite fowl and Christmas for me is absolutely wasted if I don't have a lovely little goose stuffed with chestnuts. For this dish you can use the chestnuts we've preserved if you've seen the recipe on page 28. Anyway, you need a goose, a nice young one, not too fat.

SERVES 3

3 onions
1 × 2.75 kg (6 lb) young goose, liver reserved and chopped
Butter
300 g (10 oz) veal and pork, minced
Few sprigs parsley
1 kg (2 lb) cooked chestnuts
Dash of Cognac
200 g (7 oz) fresh breadcrumbs
125 g (4 oz) bacon
300 ml (10 fl oz) milk
Salt and pepper
1 carrot
150 ml (5 fl oz) white wine
300 ml (10 fl oz) chicken stock
1 bouquet garni

Pre-heat the oven to gas mark 5, 190°C (375°F).

Chop 2 of the onions very finely and fry with the goose liver in butter. Add the minced meat, parsley, 300 g (10 oz) crushed chestnuts, Cognac, breadcrumbs and bacon. Cover with the milk and mix with your fingers. Season with salt and pepper. Stuff the mixture into the goose and stitch up the hole. Rub some butter over the goose. Put the bird into a roasting tin with a drop of water in the bottom and cook in the oven until golden.

Pre-heat the oven to gas mark 6, 200°C (400°F).

Now add the remaining onion and carrot, chopped in small pieces, to the roasting tin, pour in the white wine and chicken stock and add the bouquet garni. Cook in the oven for about 1 hour and cover the bird with a buttered paper so as not to burn it. Fifteen minutes or so before the bird is cooked, add the remaining chestnuts to the roasting tin.

OIE à la CHOUCROUTE
Goose with Choucroute

SERVES 6 TO 8

1 goose, jointed
Goose or chicken fat
2 onions, chopped
1 kg (2 lb) choucroute
(pickled cabbage), well
rinsed (see page 264)
1 bottle dry white wine
600 ml (1 pint) chicken
stock

2 cloves garlic, crushed
2 bayleaves
1 clove
7 juniper berries
Potatoes, peeled and cut in
chunks

Pre-heat the oven to gas mark 5, 190°C (375°F).

In a large casserole fry the goose pieces in the fat for 30 minutes, turning frequently. Remove the goose and fry the onions. Add the choucroute, wine, stock, garlic, bayleaves, clove and juniper berries, and pop in the goose pieces. Stir well. Seal the casserole and cook in the oven for 2 hours. Thirty minutes or so before serving, add the potatoes. Add more stock if necessary. The dish should be moist, but not soupy. (From Lorraine.)

GAME

Autumn in England tumbles untidily into a murky winter of rain and squalls and it is not until the first snowfall that anything is good about it. Then you wake up hot under the heavy blankets but your nose is cold. There is no sound through the frosted window. The stream that tinkles like distant church bells in summer is silent and the cocks no longer crow. The soft Somerset slopes are thick with snow like old-fashioned plum puddings, fat and fruity under the white sauce. The slopes which years ago, blue with cold and tense with excitement, I tramped for hours with a spade, a handful of nets, a ferret and my uncle Ken. On a good day by noon, a dozen or more paunched rabbits hung stiff from the crossbars of our bikes, leaving frozen drops of blood scattered like rubies in the snow. We ate thick cheese sandwiches and pickled onions, and sipped scalding sweet tea from a flask.

I love winter. Even its food is special. You pick sprouts that are thick with frost and taste sweet and nutty. You mash swede with butter and black pepper, and mop up the sauce from a rabbit stew or a jugged hare. You roast wild duck with glazed turnips, or marinate a boned leg of pork in wine and herbs. When roasted, it tastes like wild boar. Frost and cold does much for the flavour of food. Winter perch or pike are full of vigour and colour. Fresh perch, cleaned and gutted, grilled over the embers of the Sunday fire and then pasted with anchovy butter makes a brilliant supper.

I love winter. You can stand on the touchline under heavy grey skies with a hip-flask and cheer the home team; and after the match, a mug of mulled wine in hand, you can tell them why they lost. You can trudge over the lowlands with a gun, or lie cold and cramped in a punt in the hope of partridges, snipe or wild duck. You can cast into the winter waves on some desolate beach or skilfully lure great pike from the dark reaches of the winter river. Or you can curl up before the fire, sip a glass of port and dream of the good old days.

But in Provence, when winter comes, the sky is still a brilliant blue, and it seldom snows. The church square, which was so busy in summer, its pavement cafés thronged with beautiful people, sipping and smiling, in their bold-coloured clothes, beneath the bright parasols, is now desolate. The massive walls of the church are grey and old. A priest, one hand on his beret, the other clutching a basket, struggles against the screaming Mistral across the bleak cobbled square to the sanctity of his vestry, his cassock flying like the ripped mizzen of a crabber in a storm. A cat mews against the tightly shuttered window of the bakery.

I stand with my back to the stove in the bar. Four old men, unshaven under their caps, silently flick cards onto the felt mat. There are no glasses on the table. They won't drink till five. Just play cards. The barman is talking about wild mushrooms and morilles and of course 'la chasse' – which has nothing at all to do with people in pink coats on horseback.

It's the time of year when the French skies are so full of lead shot that birds can't avoid flying into it, and the fields and hedgerows are thick with men in leather coats and bandoliers of cartridges who look like refugees from a Stallone movie!

It is a favourite time of year here, too, for me. The quiet afternoons seem to last forever as I sip coffee and dip sugar lumps into my marc. Tonight is the Grande Loto here in the Café de France. It will start with something of a feast with my friends Pierre and Monique to celebrate the game season, and then turn into a noisy drunken night with endless prizes to be won, and argued over. The prizes are already hanging outside in front of the café windows, safe in the freezing afternoon and too sacred for anyone to steal. A wild boar is suspended by its hind legs, flanked by a brace of pheasants and red furred hares. The brilliant emerald green feathers of wild duck glint and flash. A ham, peppered black, sways encrusted in its net. Rabbits next to salamis. Sprout baskets filled with bottles chink as the wind tugs at this delicious tableau.

The shops will re-open soon. The traiteur's window is also filled with game. Multi-coloured corpses, brilliant in death as in life, sombre fur and fine feather, the speckled brown and cream breasts of thrushes and neatly plucked quails with just a ruff of feathers around their necks lie to attention. Partridge and pigeons hang from the chrome rail above them. And the back shelf is piled high with tins of foie gras, truffles and pâté de grive. Signs in the window offer jugged hare, venison stew and crayfish armoricaine ready to take away. The French are so spoiled – lucky devils, I wish such places existed in Britain!

Needless to say we didn't win a single prize in the loto, but dinner made up for it. A simple repast of thrush pâté with crunchy home-pickled gherkins followed by lightly roasted pheasant with chestnut purée, goat's cheeses preserved in olive oil, and the lot washed down with some ancient Châteauneuf du Pape. Yes, I really enjoy the winter.

Rôti de Lapin à la Moutarde
Roast Rabbit with Mustard

SERVES 4 TO 6

1 plump rabbit	*100 g (3½ oz) butter*
Salt and pepper	*2 tablespoons oil*
100 g (3½ oz) Dijon	*250 ml (8 fl oz) white wine*
* mustard*	*150 ml (5 fl oz) cream*

Pre-heat the oven to gas mark 6, 200°C (400°F).

Salt and pepper the rabbit and spread with half the mustard. Put in a roasting tin with the butter and oil. Pop in the oven for 30 minutes, basting and turning frequently. Add the wine and cook for another 15 minutes or so, until the rabbit is done.

Remove the rabbit from the cooking liquid and keep warm. Reduce the cooking liquid on top of the stove and add the cream, scraping the bottom of the tin well. Add the rest of the mustard and stir. Strain the sauce over the bunny and serve immediately. (From Burgundy.)

LAPIN AU CHOU À L'AUVERGNAISE
Rabbit with Cabbage

SERVES 6

*100 g (3½ oz) lean bacon,
  cut into small pieces*
2 tablespoon oil
*1 × 1.5 kg (3 lb) rabbit,
  skinned, gutted and
  jointed*
3 carrots, sliced

1 or 2 onions, chopped
*1 cabbage, tough core and
  outer leaves removed,
  quartered*
Salt and pepper
Stock (optional)

In a large pan fry the bacon in the oil until brown. Remove the bacon and add the rabbit pieces to the fat. Remove the rabbit when browned, then fry the carrots and onions for a few minutes.

Blanch the cabbage for 5 to 10 minutes in boiling water. In a large flameproof casserole layer the cabbage with the rabbit, bacon, carrots, onions, salt and pepper. Moisten with water or stock. Cover and cook over a low heat for 1½ hours.

To serve, arrange the vegetables in a deep platter and put the rabbit pieces on top. (From Auvergne.)

Sauté de Lapin au Cidre
Rabbit Cooked in Cider

SERVES 6

1 large rabbit
1 tablespoon vinegar
125 g (4 oz) butter
50 ml (2 fl oz) Calvados
450 ml (15 fl oz) cider

750 g (1½ lb) button mushrooms, washed
1 shallot, chopped
450 ml (15 fl oz) double cream
Salt and pepper

For the marinade:

125 g (4 oz) onions, sliced
1 carrot, roughly chopped
4 cloves garlic, roughly chopped
1 bouquet garni (thyme, bayleaf, rosemary, sage, parsley)
Pinch of cayenne pepper

2 juniper berries
1 large tablespoon sea salt
Black pepper
1 litre (2 pints) cider
50 ml (2 fl oz) Calvados
50 ml (2 fl oz) wine vinegar
3 tablespoons oil

Skin, gut and joint the rabbit, reserving the head, liver and blood. Mix the blood with 1 tablespoon vinegar, then combine half of it with the marinade ingredients. Add the rabbit pieces and marinate overnight at room temperature. Drain the rabbit, reserving the marinade.

In a flameproof casserole brown the rabbit in the butter. Remove from the heat and flame with the Calvados. Cover with half the reserved marinade liquid and the cider. Add the bouquet garni and half the onions from the marinade. Cover and simmer for 1 hour.

Meanwhile, cook the mushrooms in the rest of the

marinade liquid with the rabbit liver and head split in two. Add the rest of the onions and the garlic from the marinade, and the shallot. Cover and simmer for 45 minutes.

Arrange the rabbit and its liver on a serving platter and keep warm. Add the mushrooms and their liquid to the rabbit's cooking juices. Add the cream and the rest of the blood. Stir while the mixture thickens. Adjust the seasoning. Remove the mushrooms and arrange around the rabbit. Cover with the sauce. (From Normandy.)

ROGNONNADE DE LAPEREAUX
Saddle of Rabbit Stuffed with Kidney

This dish, created by my friend Claude Arnaud at Saint Saturnin d'Apt, demonstrates perfectly how humble ingredients can be turned into gastronomic delights as long as you use fresh produce and take care.

SERVES 4

2 rabbit saddles, about
   350 g (12 oz) each, livers
   and kidneys reserved
75 ml (3 fl oz) nut oil
75 ml (3 fl oz) dry white
   wine
Salt and pepper

1 sprig thyme
1 sprig rosemary
2 pieces pig's caul (fatty
   tissue covering pig's liver)
Butter
500 g (1 lb) broccoli, cooked
   and puréed, to garnish

Pre-heat the oven to gas mark 7, 220°C (425°F).

First carefully bone the saddles, reserving the bones. Sauté the livers and kidneys in the oil for a few minutes and put to one side. In the same pan, add the bones and fry until browned. Pour in the wine and 300 ml (10 fl oz) water. Cook gently for 30 minutes. Strain through a fine sieve.

Now season the saddles with salt and pepper and the herbs. Put the kidneys and livers inside, roll both saddles into cylinders and cover each one with a piece of caul. Roast in the oven for about 15 minutes, then put to one side and keep warm. Pour off the fat from the roasting tin, taking care to keep back the little bits of juice from the rabbit which you now reduce over a brisk heat. Add the stock which you made earlier, whisking all the while. Bubble away until it is reduced by about one-third. To enrich it, whisk in a knob of butter, so that the sauce is smooth and shiny, and strain through a fine sieve.

Put a little of the sauce on each plate. Slice the rabbit and put on the plates. Garnish with the puréed broccoli.

CIVET DE LIÈVRE AUX SPÄTZLE
Jugged Hare with Tiny Dumplings

SERVES 4

1 young hare
1 teaspoon vinegar
10 small onions
3 large carrots, sliced
3 cloves garlic
2 cloves
150 g (5 oz) small pieces of lean smoked bacon
1 sprig thyme, 1 sprig rosemary, 2 bayleaves

1 small handful parsley, chopped
Salt and pepper
50 ml (2 fl oz) plum brandy, or any fruit eau de vie
2 bottles strong red wine
125 ml (4 fl oz) oil
300 g (10 oz) butter
200 g (7 oz) field mushrooms or chanterelles

For the spätzle:

500 g (1 lb) flour, sifted
4 eggs, beaten

15 g (½ oz) salt
Butter for cooking

Pre-heat the oven to gas mark 5, 190°C (375°F).

Skin, gut and joint the hare, reserving the blood and liver. Put the hare pieces, its liver and blood and the vinegar in a large bowl. Add the onions, carrots, garlic, cloves, bacon, herbs and salt and pepper. Add the plum brandy and cover with the wine. Finally add the oil. Cover and leave to marinate in the refrigerator for 48 hours.

Carefully remove the onions and fry them until golden in the butter in a large casserole. Add the hare, bacon and herbs, and strain the marinade over. Cook in the oven for at least 1 hour. After 45 minutes, add the blanched mushrooms.

Meanwhile, make the *spätzle*. Put the flour in a large bowl and add the eggs and the salt. Beat, while slowly adding

150 ml (5 fl oz) water, until the batter is smooth.

Bring 3 litres (5 pints) salted water to the boil. Pour some of the batter on to a plate and plunge the plate into the water for a few seconds. Remove and cut the dough into tiny pieces. Return the pieces to the water. They will be done when they float to the surface. Remove and rinse in cold water. Repeat the process until the dough is used up.

When the hare is ready to serve, warm the *spätzle* by tossing them in butter in a large pan. (From Alsace.)

PERDRIX AUX MORILLES
Partridge with Morels

---

1 partridge per person, plucked, gutted, giblets reserved	*Thyme*
Armagnac	*Salt and pepper*
500 g (1 lb) fresh morels	*2 tablespoons nut oil*
150 g (5 oz) smoked bacon, diced	*150 g (5 oz) butter*
1 small onion per partridge	*1 lump sugar*
	300 ml (10 fl oz) double cream

Marinate the partridge giblets overnight in Armagnac. Stuff each bird with 1 morel, 2 pieces of bacon, half an onion, a pinch of thyme, salt and pepper and sew up the opening.

Brown the partridges in the oil and butter in a large flameproof casserole. Then add the rest of the bacon and the onions. When the onions have started to colour, flame with Armagnac. Throw in 300 ml (10 fl oz) water and the rest of the morels. Simmer for about 45 minutes until the sauce is well reduced, then stir in the sugar and cream and allow to thicken. Check the seasoning and serve. (From Périgord.)

PERDRIX AU POIVRE VERT
Partridge in Green Peppercorn Sauce

SERVES 6

*3 partridges, plucked and
gutted, livers, hearts and
gizzards reserved*
Salt and pepper
125 g (4 oz) butter
*1 kg (2 lb) chanterelles, or
any wild mushrooms*
*200 g (7 oz) smoked streaky
bacon, diced*
3 sprigs thyme
3 sprigs tarragon
4 tablespoons nut oil
20 baby onions

150 ml (5 fl oz) Calvados
3 new carrots, chopped
2 cloves garlic, crushed
300 ml (10 fl oz) dry cider
*1 bouquet garni (thyme,
bayleaf, tarragon)*
*450 ml (15 fl oz) double
cream*
*50 g (2 oz) green
peppercorns*
Juice of ½ lemon
Croutons
Watercress

Salt and pepper the insides of the birds and add a small lump
of butter, a few mushrooms, some pieces of bacon and a sprig
each of thyme and tarragon. Sew up the opening.

In a large flameproof casserole brown the birds in oil and
add the remaining bacon and onions. Flame with Calvados.
Add the rest of the mushrooms, the carrots, garlic, innards,
salt and pepper. After a few minutes add the cider, 300 ml
(10 fl oz) water and the bouquet garni.

Simmer for 40 minutes, turning occasionally, and add
more water if necessary. Remove the birds and vegetables
and carefully drain. Keep warm.

Add the cream and the green peppercorns to the juices left
in the pan. Reduce by a third, stirring frequently. Add the
lemon juice and more salt and pepper if necessary.

Mix the vegetables with half the sauce and arrange around the birds. Coat the partridges with the rest of the sauce and garnish with the croutons and watercress. (From Normandy.)

FAISAN AU CHOU
Pheasant in Cabbage

SERVES 4

1 cabbage
1 pheasant, jointed
Salt and pepper
Knob of butter
1 onion, finely chopped
250 g (8 oz) smoked bacon,
    diced

1 carrot, finely chopped
4 small smoked sausages
2 cloves garlic, crushed
4 juniper berries, crushed
1 bottle Alsace Riesling

Pre-heat the oven to gas mark 5, 190°C (375°F).

First core the cabbage and blanch in boiling water until it is easy to separate the leaves. Cool rapidly and drain thoroughly.

Meanwhile, season the pheasant with salt and pepper and brown in butter. Put to one side. Now fry the onion, bacon and carrot until golden and transfer to a casserole.

Wrap each piece of pheasant in 2 or 3 cabbage leaves and set them, along with the sausages, garlic, juniper berries and Riesling, on top of the bacon mixture.

Bake in the oven for at least 1½ hours. (From Alsace.)

FAISAN FARCI À LA PÉRIGOURDINE
Stuffed Pheasant

SERVES 4

500 g (1 lb) hen pheasant,
 giblets reserved
1 medium onion, chopped
75 g (3 oz) smoked bacon,
 diced
Salt and pepper
75 g (3 oz) butter
50 ml (2 fl oz) nut oil

75 ml (3 fl oz) Armagnac
1 litre (2 pints) Verjus
1 bouquet garni (thyme,
 bayleaf and rosemary)
300 ml (10 fl oz) double
 cream
Croutons

Stuff the pheasant with the onion, its giblets, half the bacon, salt and pepper and 1 tablespoon butter. Sew up the opening and brown the bird in oil and butter with the rest of the bacon in a flameproof casserole.

Flame with the Armagnac, add the Verjus and the bouquet garni. Cover and simmer for 30 minutes.

Uncover and reduce the sauce by a third, before stirring in the cream. Allow to thicken, season, and serve with the croutons and some potatoes sautéed in goose fat. (From Périgord.)

Salmis de Palombes
Pigeon Casserole

The Basquaises are a charming lot and their food is splendid.

One of their specialities is Pigeon Casserole, and very delicious it is too. But the way they catch the pigeons leaves a little to be desired in these enlightened times. Briefly, they net the little darlings! Très folklorique, no doubt, but actually quite barbarous. Still, this is a cookbook, not a Greenpeace pamphlet. So on with the recipe.

SERVES 4

2 plump young pigeons, cut in half
Knob of butter
3 rashers fatty bacon, diced
2 onions, diced
1 glass Armagnac
2 tablespoons flour

1 large glass red wine
450 ml (15 fl oz) chicken stock
1 sprig thyme
1 bayleaf
3 carrots, diced
Salt and pepper

Melt the butter in a pan and brown the pigeons on all sides. Remove from the pan. Add the bacon and onions and fry until golden. Return the pigeons to the pan, and flame in Armagnac. Now stir in the flour over the heat until it is well absorbed into the juices, pour in the wine and stock and boil for 5 minutes.

Add the herbs, carrots and seasoning, turn down the heat and simmer for about 1½ hours. Check that the pigeons are tender, transfer them to a hot serving dish and keep warm while you bubble up the sauce to reduce it until it is thick and rich. Strain off any excess fat and pour over the birds. (From Basque Country.)

FRICASSÉE DE MARCASSIN
Fricassée of Young Wild Boar

You can use cubed leg of pork instead of wild boar, but marinate for 48 hours instead of 24.

SERVES 6

2 kg (4 lb) wild boar, cut in
bite-size chunks
Butter
50 ml (2 fl oz) Calvados

450 ml (15 fl oz) red wine
150 ml (5 fl oz) double
cream

For the marinade:

100 g (3½ oz) onions, sliced
1 carrot, sliced
2 cloves garlic, halved
1 bouquet garni (thyme,
bayleaf, rosemary,
parsley and sage)
Pinch of cayenne pepper

1 teaspoon sea salt
Black pepper
1 litre (2 pints) red wine
50 ml (2 fl oz) Calvados
50 ml (2 fl oz) cider vinegar
90 ml (3½ fl oz) nut oil

Put the meat in a large bowl with all the marinade ingredients, adding the oil last. Leave to marinate at room temperature for 24 hours, turning occasionally.

When ready, remove the meat and sauté in butter in a large heavy-bottomed flameproof casserole. When the meat has browned, de-glaze with the Calvados and flame. Add the wine and an equal amount of strained marinade to cover the meat. Purée all the herbs and vegetables from the marinade and add to the dish, then cover and simmer for 1 hour, adding more wine if it seems necessary. Remove the meat and keep warm on a serving dish.

Add the cream to the sauce and stir over a low heat. Pour the sauce over the meat just before serving. (From Brittany.)

PIGEONNEAUX AUX PETITS POIS
Pigeons with Green Peas

SERVES 4

4 pigeons

40 g (1½ oz) butter

1 tablespoon oil

250 g (8 oz) smoked streaky bacon, cut into small cubes

200 g (7 oz) small white onions

1 tablespoon flour

1 cup chicken or veal stock

1 glass white wine

1 bouquet garni

750 g (1½ lb) shelled fresh garden peas ('Where else do peas come from?' I ask myself)

Salt and pepper

Pre-heat the oven to gas mark 5, 190°C (375°F).

Brown the birds in a heavy pan in butter and oil and put into an ovenproof dish.

In the same fat mixture sauté the bacon cubes and onions for a couple of minutes until they are golden, and pop them in with the pigeons.

Add the flour to the fat in the pan and make a roux, stir in the stock and white wine and pour over the pigeons. Add the bouquet garni, the peas, salt and pepper, and cook in the oven for about 45 minutes.

Before serving, strain off any grease which may be floating on the surface.

HAM AND OFFAL

On the question of ham, much more than 30-odd miles or so of La Manche divides us from the French – we are worlds apart. Flabby, clammy slices of pink, flavourless plastic that cling disgustingly to the teeth, pre-sliced, pre-wrapped, hanging in pallid rows in the supermarket display unit. Compare this with the tenderest curls of delicately flavoured mountain-cured raw ham, shaved parchment-thin, or with the mouth-watering possibilities of a whole piece of ham served with a piquant sauce of shallots, juniper berries and wine vinegar thickened with cream, or with the happy and earthy marriage of ham and lentils . . . well, there just *is* no comparison.

The essence of French cooking, and of the French attitude to food, is that *nothing* is forgotten or overlooked, and so in the pages that follow we have sheep's trotters and stuffed cow's stomach, calf's ears and ox hearts. You, my brave gastronauts, will probably want to pass over this chapter quickly – but the loss will be yours.

LA MIQUE LEVÉE
Dumpling Poached with Ham and Vegetables

I am such a glutton for boiled ham – one of my favourite dishes is boiled ham with parsley sauce and butter beans – that I've included several boiled ham dishes, each of which is great for parties as you can serve the liquid as a soup and use up the resulting spare time to make a really good pudding.

SERVES 6

500 g (1 lb) flour, sifted
4 eggs, beaten
2 pinches of salt
1 tablespoon goose fat
50 g (2 oz) fresh yeast, mixed with a little warm water
1.5 kg (3 lb) ham hock

1 small cabbage, tough outer leaves and core removed
4 carrots
4 turnips
1 onion stuck with cloves
5 leeks
6 potatoes

Put the flour in a large bowl, make a well in the centre and add the eggs, salt, goose fat and yeast. Mix with a wooden spoon and then knead thoroughly for 20 minutes. Roll into a ball, dust with flour and leave to rise in a warm place for at least 4 hours. It should double in size and have a pitted exterior.

Pop the ham into a large saucepan filled with cold water, bring to the boil and simmer for 1 hour. Add the cabbage, carrots, turnips, onion and leeks. Simmer for a further 15 minutes before carefully dropping in the dumpling. Simmer for 1 hour, covered, turning the dumpling occasionally. Add the potatoes 30 minutes into the cooking time. Strain and arrange everything on a serving platter. The dumpling should be separated into portions with a fork. Serve the liquid separately. (From Périgord.)

Potée à l'Auvergnade
Boiled Ham and Vegetables

SERVES 8

1.5 kg (3 lb) ham shoulder	*Thyme, bayleaves, parsley*
2 kg (4 lb) ham hock	*1 onion stuck with 2 cloves*
6 carrots	*6 potatoes*
1 cabbage, tough outer leaves and core removed, quartered	*Salt and pepper*

Soak the ham in cold water for at least 6 hours, depending on how salty it is.

Put the ham in a large saucepan, cover with fresh cold water and bring to the boil. Remove any scum that accumulates. Simmer for 1½ hours, then add the carrots, cabbage, herbs and onion. After 30 minutes, add the potatoes. When the potatoes are done, drain the meat and slice it. Place the meat, surrounded by the drained vegetables, in a heated serving dish. Add salt and pepper if necessary.

The broth can be eaten separately, ladled hot over thick slices of bread and thinly sliced cheese. (From Auvergne.)

POTÉE LORRAINE
Boiled Ham with Vegetables

SERVES 4 TO 6

2 onions, chopped
4 leeks, chopped
1 tablespoon lard
500 g (1 lb) ham hock
1 green cabbage, coarse
   outer leaves removed,
   and cut in half
4 large carrots, chopped
2 small turnips, chopped
100 g (3½ oz) haricot
   beans, soaked overnight
2 cloves
1 bayleaf

1 sprig savory
4 cloves garlic, crushed
250 g (8 oz) piece lean
   smoked bacon
4 smoked pure pork
   sausages
200 g (7 oz) green beans
200 g (7 oz) broad beans
200 g (7 oz) peas
6 medium potatoes
Salt and pepper
Pinch of grated nutmeg

In a large flameproof casserole fry the onions and leeks in the lard. Lay the ham on top and cover with water. Put the lid on the casserole and cook gently for 1 hour. Then add the cabbage, carrots, turnips, haricots, cloves, bayleaf, savory, garlic and the bacon. Cook for a further 1½ hours before adding the sausages, green beans, broad beans, peas and potatoes. Add a little salt, lots of black pepper and the nutmeg. Cook for a further 30 minutes.

Slice the meat and serve with the vegetables. Serve the liquid separately as a soup with croutons. (From Lorraine.)

Soubriquet de Jambon
Boiled Ham in a Piquant Sauce

In France it's easy to buy a piece of smoked or cured ham; here it's more difficult. So you could use a piece of gammon which you have soaked in cold water for a few hours. I cooked this dish for those eighteen chefs at the Hôtel de la Cloche in Dijon that I mentioned earlier and they loved it.

SERVES 6

2 kg (4 lb) piece smoked or
   cured ham
1 onion

2 carrots
Parsley
1 bayleaf

For the sauce:

6 shallots, finely chopped
6 juniper berries, crushed
1 glass wine vinegar
2 knobs of butter
4 tablespoons flour
1 glass dry white wine

450 ml (15 fl oz) strong veal
   or chicken stock
450 ml (15 fl oz) double
   cream
Salt and pepper

Cover the ham with cold water, add the onion, carrots, parsley and bayleaf and bring to the boil. Remove any scum that has formed and simmer for about 2 hours. (Keep the stock to make a green pea or lentil soup.)

Meanwhile you make the sauce, which will take about 45 minutes. Boil the shallots, juniper berries and wine vinegar until they are almost dry. Melt the butter in a larger pan and stir in the flour to make a roux until it starts to turn light brown. Now add the vinegar reduction and the wine, stirring carefully to avoid lumps. Add the stock and simmer for about 20 minutes until you have a smooth sauce. To finish the sauce, stir in the cream over a low heat.

Adjust the seasoning, whisk in a knob of butter to enrich the sauce further and strain into a serving jug. Slice the ham on to a serving dish. (From Burgundy.)

JAMBON À LA BOURGUIGNONNE
Ham in Wine Sauce

This makes a really quick lunch – you can use a couple of slices of cooked ham, if you must. Great with a green salad and some boiled new potatoes.

PER PERSON

2 slices raw ham (preferably Bayonne)
65 g (2½ oz) butter
6 shallots, chopped

1 large glass white wine
2 tablespoons wine vinegar
Pepper

In one pan gently fry the ham in some of the butter.

In another fry the shallots in the rest of the butter until they are translucent. Add the wine, vinegar and pepper and reduce by a third. Pour over the ham slices and serve hot. (From Burgundy.)

JAMBON PERSILLÉ
Jellied Ham with Parsley

This is another dish that requires the cooperation of your friendly butcher. It is often served as an hors d'oeuvre in restaurants – but that is not practical at home, since you must make quite a large quantity. So use it as the main course for a summer lunch or picnic.

SERVES 8 TO 10

*1 kg (2 lb) leg of ham,
    soaked in cold water for a
    few hours*
*1 calf's foot, cleaned and
    blanched*
*2–3 pieces pig's skin,
    scraped*
450 ml (15 fl oz) white wine
1 carrot
1 onion
2 cloves garlic
1 bouquet garni
1 sprig tarragon
Salt and pepper
*250 g (8 oz) parsley, finely
    chopped*
2 tablespoons wine vinegar

In a large saucepan place the ham, the calf's foot, pieces of pig's skin, wine, carrot, onion, garlic, bouquet garni, tarragon and seasoning. Add enough cold water to cover and bring to the boil. Reduce the heat and simmer for 2 hours. Allow to cool in the cooking liquid.

Remove and drain the meats, reserving the cooking liquid. Chop the pig's skin finely and mix with half the parsley and all the vinegar.

Cut the ham into chunks. In a large bowl alternate a layer of ham with a layer of the parsley mixture, continuing until the bowl is full. Finish with a layer of plain parsley. Strain the cooking liquid and pour enough over the ham nearly to cover it. Put a weighted plate on top and refrigerate until the jelly is set. Serve in slices cut in the bowl. (From Burgundy.)

PETIT SALÉ AUX LENTILLES
Smoked Ham Ribs and Lentils

Make sure that this dish is well cooked; the lentils must be very tender and juicy. Make some fresh strong mustard for the ham. It's truly a dish that will make friends with your tummy.

SERVES 4

750 g (1½ lb) smoked bacon ribs (or a smoked hock), soaked overnight in cold water

300 g (10 oz) green lentils, soaked overnight in cold water

2 tablespoons pork or goose fat

1 tablespoon butter

1 onion, chopped

2 carrots, chopped

2 cloves garlic, crushed

Salt and pepper

Parsley, chopped

Simmer the ham for 1 hour in fresh cold water. Drain.

Put the lentils in a saucepan and cover with fresh cold water. Bring to the boil, drain and rinse in fresh hot water.

In a saucepan melt the pork or goose fat and butter and sauté the onion and carrots. Add the lentils, garlic and ham. Cover with cold water. Bring to the boil and simmer for about 1 hour until tender. Add pepper and salt if necessary.

Serve on a warmed serving platter, scattered with the chopped parsley. (From Auvergne.)

POTÉE AUX LENTILLES
Ham and Lentil Stew

SERVES 4

1 onion	1 clove garlic
Olive oil	Parsley
500 g (1 lb) green lentils	1 bayleaf
4 smoked sausages	Thyme
1 × 250 g (8 oz) piece smoked bacon or fatty ham	2 tomatoes
	Salt and pepper

Fry the onion in olive oil until it is golden. Add the lentils, sausages and smoked bacon, the garlic, all the herbs and tomatoes. Season with salt and pepper. Cover with water and leave to simmer for about 1 hour.

CHOUCROUTE
Pickled Cabbage

This dish is truly a legend in its own lunchtime; and, yes, I know it looks complicated, but if French motorway restaurants and humble country inns can do it, then so can you. However, it isn't really worth attempting for fewer than ten people, and you certainly don't need to bother offering a starter or, for that matter, much of a pudding. You could, of course, buy the cabbage in tins, so that you would only have to heat it through and then pile on the cooked meats – after all, it is really only boiled and varied cuts of bacon and ham on top of a heap of pickled cabbage; so there would be nothing to stop you cooking the meats the day before and then re-heating them in stock. (That is probably what a large restaurant would do!) But if you can do the whole bit, then what follows is the real method. Which reminds me . . . I once attended the crowning of the cabbage queen at a drunken festival of choucroute in Ribeauville – very pretty girl she was, too. Or was I looking through framboise-tinted glasses?

2 firm white cabbages, tough
outer leaves and core
removed

Sea salt
Black peppercorns
Bayleaves

Shred the cabbages on the coarse-cut blade of a food processor. Sprinkle some sea salt in the bottom of a large glass, china or earthenware pot and put in a layer of the grated cabbage. Sprinkle with salt again and repeat the process till all the cabbage has been used up. Pop in a few peppercorns and a couple of bayleaves and then cover with a teatowel. Stick a great weight on the top so that the cabbage is compressed very tightly. Leave in a cool, dry place for at least 2 weeks and then proceed with the recipe that follows.

CHOUCROUTE AUX QUENELLES DE FOIE
Alsace Choucroute with Liver Dumplings

You can ignore the liver dumplings! Or you can ignore the
choucroute and just serve the dumplings with fried and
slightly caramelised onion rings and homemade *Tomato
Ketchup* (see page 26).

SERVES 12

For the meats:

1 small ham hock

*500 g (1 lb) smoked pork
belly*

*500 g (1 lb) lean smoked
bacon, cut in 6 mm
(¹/₄ in.) slices*

*1.5 kg (3 lb) smoked pork
loin*

*1 pig's caul (fatty tissue
covering pig's liver)*

6 pairs Strasbourg sausages

For the choucroute:

*2.25 kg (5 lb) mild
choucroute (pickled
cabbage)*

1 large onion, chopped

*150 g (5 oz) goose fat or
lard*

*2 garlic cloves, crushed,
10 juniper berries,
crushed, 10 whole juniper
berries (in a small
bouquet garni bag)*

*1 large onion stuck with
2 cloves*

600 ml (1 pint) Riesling

Salt and pepper

*2.25 kg (5 lb) potatoes,
peeled*

For the liver dumplings:

1 clove garlic

1 large onion, finely chopped

150 g (5 oz) goose fat or lard

200 g (7 oz) pig's liver, finely chopped

100 g (3½ oz) smoked pork fat, finely chopped

15 g (½ oz) chervil, chopped

15 g (½ oz) parsley, chopped

75 g (3 oz) white bread, crusts removed, soaked in milk and squeezed dry

2 large eggs, beaten

40 g (1½ oz) fine semolina

Salt, pepper and nutmeg

Put all the smoked pork in cold water for a couple of hours to remove some of the salt.

Pre-heat the oven to gas mark 5, 190°C (375°F).

To prepare the *choucroute*, wash in cold water and drain well. Fry the chopped onion in the goose fat in a large lidded flameproof casserole until translucent. Add the *choucroute*. Put in the bag of juniper and garlic and the onion stuck with cloves. Pour in equal amounts of Riesling and water to come about half-way up the choucroute. Add salt and pepper, remembering that the meat will already be quite salty. Bring to the boil.

Bury all the smoked pork in the choucroute. Cover with the pig's caul and the lid. Cook in the oven for 1 hour. Check that there is always at least 2.5 cm (1 in.) of liquid in the bottom of the casserole.

Turn the oven to low (gas mark 3, 160°C (325°F)) and cook for a further 2 hours. Check the liquid level occasionally: the *choucroute* must not dry out. Thirty-five minutes before the end of the cooking time put the potatoes on top of the steaming *choucroute* and return to the oven.

While the *choucroute* is cooking, prepare the liver dumplings. Crush the garlic in a pestle and mortar. Fry the chopped onion in the goose fat until translucent and add to the garlic. Add the chopped liver, pork fat, chervil and parsley to the mortar and work to a paste. Mix it all with the bread, eggs, semolina and salt, pepper and nutmeg. (You can use a food processor to mix the dumplings if you wish.) Allow the mixture to rest while you bring to the boil a large saucepan of salted water. Put the liver mixture on a floured board and shape into ovals. Gently slide these into the simmering water and poach for 10 minutes. Remove and drain on a teatowel. Keep warm and use to garnish the cooked choucroute.

When the *choucroute* is ready, remove the bag of garlic and juniper. Put the meats and potatoes aside. Slice the ham hock and pork belly. Drain the *choucroute* and pile it on a heated serving platter. Poach the Strasbourg sausages in the juice left in the bottom of the casserole. Surround the *choucroute* with the pork sausages, liver dumplings and potatoes. Serve immediately. (From Alsace.)

TRIPES À LA MODE DE CAEN
Tripe

Tripe is not exactly popular in Britain, probably because of its war-time austerity associations and because of the natural reluctance of the British to eat offal at all – which is a shame, because it's really good. Butchers' shops in France cook tripe in vast quantities and display it cold and jellified like slabs of ornamental mosaic – you simply buy a cube of it to take home and heat gently through. And it is not a 'make do' meal for the less well-off but an esteemed gastronomic treat. Try it.

SERVES 6

6 medium onions, chopped
2 leeks, chopped
2 cloves garlic, chopped
3 large carrots, sliced
8 tablespoons nut oil
1 kg (2 lb) blanched tripe
    (the butcher will have
    blanched it), cut in bite-
    sized pieces

2 calf's feet, halved
Salt and pepper
½ teaspoon allspice
4 cloves
1 bouquet garni (thyme,
    bayleaf, parsley, sage)
75 ml (3 fl oz) Calvados
1 litre (2 pints) dry cider

Pre-heat the oven to gas mark 4, 180°C (350°F).

In a large lidded flameproof casserole sweat the onions, leeks, garlic and carrots in the oil until the onions are translucent, but not brown. Add the tripe, the calf's feet, salt, pepper, spices and bouquet garni. Flame with the Calvados and cover with cider. Bring to the boil and simmer for 7 minutes. Cover and seal the lid with flour and water. Cook in a medium oven for a good 2 hours. Remove the bones and bouquet garni before serving. (From Normandy.)

CAILLETTES
Provençal Faggots

I have to say that, delicious though these faggots are, especially eaten cold at a picnic, they are but a pale imitation of the properly made great British faggot. On the other hand, they leave the mass-manufactured ones far behind.

SERVES 4 TO 6

*1 kg (2 lb) pig's liver,
  minced*
250 g (8 oz) pork, minced
250 g (8 oz) bacon, minced
8 cloves garlic, crushed
*4 tablespoons parsley,
  chopped*

*2 tablespoons fresh sage,
  chopped*
Salt and pepper
*1 large piece pig's caul
  (fatty tissue covering pig's
  liver)*

Pre-heat the oven to gas mark 7, 220°C (425°F).

Put all the ingredients except the caul into a bowl and mix well together. Roll this preparation into balls a bit smaller than tennis balls.

Divide the caul into pieces large enough to cover each faggot. Wrap each faggot in caul and place on an oiled baking tray. Roast in the oven for about 45 minutes. Allow to cool and eat cold. (From Provence.)

PIEDS ET PAQUETS
Sheep's Trotters and Stuffed Tripe

You will drive through a dark green tunnel of plane trees which block the harsh sun like a total eclipse of the heart, before entering the town where water wheels turn lazily and willows droop to the clear swift water. A blue fence barricades the tables on the *place* where the river and market-place meet. And at the Restaurant de la Gare you might eat melon from *Cavaillon* with *Muscat de Beaumes de Venise*, and follow with *Pieds et Paquets*, a stew of sheep's tripe and trotters. And you'll be pleased that you chose the speciality – although you didn't really like it.

But, my dear gastronauts, you were double-conned, because the charming little place was only re-heating this supreme dish from tins made in another part of France, especially designed to rip you off in the summer. If you really want to enjoy this brilliant offal delight, you must know where your butcher is coming from or cook it yourself. And, in fact, it is a winter dish, so in summer stick to the grilled pork with herbes de Provence – unless you have first-hand experience of the provenance of the trotters and tripe!

SERVES 6

1.5 kg (3 lb) sheep's tripe, well washed and cut in 10 cm (4 in.) squares
250 g (8 oz) lean bacon, diced
1 small handful parsley, chopped
3 cloves garlic, finely chopped

1 onion, finely chopped
1 carrot, chopped
2 tablespoons oil
750 g (1½ lb) tomatoes, peeled, de-seeded and chopped
Salt and pepper
6 sheep's trotters
2 glasses dry white wine

Stuff each square of tripe with a mixture of bacon, parsley and some of the garlic. Roll up and tie together with butcher's twine.

In a large saucepan fry the onion and carrot in oil with the tomatoes, remaining garlic and salt and pepper. Allow to simmer for 10 minutes. Blanch the tripe 'packets' in simmering water for 3 minutes and drain well. This will help to keep them sealed. Add them to the saucepan along with the sheep's feet, then add the wine and about 150 ml (5 fl oz) water.

Cover and simmer for 3 hours, adding more water if necessary; however, the sauce should be thick. (From Provence.)

OREILLES DE VEAU À LA GENEVOISE
Calf's Ears in Kidney Sauce

This dish truly takes us from the ridiculous to the sublime. Just imagine the frozen smiles of appreciation on the well-preserved faces of your friends when, delicately wiping an imaginary morsel from the corner of their mouth with one of your finest napkins, they say, 'Delicious darling. What was it?'

And you tell them.

But I do not jest. This is a quite delicious dish and, if you will pardon the mixed metaphor and pun, it really is making a silk purse out of a sow's ear.

SERVES 8

6 calf's ears, trimmed into rectangles so that they look *like beaten escalopes of veal or pork!*	1 large onion stuck with 2 cloves
	6 freshwater crayfish
	Court bouillon
450 ml (15 fl oz) dry white wine	150 g (5 oz) mushrooms
Vinegar	1 veal kidney, finely chopped
Salt and pepper	Butter
1 bouquet garni (thyme, bayleaves)	Capers
	2 egg yolks

Put the trimmed calf's ears in a large saucepan and cover with a mixture of white wine and water. Add 1 tablespoon vinegar, salt, pepper, the bouquet garni and the onion stuck with cloves. Cover and simmer for 2 hours.

Meanwhile, poach the crayfish for 10 minutes in a *court*

bouillon. Strain and reserve for garnishing the finished dish.

Thirty minutes before the ears are done, poach the mushrooms in boiling water with a little vinegar for 20 minutes. Strain and keep warm.

To prepare the sauce, fry the chopped kidney in a little butter, add some of the stock from the calf's ears and simmer for 5 minutes. Drain the ears and arrange on a serving platter with the mushrooms and capers. Stir the egg yolks into the kidney mixture over a low heat, whisking rapidly so that it does not curdle. Pour over the ears and garnish with the crayfish. (From Savoy.)

Brochettes de Génisse
Ox Heart Brochettes

These super little kebabs are especially popular in southern France. They are cooked over charcoal fires outside cafés everywhere, and make a super snack while you sit on the pavement, sipping chilled rosé and watching the Sunday evening world walk by. They don't taste any good, however, if you don't cook them over a charcoal grill.

All you have to do is buy a chunk of ox heart from the butcher. Ask him to remove all the bits of tube and unpleasantnesses, so you have just a nice piece of meat.

SERVES: DEPENDS HOW MANY YOU ASK TO EAT IT

Ox heart, trimmed and cut into 1 cm (½ in.) cubes	Herbes de Provence
Olive oil	2 slices pork fat or speck, cut into 1 cm (½ in.)
Salt and pepper	squares

Put the heart into a mixing bowl with a couple of dashes of olive oil, salt and pepper and a pinch of herbes de Provence, and leave to marinate for 30 minutes or so. Drain.

Thread the cubes of heart and squares of fat alternately on to skewers and grill quickly, turning from time to time, over very hot coals. Just before serving, sprinkle a few herbes de Provence over the coals.

Serve with fresh bread, a little dish of hot chilli paste and a little dish of soft French mustard.

RIS DE VEAU AUX TRUFFES
Sweetbreads with Foie Gras and Truffles

An extravagant little dish, but well worth the expense and trouble, I reckon.

SERVES 4

1 small onion stuck with
  1 clove
1 bayleaf
1 small carrot
750 g (1½ lb) calf's
  sweetbreads
Flour
Butter
Salt and pepper

1 × 100 g (4 oz) tin foie
  gras (goose liver)
1 large truffle – more if you
  can afford it
1 shallot, finely chopped
1 large glass dry white wine
300 ml (10 fl oz) chicken stock

The day before you prepare this meal, you must put 1 litre (2 pints) water in a saucepan with the onion, bayleaf and carrot and bring to the boil. Pop in the sweetbreads, then turn down the heat and allow to simmer for 30 minutes. Remove from the heat and allow the sweetbreads to cool in the liquid.

Once they are cool, carefully peel off the thin skin or membrane which surrounds the sweetbreads. Lay them on a flat surface, such as a teatray, put another teatray on top and load up with weights (tinned food or anything heavy) so that the sweetbreads are pressed. Leave for 3 or 4 hours. Now you have done the boring bit, preparing the dish next day will be fun and it only takes a little while.

First, cut the sweetbreads into four portions and dust lightly with flour. Melt some of the butter in a pan and fry the sweetbreads on both sides for about 15 minutes. Season with salt and pepper. They should be slightly golden on the outside and firm and not spongy. Put to one side in a warm place and lay a thin slice of foie gras on each one.

Meanwhile, in the same pan fry thin slices of truffle very gently with the shallot. Pour in the white wine and bubble furiously for a moment or two. Then add the chicken stock and continue bubbling. Leave this mixture bubbling, but lift out the truffle slices and scatter them over the sweetbreads. Reduce the liquid in the pan to about a half. Whisk in a knob of butter so that the sauce is smooth and shiny. Adjust the seasoning and strain the sauce over the sweetbreads. If necessary, pop the prepared dish under the grill for a second or two, just to make sure that it is really hot.

PÂTÉ DE FOIE GRAS AUX TRUFFES
Fresh Foie Gras with Truffles

Foie gras is the food of kings and Arab princes – and also the French, especially at Christmas time. Sadly, the method of preparing this great delicacy is rather barbaric (the force-feeding of the geese to produce the abnormally large liver). The farmers, of course, deny any cruelty. And I must admit that it has never stopped me from enjoying it. Sorry.

SERVES 8

1 large pink foie gras (goose liver), skinned, blood vessels removed
½ glass good Cognac
15 g (½ oz) salt for each 500 g (1 lb) foie gras
White pepper
200 g (7 oz) pork fat
1 truffle, well washed and finely sliced

Put the goose liver in a bowl and add half the Cognac, salt and pepper. Gently knead it to allow the Cognac to penetrate. Chill for 24 hours. Add the rest of the Cognac and return to the refrigerator for 1 hour.

Pre-heat the oven to gas mark 6, 200°C (400°F).

Meanwhile, line a terrine with the pork fat. Push the liver into the terrine. Slice the liver down the middle lengthways with a very sharp knife and push the truffle slivers about half-way down into it. Close the liver opening and cover with pork fat. Cover the terrine and cook in a bain-marie in the oven for 35 minutes. The water temperature should not exceed 80°C (176°F). Refrigerate and serve completely cool. (From Périgord.)

DESSERTS

The French hostess is in the enviable position of being able to pop into her local *pâtisserie* when she needs to pull out all the stops with a grand finale pastry confection of great complexity or with a magnificent, multi-layered gâteau of various-flavoured creams and luscious fillings. So you'll find none of those here. Instead I've chosen the sort of everyday puddings or tarts, usually fruit-based, that the regional cook or French house-wife of reasonable competency has in her repertoire of well-tried recipes. All of them are personal favourites of mine as well, and I do urge you to try them – you'll find them a marvellous change from raspberry cheesecake or Black Forest gâteau (and so will your guests!).

BOURDELOTS
Baked Apples in Pastry

For the pastry:

350 g (12 oz) flour, sifted   Butter at room temperature

Pinch of salt

For the filling:

7 cooking apples, peeled and cored

6 teaspoons brown sugar

6 teaspoons butter

6 pinches of nutmeg

6 teaspoons ground walnuts

6 teaspoons blackcurrant jelly

2 egg yolks, beaten with 1 teaspoon sugar

125 ml (4 fl oz) double cream, whipped

First make the pastry – preferably the day before you intend to make the dish. Pour the flour into a large bowl. Make a well in the centre, add the salt and enough water to make a smooth dough. Roll into a ball and allow to rest for 15 minutes. On a floured surface, knead the dough for 5 minutes, weigh it and allow to rest for a further 30 minutes. Meanwhile, weigh an equal amount of butter to dough and cut into small pieces.

Roll out the pastry in one direction, until you have a rectangle 1 cm (½ in.) thick. Dot two-thirds of the surface with the butter. Fold the unbuttered third on to a buttered third, and the other buttered third on to that.

Roll out the dough three more times very lightly, folding in thirds each time. Refrigerate for 20 minutes.

Roll out again until you have a rectanagle 1 cm (½ in.) thick. Fold as before, roll three times and refrigerate. Repeat this operation a total of six times. Keep the pastry wrapped in greaseproof paper in the refrigerator until needed.

Pre-heat the oven to gas mark 6, 200°C (400°F).

Plug 6 of the apples with a piece from the 7th and stuff with a mixture of the sugar, butter, nutmeg and ground nuts, topped with the blackcurrant jelly.

Roll out the pastry until 1 cm (½ in.) thick and cut out circles with a diameter of three times the height of the apples. Wrap each apple in pastry, leaving a small hole at the top for the cooking steam to escape. Decorate with pastry leaves and paint with the egg yolk mixture. Bake in the oven for 35 to 40 minutes. Serve with the whipped cream. (From Normandy.)

POMPE AUX POMMES DU PÉRIGORD
Apples and Almonds in Flaky Pastry

---

2 cooking apples, peeled,
  cored and finely sliced
250 g (8 oz) almond slivers
200 g (7 oz) sugar
75 ml (3 fl oz) oil

Pinch of salt
1 egg, beaten
350 g (12 oz) puff pastry
  made with butter

Pre-heat the oven to gas mark 5, 190°C (375°F).

Save 1 tablespoon of the almonds and 1 of the sugar before mixing all the other filling ingredients carefully together.

Roll out the pastry and cut into four equal-sized rectangles. Spread the apple and almond mixture evenly over the first three pieces. Now stack one on top of the other. Place the fourth piece on top and sprinkle with the reserved almonds and sugar. Squeeze all the edges together a bit and bake in the oven for 20 to 30 minutes. (From Périgord.)

Pompe aux pommes
Apple Pie

For the pastry:

350 g (12 oz) flour, sifted
Pinch of salt

175 g (6 oz) butter, cut in
  pieces

For the filling:

Juice of 1 lemon
5–6 apples, peeled, cored
  and finely sliced

5–6 tablespoons sugar
1 egg yolk, beaten

First make the pastry. Mix the flour, salt and butter together with your fingertips. Add enough water to make a firm but not sticky dough. Don't handle any more than necessary. Roll into a ball and leave in the refrigerator for 1 hour.

Pre-heat the oven to gas mark 7, 220°C (425°F).

Pour the lemon juice over the sliced apples and toss until each slice is coated.

Roll out two-thirds of the dough on a floured board and carefully line a pie dish with it. Arrange the apple slices on top and sprinkle on the sugar. Roll out the rest of the dough and cover the apples with it. Make sure that the edges of the pastry are well pinched together. Cut slits in the top to allow the cooking steam to escape. Paint with egg yolk.

Pop into the oven for approximately 45 minutes, until the pie is nicely browned. Allow to cool before turning out. (From Auvergne.)

PASTIS
Apple Cake

---

500 g (1 lb) flour, sifted
1 egg
2 pinches salt
1 tablespoon nut oil
125 g (4 oz) butter, melted

200 g (7 oz) caster sugar
½ glass Armagnac
1 cooking apple, peeled,
    cored and thinly sliced

Put the flour into a bowl and make a well in the centre. Add the egg, salt, oil and enough water to make a soft dough. With your fingertips, carefully incorporate the flour, little by little. Thoroughly knead the dough on a floured surface. Beat it with a rolling pin and throw it down several times. When the pastry is quite smooth and stretches without cracking, it is ready. Roll it up, oil it lightly and refrigerate for at least 4 hours.

Pre-heat the oven to gas mark 5, 190°C (375°F).

Cover a large table with a floured cloth. Shape the dough into a long baguette and then pull it into a large rectangle, with the dough as thin as possible. Allow to dry for 10 minutes. Paint it with some of the melted butter and sprinkle all over some of the sugar and Armagnac.

Butter a cake tin. Cut the pastry into six rounds slightly bigger than the tin. Line the tin with three layers of pastry and then the apple slices, sprinkled with more sugar and Armagnac. Cover with the other three rounds. Paint the surface with melted butter and dust with a little sugar. Cut the pastry remains into strips and use them to decorate the cake. Sprinkle with sugar and Armagnac and paint with butter. Bake for 30 minutes in the oven. (From Périgord.)

TARTE CHAUDE NORMANDE
Normandy Tart

For the pastry:

200 g (7 oz) flour, sifted

100 g (3½ oz) ground
almonds

150 g (5 oz) butter, softened
and cut in pieces

15 g (½ oz) salt

1 tablespoon caster sugar

1 egg, beaten

For the filling:

2 kg (4 lb) cooking apples,
half peeled, cored and
finely sliced; the other
half cooked with butter,
150 g (5 oz) sugar and a
vanilla pod

75 ml (3 fl oz) Calvados,
warmed

1 egg yolk, beaten

For the caramel:

200 g (7 oz) sugar

50 ml (2 fl oz) Calvados

Make the pastry. In a large bowl mix the flour and ground almonds. Add the butter, salt, sugar, egg and about 150 ml (5 fl oz) water. Mix together with your fingertips. Roll into a ball and carefully knead, bit by bit, until you have a smooth dough. Refrigerate for a few hours wrapped in a floured teatowel.

Pre-heat the oven to gas mark 5, 190°C (375°F).

Roll out the pastry to 6 mm (¼ in.) thickness on a floured board. Carefully butter a large flan/tart dish and line it with pastry. Bake blind in the oven for 30 minutes.

Fill the pastry shell with the cooked apples and top with the sliced apples. Sprinkle with 75 ml (3 fl oz) of warmed Calvados and flame. Paint the pastry with egg yolk and bake for a further 30 minutes.

Meanwhile, make the caramel. Heat 50 ml (2 fl oz) Calvados and sugar together in a heavy-bottomed pan until the mixture turns golden brown. Pour the caramel over the tart and serve with whipped cream. (From Normandy.)

LE MILLARD
Auvergne Cherry Cake

---

3 eggs, beaten
4 tablespoons caster sugar,
   plus extra for dusting
125 g (4 oz) flour, sifted

1 teaspoon dried yeast
Milk
500 g (1 lb) cherries, stems
   and stones removed

Pre-heat the oven to gas mark 7, 220°C (425°F).

Beat the eggs and sugar together. Slowly add the flour, then the yeast. Mix well. Add enough milk to make a smooth and not too thin pancake batter. Butter a flan dish and pour in the batter. Arrange the cherries on top.

Bake in the oven for 30 to 45 minutes. The cake will be done when it is golden brown and when a knife pushed into the middle comes out clean. Dust with sugar and serve either warm or cold. (From Auvergne.)

GÂTEAU AU NOIX
Nut Tart

For the pastry:

250 g (8 oz) flour, sifted
100 g (3½ oz) butter,
  softened

50 g (2 oz) caster sugar
2 egg yolks
Pinch of salt

For the filling:

125 g (4 oz) fresh walnuts,
  chopped, or dried
  walnuts, ground
300 ml (10 fl oz) double
  cream

½ teaspoon vanilla essence
100 g (3½ oz) caster sugar
1 egg white, beaten until
  stiff
Pinch of salt

For the icing:

50 ml (2 fl oz) Armagnac
100 g (3½ oz) icing sugar

10 walnut halves

Mix the pastry ingredients into a firm ball. Refrigerate for 1
hour before rolling out to 1 cm (½ in.) thick.

Pre-heat the oven to gas mark 4, 180°C (350°F).

Line a pie dish with the pastry and pop into the oven until
it hardens, without browning.

Meanwhile, combine all the filling ingredients and fill the
pie shell with the mixture. Return to the oven at gas mark 5,
190°C (375°F), for 35 minutes. While the tart is cooking, mix
the icing sugar with the Armagnac. When it is cooked, allow
to cool, then ice it with this mixture and decorate with the
walnut halves. (From Périgord.)

TARTE AU LAIT CAILLÉ
Curd Pie

For the pastry:

250 g (8 oz) flour, sifted   Pinch of salt
125 g (4 oz) butter, softened
  and cut in pieces

For the filling:

750 ml (1¼ pints)   100 g (3½ oz) icing sugar
  unpasteurised milk   Few drops of vanilla
Rennet   essence
300 ml (10 fl oz) double   2 egg yolks, beaten
  cream   2 whole eggs, beaten

The day before you intend to make the tart, warm the milk to blood temperature and add a few drops of rennet. Stir and allow the milk to curdle in a warm place for 4 to 5 hours. Then drain the curds either through a fine sieve or in a colander lined with muslin for 12 to 18 hours. If you can't be bothered with any of this, just buy curd cheese!

Make the pastry. Mix the flour, butter and salt together with your fingertips. Add enough water to make a firm dough. Roll up and leave in the refrigerator for an hour.

Pre-heat the oven to gas mark 7, 220°C (425°F).

In a large bowl combine the drained curds with the cream. Add the sugar and vanilla. Beat well and add the egg yolks and whole eggs. Keep beating until you have a mixture rather like whipped cream.

Line a pie dish with the pastry. Prick all over with a fork and bake blind for 10 minutes. Pour in the filling and return to the oven for 20 to 30 minutes. (From Auvergne.)

TARTE AUX QUETSCHES
Alsatian Plum Tart

———

Bilberries can also be used, in which case omit the cinnamon.

For the pastry:

300 g (10 oz) wheat flour,
    sifted
150 g (5 oz) butter, cut in
    small pieces

7–15 g ($^{1}/_{4}$–$^{1}/_{2}$ oz) fine salt
1 tablespoon caster sugar
1 egg, beaten

For the filling:

2 eggs
50 ml (2 fl oz) milk
1 teaspoon vanilla essence
125 g (4 oz) caster sugar

1 kg (2 lb) firm plums,
    stoned and halved
    lengthways
$^{1}/_{4}$ teaspoon cinnamon

Put the flour into a large bowl, make a well in the centre, add the butter, salt, sugar and egg. Mix with your fingertips until well amalgamated and roll into a ball. Knead on a floured board until smooth. Wrap in a floured cloth and refrigerate for a couple of hours.

Pre-heat the oven to gas mark 5, 190°C (375°F).

When the pastry is well rested, roll it out on a floured board to an approximate thickness of 6 mm (¼ in.). Liberally butter a flan dish (best to use one with a removable base) and line it with the pastry. Prick the bottom all over with a fork and bake blind in the oven for 20 minutes.

While the pastry is cooking beat the eggs, milk, vanilla and 25 g (1 oz) of the sugar together. Pour into the pastry shell and return to the oven. Allow the custard to set but not to discolour.

Remove the tart from the oven and arrange the plums in concentric circles on the custard, some skin side up, some down. Return to the oven at gas mark 7, 220°C (425°F), for 20 minutes.

Remove and sprinkle with the remaining sugar. Pop back in the oven for a final 5 minutes. Cool and dust with the cinnamon before serving. (From Alsace.)

TARTE AUX MIRABELLES
Plum Tart

---

350 g (12 oz) shortcrust or
  puff pastry
1 tablespoon granulated
  sugar

350 g (12 oz) plums, stoned
1 tablespoon caster sugar

For the sauce:

1 tablespoon Mirabelle jam

1 tablespoon Mirabelle eau
de vie

Pre-heat the oven to gas mark 6, 200°C (400°F).

Line a pie or flan dish with the pastry and prick the bottom all over with a fork. Sprinkle with the granulated sugar. Arrange the plums in concentric circles and pop into the oven for 25 minutes. Allow to cool, then dust with caster sugar.

Warm the sauce ingredients together with 1 tablespoon water until syrupy. Serve separately. (From Lorraine.)

TARTE AUX QUETSCHES SOUFFLÉE
Souffléed Plum Tart

---

350 g (12 oz) shortcrust
  pastry
350 g (12 oz) plums, stoned
  and quartered
40 g (1½ oz) butter
40 g (1½ oz) sugar

1 egg, separated
75 g (3 oz) fine semolina
75 ml (3 fl oz) cream
50 ml (2 fl oz) milk
Caster sugar and cinnamon

Pre-heat the oven to gas mark 6, 200°C (400°F).

Line a pie or flan dish with the pastry. Arrange the plums on the pastry in concentric circles. Beat the butter, sugar and egg yolk together until fluffy. Stir in the semolina, cream and milk. Beat the egg white until stiff and fold into the mixture. Pour over the plums and pop in the oven for 25 minutes. Dust with caster sugar and a little cinnamon. (From Lorraine.)

TARTE MOIRANDELLE AUX PRUNEAUX
Prune Tart

For the pastry:

500 g (1 lb) flour, sifted
2 eggs, beaten
Pinch of salt

1 glass cream
250 g (8 oz) butter, softened
  and cut in pieces

For the filling:

1 kg (2 lb) stoned prunes,
  cooked with sugar

3 tablespoons sugar

Put the flour in a large bowl. Make a well in the centre and pour in the eggs, salt and enough cream to make a dough, and add the butter bit by bit. Mix well, roll up and leave in the refrigerator for about 2 hours.

Pre-heat the oven to gas mark 6, 200°C (400°F).

Roll out the pastry on a floured board and line a pie dish with about two-thirds of it. Squash some of the prunes together and put them in the pie shell. Arrange the rest of the prunes on the top. Cut the remaining pastry in 1 cm (½ in.) strips and criss-cross the tart with them.

Bake in the oven and, when nearly done, dust the tart with the sugar then return to the oven to brown.

The tart can be eaten hot or cold. (From Burgundy.)

TARTE À LA RHUBARBE
Rhubarb Tart

---

1 kg (2 lb) rhubarb, peeled and cut into small chunks	*2 eggs*
	2 tablespoons vanilla sugar
175 g (6 oz) sugar	*75 ml (3 fl oz) milk*
350 g (12 oz) shortcrust pastry	*300 ml (10 fl oz) cream*

Put the rhubarb in a sieve and dust with half the sugar. Leave for 1 hour.

Pre-heat the oven to gas mark 5, 190°C (375°F).

Line a flan dish with the pastry and cover with the rhubarb. Break the eggs into a bowl and beat with the rest of the sugar, and the vanilla sugar. Stir in the milk and cream.

Pour the mixture over the rhubarb and cook in the oven for 25 minutes. (From Lorraine.)

Tartes aux Poires et Raisins
Pear and Raisin Tarts

For the filling:

500 g (1 lb) pears, peeled,
  cored and quartered
125 g (4 oz) sugar
4 cubes dark chocolate

150 g (5 oz) raisins
Finely grated rind of 1
  orange

For the pastry:

200 g (7 oz) flour, sifted
125 g (4 oz) butter, cut in
  small pieces

3 egg yolks, beaten
Pinch of salt

Cook the pears in 300 ml (10 fl oz) water with the sugar, chocolate, raisins and orange rind, until you have a thick compote.

Meanwhile, make the pastry. Put the flour in a bowl and make a well in the centre. Add the butter and 4 tablespoons water, 2 of the egg yolks and salt. Mix together and knead until you have a firm, elastic dough – add more water if necessary. Allow to rest for 30 minutes.

Pre-heat the oven to gas mark 6, 200°C (400°F).

Roll out the pastry into a rough square, approximately 6 mm (¼ in.) thick. Cut rounds in the pastry with a cutter or glass and put a small dollop of compote on each. Fold in two and seal the edges with water.

Paint with the remaining egg yolk and place on a buttered baking sheet. Pop into the oven for about 20 minutes. (From Savoy.)

TARTE AU FROMAGE BLANC
Alsatian Cheese Cake

---

1 pastry pie shell as for Alsatian Plum Tart (see page 286),
   baked blind for 20 minutes

For the filling:

400 g (14 oz) fromage blanc
   (minimum 60 per cent fat
   content)
100 g (3½ oz) caster sugar

5 eggs, separated
50 g (2 oz) flour, sifted
Juice of 1 small lemon
1 teaspoon vanilla essence

Pre-heat the oven to gas mark 7, 220°C (425°F).

While the pastry is cooking, beat the fromage blanc, sugar, egg yolks, flour, lemon juice and vanilla essence together. Beat the egg whites until stiff and gently fold into the mixture. Pour into the pre-cooked pastry shell and return to the oven for 30 to 40 minutes until a rich brown all over. Slide out on to a cooling rack and leave upside down until cool. This will keep the surface smooth. Serve right side up. (From Alsace.)

GÂTEAU BRETON
Breton Cake

---

150 g (5 oz) butter, melted
150 g (5 oz) caster sugar
150 g (5 oz) flour, sifted
4 eggs, separated

15 g (½ oz) live yeast,
   mixed with 75 ml (3 fl oz)
   warm milk
1 teaspoon orange water

In a bowl combine the butter, sugar, flour and egg yolks. Add the yeast mixture and the orange water. Allow the batter to rest for an hour or so in a warm place.

Pre-heat the oven to gas mark 5, 190°C (375°F).

Butter a 20-cm (8-in.)-square, 5-cm (2-in.)-deep cake tin. Beat the egg whites into stiff peaks and fold into the batter. Pour into the tin and bake in the oven for 40 minutes without opening the door. (From Brittany.)

KUGELHOPF
Alsatian Sponge Cake

---

20 g (³/₄ oz) fresh yeast
150 ml (5 fl oz) milk, warmed
500 g (1 lb) flour, sifted
3 eggs
15 g (¹/₂ oz) fine salt
75 g (3 oz) caster sugar

250 g (8 oz) butter, creamed
100 g (3¹/₂ oz) raisins, soaked overnight in 90 ml (3¹/₂ fl oz) water
20 blanched almonds
Icing sugar to dust

In a small bowl mix the yeast with the warm milk and add enough flour to make a light batter. Cover with a cloth and leave in a warm place. Allow to double in size.

Now prepare the cake mixture. Put the rest of the flour in a large bowl, make a well in the centre and add the eggs, salt and sugar. Beat thoroughly for 15 minutes, incorporating as much air as possible. Add the butter. Mix until smooth but not too sticky. Add the yeast mixture. Mix well, cover with a floured cloth and leave to double in size in a warm place (about 1 hour). Knead the dough until it retains its original size. Incorporate the raisins, carefully dried.

Pre-heat the oven to gas mark 5, 190°C (375°F).

Liberally butter a kugelhopf mould. Arrange the blanched almonds over the base. Add the cake mixture. Allow to rise again in a warm place until it just peeps over the top of the mould.

Bake in the oven for 45 minutes – cover with aluminium foil if it seems to be browning too quickly. Unmould. Allow to cool and dust with icing sugar. (From Alsace.)

LA GALETTE CHARENTAISE
Charente Cake

---

250 g (8 oz) flour, sifted
2 tablespoons vanilla sugar
15 g (½ oz) dried yeast
125 g (4 oz) butter, melted
1 egg, beaten

125 g (4 oz) sugar
15 g (½ oz) preserved
  angelica, chopped
1 egg yolk, beaten

Pre-heat the oven to gas mark 5, 190°C (375°F).

Put the flour in a large bowl and make a well in the centre. Add the vanilla sugar and yeast. Add the butter and egg with the sugar. Knead well and add the angelica. Push the dough into a pie pan and glaze with the egg yolk. Make a criss-cross pattern all over with a fork. Cook for 20 minutes. (From Charente.)

LE MILLA
Charente Vanilla Cake

---

1 cup cornflour, sifted
1 cup plain flour, sifted
1½ cups milk
1½ cups caster sugar
25 g (1 oz) dried yeast

2 packets vanilla sugar
¼ glass Cognac
Pinch of salt
125 g (4 oz) butter, melted
2 eggs, beaten

Pre-heat the oven to gas mark 7, 220°C (425°F).

Mix everything together well, adding the butter and eggs last. Pack the mixture into a pie dish, drizzle a little melted butter over the top and sprinkle with a little flour. Bake in the oven for 35 minutes. (From Charente.)

TARTE À LA MIE DE PAIN
Bread Dough Pie

For the pastry:

250 g (8 oz) flour, sifted
Pinch of salt

125 g (4 oz) butter, softened
Milk

For the filling:

150 g (5 oz) fresh white
  breadcrumbs
300 ml (10 fl oz) milk
125 g (4 oz) caster sugar

30 g (1¼ oz) ground
  almonds
5 eggs, separated
3 tablespoons kirsch

Make the pastry. Put the flour and salt in a bowl. Add the butter little by little and enough milk to make a firm dough.

Roll up and keep in the refrigerator for 2 to 3 hours.
Pre-heat the oven to gas mark 5, 190°C (375°F).

In a large bowl put the breadcrumbs and enough milk to soak the bread. Add the sugar, almonds, egg yolks and kirsch. Beat the egg whites until stiff and fold into the mixture.

Line a pie dish with the pastry and pour in the filling. Pop into the oven for 30 to 40 minutes. (From Burgundy.)

GÂTEAU BASQUE
Basque Cake

---

1 free-range egg and 4 egg yolks	Finely grated rind of 1 lemon
200 g (7 oz) unsalted butter, softened	350 g (12 oz) flour, sifted
250 g (8 oz) caster sugar	300 ml (10 fl oz) rich milk (not that de-creamed stuff), warmed
Pinch of salt	

Beat 1 whole egg and 2 yolks in a mixing bowl, then beat in the softened butter, 200 g (7 oz) of the sugar, the salt, lemon rind and finally 325 g (11 oz) of the flour, until you have a smooth and shiny mix. Leave this for 1 hour in a cool place.

Beat the remaining sugar and flour with 2 egg yolks in a saucepan. Over a low heat stir in the warmed milk. Keep stirring until you have a thick custard. Allow to cool.

Pre-heat the oven to gas mark 6, 200°C (400°F).

Butter a shallow cake tin and put in two-thirds of the cake mix, then the custard, and cover with the remaining cake mix. Bake in the oven for about 40 minutes.

Allow to cool before tipping out of the cake tin. (From Basque Country.)

GÂTEAU DE SAVOIE
Savoy Cake

---

3 eggs, separated
150 g (5 oz) flour, sifted
200 g (7 oz) caster sugar

15 g (½ oz) yeast
Finely grated rind of
1 lemon

Pre-heat the oven to gas mark 5, 190°C (375°F).

Beat the egg yolks in a mixing bowl and whisk in, little by little, 75 g (3 oz) of the flour, the sugar, yeast and lemon rind. Put to one side.

Meanwhile, beat the egg whites until stiff and carefully mix in the rest of the flour.

Now mix the two preparations together. Put into a buttered cake tin and bake in the oven for about 1 hour. (From Savoy.)

BRIOCHE ST DENIS
Praline Cake

---

15 g (½ oz) fresh yeast
500 g (1 lb) flour, sifted
Salt
6 eggs

25 g (1 oz) sugar
350 g (12 oz) butter, cut in
pieces
200 g (7 oz) pralines

The night before you make the cake, mix the yeast with a little warm water and leave in a warm place.

Put the flour and salt on a pastry board and make a well in the centre. Beat the eggs with the sugar and pour on to the flour with the yeast. Knead the dough until it is completely smooth. Add the butter little by little, until the dough is smooth again. Allow to rest until it is well risen. Beat it down and allow to rest in a cool place overnight.

The following day pre-heat the oven to gas mark 5, 190°C (375°F).

Stir 125 g (4 oz) of the pralines into the dough. Butter a cake tin and put in the dough. Cover with the rest of the pralines. Pop in the oven for 40 minutes. (From Savoy.)

GÂTEAU AU CHOCOLAT
Rich Chocolate Cake

---

4 eggs	2 tablespoons vanilla sugar
The eggs' weight of each of the following: plain chocolate, butter and caster sugar	75 g (3 oz) ground almonds
	1 tablespoon potato flour (or cornflour)

Pre-heat the oven to gas mark 5, 190°C (375°F).

Separate the eggs. Put the chocolate in a mixing bowl over a pan of simmering water. When it has melted, whisk in the butter, sugar and vanilla sugar, egg yolks and ground almonds. Next add the potato flour and fold in the egg whites, stiffly beaten.

Pour the mixture into a buttered shallow tart tin and bake in the oven for about 40 minutes. Let the cake cool in the tin before turning out. (From Lorraine.)

POMPE À L'HUILE
Christmas Dessert Cake

The traditional Provençal Christmas dessert consists of an arrangement of dried fruits, walnuts, almonds, dried figs, raisins, pistachios and prunes, fresh fruits (apples, pears, oranges and pomegranates), white and black nougat and fruit jellies. The most important part of the display is the cake.

500 g (1 lb) flour, sifted
25 g (1 oz) fresh yeast
150 ml (5 fl oz) olive oil
125 g (4 oz) moist light brown sugar
Few drops of orange flower water

Mix half the flour with the yeast and a little warm water. Cover with a cloth and allow to rise overnight in a warm place.

Mix the rest of the flour with the olive oil and brown sugar. Add the yeast mixture and the orange flower water. Knead well and allow to double in size, covered with a damp cloth.

Pre-heat the oven to gas mark 7, 220°C (425°F).

Divide the dough into six equal parts and shape each piece into a ring. Link them all together like a chain. Place on an oiled baking sheet and allow to rise for a further hour. Pop in the oven for 20 minutes or until a deep golden brown. (From Provence.)

BABAS AU RHUM
Rum Babas

---

15 g (½ oz) yeast
150 ml (5 fl oz) milk,
  warmed
250 g (8 oz) flour, sifted
3 eggs

40 g (1½ oz) sugar
Pinch of salt
75 g (3 oz) butter, softened
75 g (3 oz) raisins

For the syrup:

250 g (8 oz) caster sugar
300 ml (10 fl oz) rum

75 ml (3 fl oz) prune eau de
  vie

First dissolve the yeast in the warm milk. Put to one side.

Put the flour into a mixing bowl and beat in the eggs, sugar, salt, the milk and yeast mixture and the softened butter. Mix well until you have a smooth paste and it begins to fall away from the sides of the mixing bowl. Cover the bowl with a teatowel and leave the paste to rise for about 1 hour.

Pre-heat the oven to gas mark 5, 190°C (375°F).

Now butter some rum baba moulds. Mix the raisins into the paste and half-fill each mould with the mixture. Leave until the mixture rises to fill the moulds. Bake in the oven for about 20 minutes.

Meanwhile, make a syrup with 450 ml (15 fl oz) water and 250 g (8 oz) caster sugar and boil for 5 minutes. Turn off the heat and add the rum and eau de vie. When the babas are cooked, soak them in this liquid. Eat cold with whipped cream. (From Lorraine.)

MADELEINES

These are the classic little snacks that all kids raid the larder for when they come home from school. They are brilliant if they are fresh.

125 g (4 oz) sugar
4 eggs
125 g (4 oz) butter, melted

Couple of dashes of orange
   flower water
125 g (4 oz) flour, sifted
15 g (½ oz) dried yeast

Pre-heat the oven to gas mark 5, 190°C (375°F).

Whisk the sugar and eggs together until fluffy. Now whisk in the melted butter and the orange flower water, and when that's well mixed add the flour and yeast.

Butter a tart tray and put a couple of tablespoons of the mixture into each hole. Cook for about 25 minutes in the oven. Allow to cool and gobble them up! (From Lorraine.)

LE PAIN D'ÉPICES AU MIEL
Gingerbread with Auvergne Honey

125 g (4 oz) honey, thinned
   with 300 ml (10 fl oz) hot
   water or milk
125 g (4 oz) sugar
½ teaspoon ground aniseed

½ teaspoon ground ginger
1 teaspoon bicarbonate of
   soda
250 g (8 oz) flour, sifted

Pre-heat the oven to gas mark 6, 200°C (400°F).

Put the honey mixture into a big bowl, add the sugar and

spices and the bicarbonate of soda. Beat well. Slowly add the flour. Mix well until smooth.

Butter a cake tin and dust with flour. Pour in the batter. The cake tin should be three-quarters full. Bake in the oven for 1 hour or until a knife inserted in the middle comes out clean. (From Auvergne.)

SOUFFLÉ AU KIRSCH
Kirsch Soufflé

SERVES 4 TO 6

300 ml (10 fl oz) milk
100 g (3½ oz) sugar
1 teaspoon vanilla essence
75 g (3 oz) butter
50 g (2 oz) flour

5 egg yolks, beaten
75 ml (3 fl oz) kirsch
    d'Alsace
6 egg whites, beaten to soft
    peaks

Pre-heat the oven to gas mark 5, 190°C (375°F).

Bring the milk, sugar and vanilla to boiling point.

Melt the butter in a large heavy-bottomed saucepan. Sift in the flour little by little, stirring well. When the mixture is bubbling, add the boiling milk in a steady stream; bring back to the boil and beat all the time until thick and smooth. Remove from the heat and allow to cool a little. Beat in the egg yolks and the kirsch.

Liberally butter a soufflé dish and dust with sugar. Carefully incorporate the egg whites into the soufflé mixture and pour into the mould. Pop into the oven for 20 to 25 minutes. Serve immediately. (From Alsace.)

CRÈME CARAMEL

This classic and popular dessert is also sometimes known in France as a flan.

In these days of mass-produced puddings, it has become something of a bad cliché; but, in fact, properly prepared, it is one of the nicest ways to finish a meal. Here is a typical recipe.

SERVES 6

75 g (3 oz) plus 2 tablespoons caster sugar
1 vanilla pod

600 ml (1 pint) Channel Island milk (really rich stuff, none of this pasteurised nonsense)
2 whole eggs and 2 egg yolks

Pre-heat the oven to gas mark 5, 190°C (375°F).

Melt the 75 g (3 oz) caster sugar in a saucepan and, when it begins to change colour, stir from time to time until it is golden brown and runny. Pour a little of this on to the bottom of each of six ramekins.

Put the vanilla pod into the milk and bring to the boil. Simmer for 2 or 3 minutes and remove the vanilla pod.

Meanwhile, whisk the eggs, egg yolks and 2 tablespoons sugar together in a bowl. Then, whisking the while, pour in the hot milk. Fill each ramekin with this mixture. Put the ramekins into a roasting tin half-filled with water and cook in the oven until they are set.

Leave to cool before turning them out and eating.

LES CAILLEBOTTES
Curds

These are jolly good with fresh raspberries and Guernsey cream!

SERVES 6

1 litre (2 pints) unpasteurised milk	*½ teaspoon vanilla essence*
4 tablespoons caster sugar	*1 tablespoon rennet*

Bring the milk to blood temperature, add the sugar and vanilla and stir well. Pour into a shallow dish and add the rennet, stir a few times and allow to set for 45 minutes in a warm place.

Break up the curds with a knife and pour into a saucepan, bring to the boil and immediately remove from the heat. Allow to cool and eat as soon as possible. (From Charente.)

Nougat glacé à l'orange
Nougat Ice Cream with Orange

SERVES 8

100 g (3½ oz) granulated
   sugar
200 g (7 oz) honey
50 g (2 oz) glucose
8 egg whites
1 litre (2 pints) double
   cream, whipped

500 g (1 lb) orange
   marmalade
400 g (14 oz) nougat,
   broken into small pieces
50 ml (2 fl oz) orange
   liqueur

Melt the sugar, honey and glucose in a saucepan. Whisk the egg whites until stiff and pour the melted sugar mixture over them. Mix carefully together. Allow to cool.

Add the whipped cream to the cooled mixture along with the marmalade, nougat and liqueur.

Put into a mould and leave to set in the freezer for about 12 hours.

Poires belles dijonnaises
Pears with Blackcurrant Sorbet

SERVES 6

250 g (8 oz) sugar
1 vanilla pod
1.5 kg (3 lb) pears, peeled,
   with stalks left on
300 ml (10 fl oz) double
   cream

500 ml (17 fl oz)
   blackcurrant sorbet,
   softened
250 g (8 oz) fresh
   raspberries, puréed
Toasted slivered almonds

Put the sugar and vanilla pod in a large pan with 1 litre (2 pints) water and bring to the boil, stirring until the sugar dissolves. Poach the pears for 15 minutes in the vanilla syrup. Remove and cool. Put in a serving bowl. Mix the cream with the sorbet and dollop over the pears. Pour over the raspberry purée and scatter with the toasted almonds. (From Burgundy.)

CRÊPES SAVOYARDES
Savoy Pancakes

SERVES 6

250 g (8 oz) flour, sifted	*Pinch of salt*
2 eggs	*450 ml (15 fl oz) milk*
1 tablespoon nut oil	*Oil for frying*

Put the flour into a large bowl and make a well in the middle. Break in the eggs, add the oil, salt and half the milk. Beat until smooth, before slowly stirring in the rest of the milk. Allow to rest for 1 hour.

Oil a frying pan. When it is hot, pour on the batter in batches, turning to cook both sides. Serve with sugar or jam. (From Savoy.)

EPILOGUE

L eo is looking grey and old like the walls of the church you can see through the dirty windows of the Café de France. We embrace. He smells old but his eyes twinkle as he pulls down the handle on the coffee machine. 'Ça va, mon beau?' 'Yes. And you?' He shrugs and rolls his eyes. 'Oui, ça va.'

I haven't seen him for a long time. Not since I lived in this village which, twice a year, at Easter and in August, is dominated by the largest antiques fair the South of France can boast. Then I coaxed an ailing lorry overladen with Lloyd loom chairs, stripped pine and pretty English china tea services down the awful autoroute du soleil and unloaded the cheap treasures to a clamouring crowd of dealers who swooped like cormorants, avaricious and unscrupulous behind a slow trawler. To return years later, footloose and fancy free of the burdens of commerce, gives me that wonderful feeling of detached belonging. Being there.

I sip the strong coffee and Leo splashes a dash of rum into the cup. My eyes are gritty and my back aches after driving 500 mad miles through the night to descend from the hell of the autoroute to the heaven that is Provence. A plump woman wearing an apron and overcoat is setting up a trestle table in front of the café door. She unloads baskets of chives, salad and dandelion leaves from a rusty corrugated can, levels off her scales and waits for the first customer and the sun. The church clock chimes seven. Quietly the café begins to fill with men, some on the way to work, others just coming to sit away the day, playing cards or gazing with faded eyes

306

through the windows at the church. Outside, a swarthy man in a tracksuit on a white bicycle is buying a dark green salad with red-tinged leaves. Eight o'clock strikes as the sun bathes the old ochre roofs in a soft warm light. It is time to move off and find breakfast with my friend Eva who once rented her balcony in Aix en Provence to friends to witness France's last public execution in 1938.

I eat in her sunny garden from a table of plenty. Thin slices of cured ham, pink, fiery radishes, soft, creamy goat's cheeses. Warm bread spread with *tapenade*, the black butter of Provence – a smooth paste of olives, slightly bitter on the tongue, but good with the scented red wine that René says is the best for miles. Eva is already sipping a pastis, since she ate long ago after feeding the ducks and chickens. She says that her husband René is getting lazier by the day. 'Not so, I shot a rabbit yesterday, and who knows, maybe today I'll skin it for you.' She brushes imaginary crumbs from her floral apron, stoops for her empty feed buckets and goes into the house. She's not cross, but, like most Provençal women, she's the boss. René and I finish the wine and drink a coffee and a marc. The day has started well. And I remember the day we ate aïoli and snails and roast goat (that Eva had nursed with love till it was time to be eaten), and we played 'boules' till dusk one hot August night.

A banner draped from the plane trees proclaims the 26th Easter Antiques Fair. Hordes throng the streets, gawking and poking at mountains of bric-a-brac piled high under canvas-covered stalls. The sky is blue and the world jostles by in shirt sleeves and T-shirts, yet the grey, cold trees on the avenue have no leaves. They have been so severely pruned that they stand like a guard of scarecrows, old and stunted. It is hard to believe that in just a few weeks they will burgeon into a thick green tunnel, where you can sit out of the blazing sun, dangle your toes in the ice clear water of the River Sorgue and watch the huge water wheels turn. Just the spot to sit and speculate if I was in my right mind when I decided to quit this place and return to England.

I leave the stallholders – afraid to miss a sale – to unpack picnics of garlic sausage, cheese, bread and wine and cross the bridge by the basin, where the river divides to encircle the town, and walk on to Pichelin's bar. The proprietor, brash and noisy, hits me on the back of the head and insults me. With glorious vulgarity he kisses me on both cheeks and hands me a diabolically strong pastis before ordering my lunch, the choice of which I am not permitted to influence. I tuck into a bowl of salade composée: sweet, bright green leaves of endive, crisp wisps of pale green curly endive, so fresh that they spring back as you plunge in your fork, mixed with hard-boiled eggs, thick anchovy fillets, black olives, blood red tomatoes and rich virgin olive oil. Guy Pichelin, standing back on his heels, watches me eat; touches his mouth with his finger and thumb. I nod back. Yes, it's great.

Next, a tarnished stainless steel platter piled high with boiled salt cod, small, dark green artichokes, tinged purple at the edges, bright orange carrots, boiled potatoes, steamed clams and a chipped bowl of yellow garlic mayonnaise. Pichelin joins me for cheese, while his wife, buxom and blonde, sweats in the tiny kitchen. My meal is under £7. I make a note to write a letter of complaint to the ferry company that ripped me off for disgusting food the night before. But first it's siesta time in my shuttered hotel room.

I open the window to see the early evening crowds, and the children's roundabout spinning playfully in the street below, next to the brochette vendor's charcoal grill that perfumes the cool evening air with ox hearts and herbes de Provence. I adjust my tie in the foyer before setting out for the parties on this last night of the fair, and the hall porter gives me the bad news: 'The garage phoned. Your car needs parts from Marseille. It may take several days.' Just one of life's little setbacks. 'Too bad,' I say. At least I can enjoy the party that Thierry and Lizzie are throwing to open their new shop – it's only walking distance from here.

Thierry started selling tin toys from a carpet on the floor of the Sunday street market. Now he deals in Art Deco in the rue de Quatre Hôtages, drinks champagne and wears designer clothes. I push open the door and enter the party. A marathon of kissing and handshaking is endured before I can get a drink.

In a brilliant mirrored room, pink, blue, crimson and yellow women with spectacles on jewelled strings sip champagne through vermilion lips, while men in tweed jackets, collars up and cuffs rolled back, adjust their silk bootlaceties. Thierry pirouettes, arms akimbo, through the babbling crowd, catalogue in hand and clients in tow. I stand in a corner with a whisky and nibble on miniature puff pastry whirls, tangy with anchovy, while the Japanese girl from the PR agency tells me in her soft American accent that this is one of the finest collections of Deco glass. 'Not only very beautiful, but a good investment too.' It is very hot and the whisky tastes fine as these decorated birds wheel and deal, husbands for lovers and francs for glass.

'OK gang, let's go,' Thierry says, pointing to the back door. We troop unsteadily out and across the gravel to a sombre house behind a wrought-iron fence where a banquet of langoustines and rare roast beef awaits us in the sepulchral gloom of a huge, derelict dining room, presided over by a stuffed bear. Albert Gassier, tall and hospitable, president of the antiques fair and an old friend, embraces a crowd of us with ease between his great arms.

'My friends. Welcome. Let us eat. Let us drink. Let us drink champagne. Yes, champagne. But,' he lets slip two or three wriggling women, 'but for you, Floyd, I have the best whisky. The best whisky.' And then in English: 'How do you say? Time is money, yes?' And roars with laughter. Funny lot the French. They always say, 'How do you say? Time is money, yes?' when they are wide-eyed and legless.

They are taking down the stalls and loading up the vans, trucks, cars and lorries with unsold junk. Some whistling happily as they prepare to return home to celebrate a profitable fair, others packing up in silence. Under the bare scaffolding that supported the brightly coloured canvas *bâches*, an unshaven man fries deep yellow-yolked eggs on a camping gas stove and slides them on to a plate, swills the smoking pan with a dash of vinegar which fizzes in the butter, and tips it out over the eggs. He pours a mug of red wine and eats.

The morning sun shimmers off the pale green olive trees and the mountains are nearly black across the valley. Neat rows of cherry trees, just blossoming, stand clean from the immaculately tilled red soil. A village, high and proud, carved from soft yellow nougat, reflects this big bright sun as I speed in my noisy French hire car through the mist to lunch. I drive on towards the bleeding rocks of Apt and Roussillon from whence come the crystallised cherries that adorn your Christmas cake.

I enter this modest hill village, huddled tight under the ruins of a medieval château, where the Hôtel Saint Hubert is lifeless behind plain green painted doors and neat net curtains. I push softly on the door. In the airy dining-room I sip champagne and myrtleberry liqueur on this holiday Monday, as ruddy-faced farmers, in neat suits that no longer fit, slurp soup from heavy silver spoons, half-hidden by huge fists, while their grey-faced wives break morsels from the crisp loaves and munch self-consciously with pursed lips.

The waitress places a plate of wild mushrooms with asparagus, like white roman candles, before me. The room is humming harder as the farmers fade away and the boned rabbit, stuffed with its kidneys, is served with a broccoli purée: it has been cooked in heaven, easily visible through the clear windows of this hotel. Claude and Katie, now that the service is over, sip Marc de Provence with me and we talk of old times. I say he is still the best cook I know and he gets embarrassed. We drink one more and then I must go.

Big sign says Arles, Nîmes and Marseille above the red traffic light as I turn right by the illuminated city walls into the railway station. I wander into a crowded bar, filled with red-faced lovers going home; a drunk sleeps under a destination board that reads Metz, Barcelona, Paris and Kiel. A gaggle of rucksack-carrying American schoolgirls haggle hopelessly over the price of a Coke. My waiter perfunctorily wipes the table and crashes down a foaming demi of iced beer. My mouth is stale and the beer tastes good. An Arab idly sweeps the tiled floor. The Paris train leaves. The Americans and soldiers have gone. The angry bartender pulls down the guard over the counter. And me? I am sitting – another fallen star – waiting for the early train. But happy.

INDEX

INDEX

INDEX

INDEX